A Short History of Rome

THE ROMAN FORUM TODAY

A SHORT

HISTORY OF ROME

BY

FRANK FROST ABBOTT

PROFESSOR IN PRINCETON UNIVERSITY. AUTHOR OF
"ROMAN POLITICAL INSTITUTIONS"

SCOTT, FORESMAN AND COMPANY
CHICAGO   ATLANTA   NEW YORK

PREFACE

The primary purpose of this volume is to give the important facts of Roman history, and to bring out clearly their connection with one another. The author has also aimed to put the material in a form simple and compact enough to enable teachers who use the book to cover the entire period to the reign of Charlemagne in the time commonly given to this branch of history.

Besides showing the qualities which every historical narrative should have, an introductory manual should, in the first place, be concrete, and, in the second place, it should present the facts in such a way that their logical sequence will be apparent at once. It can be made concrete by avoiding abstract statements, where it is possible, and by using the personality of a great leader, like Sulla, or Caesar, or Charlemagne, in describing the movement with which he was associated. In like manner the atmosphere of the times may be reproduced by quoting freely from the sources. The second quality mentioned, unity in the story, is still more important. The student, as he reads, should feel that each new development was the natural outgrowth of the situation which preceded it. This method of treating the subject not only gives him some idea of the real meaning of history, but it relieves him from the painful task of memorizing a series of loosely connected incidents. Furthermore, a history of Rome should include in its logical treatment not only the story of political development but all sides of the people's life. The literature, the religion, and the social life of a particular period reflect its temper as clearly as the form of government or the political policy, and should not be treated as separate topics, but should be made a part of the main narrative. In this method of presentation the reader will see clearly

a

that the form which these phases of Roman life took from generation to generation was a natural expression of the tendency of
the times. An earnest effort has been made to follow these
cardinal principles in the preparation of this book.

The maps in black and white show the scene of operations for
each of the important wars, giving only those places which are
mentioned in the text. The colored maps illustrate the growth
of the Empire from one period to another, its disintegration, and
the ultimate reorganization of western Europe. It is hoped that
the series last mentioned will let the student see at a glance the
line of development or contraction, as the case may be, and some
of the reasons which determined it. To assist him in keeping
the general trend of events clearly in mind, each chapter has a
brief analysis at the beginning and a summary of its contents
at the end. The illustrations, unless otherwise indicated, are
from photographs. The reproduction of a Roman galley is taken
from Herschel's *Frontinus* with the kind permission of the author.
The two designs on the front cover symbolize respectively the
two great periods of Roman history—the development of pagan
Rome with its conquest of the world by the force of arms, and
the triumph of Christianity, culminating in the coronation of
Charlemagne by the Pope in St. Peter's. The Roman eagle is
copied from a sepulchral monument now in the Palazzo Albani
at Rome; the monogram of Christianity, which is made up of
the first two letters of the Greek form of Christ's name standing between Alpha and Omega, is taken from a gem belonging
to the period subsequent to Constantine.

This volume is intended primarily for the pupil, and it is
believed that he will find no difficulty in using without aid all
the material which is found in it. Issued simultaneously with it
is a small *Handbook* which contains hints, questions, and other
helps for teachers.

For many valuable criticisms and suggestions in preparing
this volume the author is greatly indebted to Miss Victoria Adams
of the Calumet High School and to Mr. A. F. Barnard of the

University High School, Chicago, to Mr. W. E. Moffatt of the Toledo High School, to Dr. Mary B. Peaks of Vassar College, to Professor H. W. Johnston of Indiana University, and to Mr. B. L. Ullman, Dr. R. J. Bonner, and Professor Edward Capps of the University of Chicago, and to all of them he wishes to express his thanks for the assistance which they have rendered him.

FRANK FROST ABBOTT.

Chicago, June, 1906.

CONTENTS

MAPS AND PLANS

(Based in Part on Putzger, Spruner-Sieglin, Murray, and Freeman)

COLORED MAPS

SKETCH MAPS AND PLANS

   * The maps marked with a star show the expansion of Roman territory
from one period to another, until the empire reached its greatest extent.

9

ILLUSTRATIONS

10

CHAPTER I

How Rome developed out of a city-state into an empire, and how her history concerns us.

1. The Conquests of Rome. The history of Rome is the story of the development of a city-state into an empire of world-wide extent, which finally of its own weight broke into pieces. In the first stage of her growth this single city on the Tiber makes herself a leader among the neighboring towns which lie in the low country known as Latium, to the south of the river. Using these towns as her allies and dependents, she conquers the Etruscans to the north, and the Samnites in the hills to the east. In this way she has scarcely become mistress of central Italy when the fortunes of war bring her into conflict with the peoples of Magna Græcia, as southern Italy was called, and their champion Pyrrhus. The conquest of southern Italy follows.

Rome now controls the whole peninsula and is a world-power. Her outlook is towards the West and the trend of events plunges her into a struggle with Carthage, the other great power of the West. She crushes Carthage and strips from her Sicily, Sardinia, and Spain. Then she turns for the first time toward the East and forces Greece, Macedonia, and Asia Minor to yield to her. Her great leader, Julius Cæsar, conquers central Europe and begins the subjugation of Britain. In this way the limits of her empire are steadily pushed forward until throughout the civilized world, from the Atlantic on the west to the Euphrates on the east, from the Sahara on the south to the Rhine and the Danube on the north, the authority of Rome is recognized, the Latin language is spoken, and Roman institutions are firmly established.

2. Rome a City-state. For this vast area the seat of government was located at Rome. There the consuls and emperors fixed their official residences; there the senate met, and thence officials were sent out to govern the provinces. But Rome was not simply a capital, like Washington or London. It was more than that. A citizen of the United States or a British subject living in any small town whatsoever has the same political powers and privileges as one who resides in the capital city, because he can cast his vote in his native town and have the representatives thus chosen pass the laws which he wishes. Not only was the city on the Tiber the seat of legislative and administrative activity, but meetings of the popular assemblies to choose magistrates and enact laws could be held nowhere else. This left the power of electing magistrates and making laws to those who lived in Rome or near enough to the city to go there to deposit their votes. In other words the government of the world, even after the franchise had been granted to towns throughout Italy, was left to the city of Rome. When the city-state became an empire and the right of electing magistrates and of voting on laws passed out of the hands of the people, as it at last did, the city was reduced to the position of a modern capital, and finally lost even this distinction, when the empire which had brought the different sections of the world within its limits began to fall to pieces.

3. Internal Struggles. For several centuries the government rested in the hands of the few, while the great mass of the people were excluded from the offices, and gained the right to hold them only as the result of a long and painful struggle. With this great contest for equality between those who enjoyed political privileges and those who were deprived of them, there was interwoven the struggle between the rich and the poor; a struggle which was intensified when the great mass of the people—the plebeians as they were called—had secured political equality.

4. Changes in the Form of Government. Meantime the growth of the empire had an influence upon the political and social development of the city. The great armies which were needed in acquiring new territory, and in maintaining order throughout the territory already acquired, secured a controlling influence in domestic affairs, for the consuls and the senate could not enforce their authority successfully against a Marius, a Sulla, a Pompey, or a Caesar. So in time the reins of government passed from the annually elected consul and the senate, both of whom reflected the wishes of the people of Rome, to the emperor, who represented better the interests of the empire; and the government of the world for the benefit of a single city gradually gave way to a policy which was better adapted to the interests of the whole Roman world. The form of government has passed through a complete cycle in its development. The monarchy gives way to a republic; the republic is transformed into a democratic empire, and out of the latter develops an autocracy, or state in which one man holds the supreme power.

5. Social Changes. The social changes which Rome and Italy underwent were as marked as the political. At the beginning the people were tillers of the soil, of simple tastes, possessed of the bare necessities of life, and inured to warfare. As trade developed, and tribute came to them from the provinces, their wealth increased, and with wealth came a taste for luxury, and a loss of the physical and moral strength which had brought them their earlier successes. They enrolled barbarians in the army to fight for them, and imported hordes of slaves to till their fields. In their weak and helpless state they were no longer able to hold back the Germanic peoples of northern Europe who steadily pushed on to the south and finally made themselves masters of the western part of the empire. Then the process of conquest and unification begins again, this time under the Franks, and is carried to completion by their great leader Charlemagne.

6. The Task of the Historian. It is our object to see how this great territory was acquired and governed, how the city-state developed into an empire, how the great mass of the Ro-

mans gained their political rights, how the character and mode of living of the people gradually changed, and finally to ask ourselves how and why the vast structure disintegrated and society reformed itself into the states of Medieval Europe.

7. Significance of Roman History.   Our inheritance from Rome has been so large, and her law, her institutions, and the Latin language, are so interwoven in the fabric of our own public and private life that we cannot understand modern civilization without a knowledge of Roman history.   But to us Anglo-Saxons the story of Rome will always appeal with peculiar force because it is the history of a people who showed, as we have shown, a steadfastness of purpose, a knowledge of practical affairs, a skill in adapting means to an end, and a regard for tradition. It is the history of a people whose success in colonizing other lands and in moulding other civilizations into a likeness to their own, finds perhaps no other parallel than that which the history of the Anglo-Saxon people offers.

ITALY
about 500 B.C.

Greek Colonies and Settlements are shown in red.
A = Æolian or Achæan colony.
D = Dorian colony.
I = Ionian colony.

Phœnician Settlements are underscored thus:
Panormus

The name Italia or Œnotria was first applied to the southernmost part of the peninsula only.

Italian territory yellow.

CHAPTER II

THE LAND AND THE PEOPLE

How the geography of Italy tended to bring her territory and inhabitants under one government, notwithstanding the fact that at the outset the peninsula was occupied by different peoples, and had a variety of climates and products — How Rome was geographically the natural capital — How the Italians lived.

8. The Peoples of Italy. We have just taken a bird's-eye view of the story of Rome, and have noticed some of the questions which the student of Roman history asks himself. To answer these questions we must first know something of the antecedents and character of the Roman people, something of their country and of the peoples about them. When our interest in Italy begins there were three races represented within its limits with whom we are especially concerned: the Etruscans, the Greeks, and the Italians.

9. The Etruscans. Whence the Etruscans came, how they entered Italy, or with what people they were related, is still a mystery, but in early times, at the height of their power, their territory to the north included the valley of the Po, and to the south extended into Campania, possibly including Latium. The southern countries, however, threw off their yoke in the fifth century B. C. and the pressure of the Gauls robbed them of their northern possessions, so that in time Etruria proper extended only from the Arnus to the Tiber.

10. Their Influence on the Italians. Etruria played an important part in the development of Italian civilization by introducing a knowledge of Greek art and Greek institutions. Her merchants visited the cities of Greece; she had a rich, firmly established nobility, which fostered the arts, and the Etruscans lived in cities and were not simple herdsmen or farmers, like the Italians. All these circumstances led them to ac-

17

cept eagerly and to develop the material side, at least, of Greek civilization, and through the Etruscans Greek culture made itself felt in some measure in Italy long before the Italians were brought into direct contact with the Greeks.   From them the Romans learned, for instance, the construction of the arch which they used so effectively later in their public buildings and

AN ETRUSCAN SARCOPHAGUS

aqueducts.   From them they acquired some skill and taste in the manufacture, from clay and metal, of articles of use and ornament.   Dancers and pipe players found their way from Etruria to Rome, and from the Etruscans the Romans borrowed the practice of celebrating festivals with gladiatorial combats.

11. The Greeks. The most important Greek settlements in Italy were Cumæ, Posidonia or Pæstum, Thurii, Rhegium, Croton, Metapontum, and Tarentum.   If we look at the location of these towns on the map, we see that the main Greek colonies are all on or near the seaboard, and run from Campania, southward along the western coast and northward to the head of the Gulf of Tarentum along the east side of the great promontory which runs down toward Sicily. The earliest of these settlements, Cumæ, was as old as the city of Rome itself. Situated on the Bay of Naples, with the rich plains of Campania behind it, its growth was rapid, and it became a very prosperous town. It was the nearest to Rome of any of the Greek colonies, and maintained friendly relations with that city, so that it is not surprising that from an early period it should have exerted a great influence on the Latins. Frequent references to the Cumæan oracle in early Roman tradition, and the introduction

A GREEK TEMPLE AT PÆSTUM

into Latium of the Cumæan alphabet, testify to this fact. Rhegium owed its importance largely to its location. With its sister-city Messana, on the coast of Sicily opposite to it, it controlled the Strait of Messina. But of all the cities in Magna Græcia, or southern Italy, Tarentum was the most flourishing. Its fine harbor made it the natural port of entry from Greece and the Orient, and the most important commercial and manufacturing point in southeastern Italy, and when, in the course of time, the inevitable conflict between the Greeks to the south and the Italians to the north came, it was natural that Tarentum should become the centre of resistance against the Italian invaders.

12. Their Character. All of these cities enjoyed a flourishing trade, and became prosperous and influential. They fostered the arts, and took a deep interest in philosophy and literature, and the real beginnings of literature and art in Rome date from the campaigns which the Romans carried on in Magna Græcia in the third century before our era. But it was well for the Roman people that they were not brought into contact with the Greek cities of the South at an earlier date, before Roman political ideals had become fixed and before Roman public and private character had had an opportunity to develop along their own characteristic lines, for the Greek colonies in southern Italy showed all the political weaknesses of the mother country. They not only lacked cohesion among themselves, but the several towns were constantly rent by internal dissensions, and partisan feeling ran so high in the struggles between the aristocratic and democratic factions, that a party often preferred to call in a foreigner and submit to him rather than to yield to its political opponents. This inability to act in harmony which the Greek colonies showed of course made their ultimate conquest by Rome a comparatively easy matter.

13. The Italians. The Italians proper occupied central Italy. They were divided into two branches. One was made up of the Umbrians and the Oscan-speaking peoples; the other was Latin. The Umbrians dwelt in the territory between the Tiber and the Apennines. The most powerful of the Oscan-speaking peoples were the Samnites, some of whom dwelt in little villages in the mountains of central Italy, and lived the simple life of their fathers, while others had descended into the plains of Campania, Lucania, and southern Italy, and had adopted the mode of living of the Greek coast towns. Akin to the Samnites were certain tribes in central Italy like the Volscians, Aequians, and Hernici, the three peoples who shut in Latium, the country of the Latins, to the east and south. Latium, or "the land of the plain," was bounded on the north by the Tiber, and on the east and south by a line drawn just beyond the towns of Præneste, Velitræ, Cora, and Setia; it stretched along

the coast for sixty or seventy miles, and came at an early period
to include within its limits a large part of the country of the
Aequians, the Hernici, and Volscians, and extended along the
coast to Sinuessa.

14. Diversity of Race and of Occupation. The presence
in Italy of these different races with their diverse tastes, religions, and modes of living made against the development of
a common national life. Leaving out of account differences in
language, which create a deep prejudice, and constitute an almost insurmountable barrier between peoples, the Greeks in the
south, living in well-built cities on the coast, with their highly
developed civilization and their commercial instincts, were alien,
like the Etruscans in the north, to the Italians in central Italy,
who cultivated their fields in the lowlands, or alternated in the
hill-country between tending their flocks and raiding their neighbors. One might have prophesied with some confidence that
this racial diversity would give rise to the development of half
a dozen independent states in Italy.

15. The Peninsula and its Products. This would have
seemed all the more likely in view of the configuration of the
country and the diversity of the climate. The fertile plains
along the west coast invite to agriculture; the hills furnish excellent pasturage for flocks and herds, while the fastnesses of the
Apennines, which run from one end of Italy to the other, and
send out spurs to the east and west, offer secure retreats to bands
of brigands and freebooters. Then too, Italy is six hundred
miles or more long from north to south, and, therefore, offers
a great variety in climate. The soil in the highlands differs
radically from that in the lowlands, and this great variety of
soil and climate gives rise to a correspondingly large diversity
of products. The cultivation of the olive and the vine, the
raising of grain and fruits of almost every sort, and the rearing
of cattle, sheep, and swine, could all be carried on profitably
within the borders of the country, and could not fail to empha-
size the diversity which racial differences produced.

16. The Geography of Italy. But these influences were

more than offset by the fact that Italy is a natural geographical unit. On the only side where it touches another land the Alps form a natural frontier, and yet, although the Alps help to give Italy unity, they do not form an impassable boundary to isolate it from the rest of the world, as Spain is cut off by the Pyrenees. The sea between Calabria and Epirus was not broad enough to frighten even the timid navigators of ancient times, the islands of Sicily and Sardinia bridged over the long stretch to Africa, and still Italy was not close enough to either region to lose her own individuality. It had been otherwise with Greece. The islands scattered at convenient intervals through the Ægean Sea, brought her into too close relations with the Orient to allow her to develop a unified national life. Greece faced the Orient too, while the harbors of Italy are to the west—away from the centres of the older civilizations. The development of a country is determined in large measure by its rivers and by the trend of its mountains. River valleys are apt to be fertile and they, therefore, tempt the settler, and as trade grows up, the rivers themselves afford a convenient means of communication. Mountain chains furnish a natural defense, and a boundary beyond which a people, in its early history, at least, is not likely to extend its settlements or its conquests. If, having these facts in mind, we glance at the map of Italy, we shall see that the peninsula is divided into three great sections, the valley of the Po, the territory to the east, and that to the west of the Apennines. Each of these districts is marked off from the other and capable of independent development.

17. The Valley of the Po. The valley of the Po is shut in on the north by the Alps and on the south by the main chain of the Apennines, which runs from the Gulf of Genoa in a somewhat southeasterly direction to the Adriatic. The Po is a broad, sluggish stream, so that it is navigable and yet at the same time it can be easily forded. The Apennines separate this valley so markedly from the rest of the peninsula that its early history was quite distinct from that of Italy proper. In fact it is commonly known to the Romans as Cisalpine Gaul.

18. The Adriatic Coast. Italy itself is divided into two strips by the mountain chain which runs through the central part parallel to the coast line. The eastern section is turned toward the cold winds of the North and East; its lowlands are narrow, and its soil comparatively sterile; it is nearly cut off from communication with the rest of the world, because it is easily approached by land only from the North, it has few rivers and harbors, and in ancient times the opposite coasts of the Adriatic were inhabited by uncivilized peoples.

19. The West Coast. The plains on the west coast are broader and more fertile; they are protected by the mountains from the cold north winds; the rivers are deeper and the bays and harbors more numerous. All of these facts gave the Mediterranean side of the peninsula a great advantage over the Adriatic coast, and go far toward explaining the earlier development and the greater importance of that part of Italy. We should remember also that the Greeks made no settlements on the Adriatic side, but *did* colonize the western coast. This fact was of great moment, because the civilizing influence which they exerted and the spirit of imitation or of resistance which they aroused in the Italians west of the Apennines, tended strongly to further the development of that portion of the peninsula.

20. Location of Rome. At the centre of this favored coast, and near the mouth of the Tiber, Rome was situated. One needs only to recall the Nile, the Tigris and Euphrates, the Indus and Ganges, to appreciate how great a part rivers played in ancient times in making communities political and commercial centres. The Romans of the later period understood how much the city owed to its fortunate location. The historian, Livy, well sums up these advantages when he writes: "With great wisdom have gods and men selected this site for the city—a spot where there are health-giving hills, on the banks of a river, on which the fruits of the earth from the lands behind us may be brought hither, on which produce from abroad may come, with the sea close enough to be of service—a place not so near the coast as to be exposed to danger from hostile fleets, in the centre of Italy, and peculiarly adapted to insure the growth of a city." In brief, it may be said that the partition of Italy among several independent states to which the diversity of her races, soil, and climate seemed to point, was made impossible by the fact that her natural boundaries gave her unity, that the conformation of the country led to the development of the west coast first, and that the location of Rome on a navigable river at the middle point of this coast made her the inevitable political and commercial capital of the whole country.

21. The Italians an Agricultural People. The Latins, as well as the other Italians, probably entered Italy from the North. They were primarily an agricultural people, engaged mainly in growing grain. The vine and the fig were, however, known to them from the earliest times. The rearing of cattle too, must have been an important industry, since the earliest Latin word for wealth, *pecunia*, comes from *pecus*, cattle, and oxen and sheep formed the oldest medium of exchange. Artisans were almost unknown. The members of each household raised their own cattle and grain, made their own garments from flax or wool, and fashioned the few articles of wood or clay needed for their simple life. Only with the development of urban life came the growth of an artisan class. What we know of the primitive religion of the Italian and the Roman confirms the conclusions which we have just reached in regard to the state of society in the early period. They thought of the gods as helping or hindering them in cultivating the fields, in raising cattle, and in waging war, and to these functions the powers of most of their divinities were confined. Such a conception indicates plainly enough that the great material interests of the people did not extend beyond these three occupations. The manual arts and commerce were still undeveloped, as we see from the fact that the divinities, Minerva and Mercury, who in the later period helped and guarded the artisan and the merchant respectively, were unknown in the early Roman religion, and that Neptune had not yet become the god of the sea and of seafaring men.

22. Their Character. The whole history of the Italians

shows that they were a people of good sense, wit, self-control, and determination. They were industrious and simple in their tastes; they had remarkable powers of endurance, a great respect for authority, and a willingness to subordinate their personal interests to the common good.

23. The Family and the Clan. The family organization was very compact. Not only the slaves, but the mother and the children owed implicit obedience to the father. On the family was based the *gens* or clan, which was made up of all those who could trace their lineage back from father to father to a common ancestor. The control of clan affairs rested probably with the members of the clan, or with its old men. For mutual protection several of these clans commonly settled near one another about some fortified point, where all could take refuge in time of danger. The land originally belonged not to individuals but to the clan, and the crops from it were divided among the several households. Even after the arable land was apportioned to individual owners, the pasture-land and wood-land was held as the common property of the entire community.

24. Religion. We have noticed above, that the state of society and the character of the people in the early period is reflected in their religious system. A study of this side of their life will be of much service in helping us to understand later history, because religion was so closely interwoven with public and private affairs, that it will repay us to try to find out what the character of their gods was, what attitude the people took toward them, and what influence religion had upon the life and development of the people. What has been said in this chapter of the character and civilization of the people is true of all the Italians. In discussing religious matters, we shall confine our attention to the Romans, because we are primarily interested in them, although the religion of the other Italians did not differ essentially from theirs.

25 Sources of our Knowledge. Fortunately for our purpose the Romans, who were conservative in all matters, were peculiarly so where religion was concerned, and many practices sur vived in later years which carry us back almost to the beginning of things Roman, and show us what the people thought and did in early days.   One piece of evidence which helps us is furnished by the extant calendars of religious festivals which give us a list of the gods in whose honor public celebrations were held. The oldest of these calendars goes back, it is true, to a date only shortly before the birth of Christ, but it contains the record of ceremonies which had been observed year after year for centuries before that period.   From writers upon antiquity, like Varro and Aulus Gellius, from inscriptions upon altars, temples, and tombstones, and from tablets engraved for priesthoods, like the tablets of the Arval Brothers, which record ceremonies and prayers used by them for generations, we learn much about the way in which the gods were worshipped in the early period, as well as about the gods themselves.   Putting all this material together we have a fairly clear idea of the primitive religious system of the Romans.

26 Foreign Religions.   To appreciate one fundamental point of difference between their attitude in religious matters and our own, we must bear the fact in mind that the Romans had many gods, and that a people which itself believes in many divine beings receives the gods of other nations hospitably.   The people of Rome formed no exception to this principle.   They took the position that there were gods unknown to them, and in early days, at least, when a new community was incorporated in the state or transferred to Rome, its right to carry on the worship of its old divinities was fully recognized, and in many cases the new religion was officially adopted.   In this way the number of Roman or Latin divinities steadily increased, and it is difficult to say in all cases which were the *di indigetes*, or original gods, of the Romans, and which the *di novensides*, or naturalized deities. Of the *di novensides*, the majority came from the other Italians and the Greeks.   To the other Italians the Romans owed the worship of Diana, Minerva, Hercules, and Venus.   Of Greek origin was the worship of Apollo, Mercury, and Neptune as a god of the sea.

27. The National Deities. Most of the strictly Roman deities, the *di indigetes*, were, as we have already noticed, the gods of the herdsman, the farmer, and the warrior. Jupiter, the god of the heavens, sent rain and sunshine to nourish the crops. Juno, who is closely allied with him, exercised similar functions. Tellus and Ceres presided over the fields where the seeds were planted and over the growing crops. Saturnus was the god of the sowing; Silvanus and Faunus of the woods; Mars was the god of war, but was thought of especially as protecting the fields and the herds from the incursions of the enemy. To Vesta and the Lares and Penates was entrusted the care of the house and the household. Their altar is the hearth, the central point in the house, where the food for the family is prepared, and before a

A VESTAL VIRGIN

meal a little wine was poured out on the hearth and a little food offered to these deities who protected the household. Like the family the state also had its hearth in a temple where a fire was always kept burning in honor of Vesta, or *Vesta publica populi Romani Quiritium*, as she was called, by six Vestal Virgins chosen for this purpose. Roman deities interested themselves in Roman affairs only. They were national in the strictest sense of the word, and the Roman's religion was as purely a national institution as was his form of government.

28. The Less Important Deities. The number of deities was made very great not only by admitting the gods of other communities, but also by the Roman practice of thinking of some protecting spirit as presiding over almost every human action and natural object. One of their antiquarians calculates that in the later period the Romans had six thousand different gods. The spring of water, the forest, and the valley each had its own guardian deity. Oxen were protected by one supernatural being, sheep by another. A special god took charge of one in going out of a house, and another divinity guarded a person on his way home. We can readily see that the danger of offending some deity, since they were so numerous, was an ever present one, and made the Roman very constant in his prayers and sacrifices.

29. The Ritual Complex. His difficulties were augmented by the fact that no public or private business of any importance could be transacted without divine sanction, and that the proper observance of very complicated ceremonies was essential in winning the favor of a friendly god or in appeasing the wrath of one that was hostile. This state of things, however, had its compensatory features, since there were deities who interested themselves in every act of his life, and upon engaging in any undertaking the Roman believed that there was a particular god who concerned himself with that undertaking. He held, therefore, that the scrupulous performance of the religious acts prescribed for the purpose in hand, bound the god concerned to favor his enterprise.

30. Religious Ceremonies. The good-will of the gods was sought by offering prayers, by holding festivals and instituting processions in their honor, and by making offerings. In early times the offerings which the state made, like those of the individual, were the simple fruits of the field, garlands and cakes, and in rare cases an animal was sacrificed. One side of their relations with the gods the Romans developed to an extraordinary extent, and its development is characteristic of the practical bent of the Roman mind. The farmer could not expect a harvest from his spring sowing; the state could not prosecute a war successfully, without the help of the gods. It was very desirable, therefore, to find out before undertaking any enterprise, what the will of the gods was, and what indications they would give of the best plan to adopt in order to ensure success. Consequently a most elaborate system of divination from watching the flight of birds, inspecting the entrails of animals, and interpreting all sorts of natural phenomena, was developed—a system adapted to all the needs of public and private life.

31. The Priests. The relations between gods and men were direct, that is to say, the individual could make his prayers and his offerings directly to the deity. The intervention of a priest was unnecessary. Colleges of priests, like the Augurs or the Salii attached to the worship of Mars, were either the servants of the gods, and guarded their insignia or celebrated their public festivals, or they were the representatives of the whole community in its dealings with the supernatural powers. Neither was religion independent of the state, for the priest was subordinate to the magistrate. We may say of the position of the priests in the community, that the great number of the gods and the complex character of the ritual made them men of importance. They alone knew the necessary formulas and ceremonies to appease the gods, and yet they never formed a separate caste, as was frequently the case in the Orient.

32. Influence of this Religion. Such a religion and such a religious organization as we have outlined could not fail to exert a great influence upon the intellectual and moral life of the people. The gods of the Greek were exalted human beings, endowed with all the faculties of men and women, but they were free from disease and pain and the other physical imperfections and limitations from which mortals suffer, and were perfect in form and beauty. They furnished the philosopher, the poet, and the artist, therefore, with their ideals of power, beauty, and wisdom. Poetry, art, and philosophy among the Greeks all sprang from religion. The colorless conceptions which the Italians had of their gods, lacking the elements of personality, furnished no such inspiration to the poet. Their history, carrying him no farther back toward the beginning of things than did the founding of his own state, failed to stimulate his interest in the broader questions of man's origin, his place in nature, and the meaning of human life. Consequently his thoughts were directed only to the affairs of everyday life. The practical bent of his mind, which of course determined the form of his religion, was in turn emphasized by that religion itself. So far as character was concerned, his gods were scarcely vested with moral qualities, his religion did not hold up exalted ethical standards, nor did it appeal to spiritual motives of a high order, but it did enforce the observance of good faith, it inculcated a spirit of discipline, a high regard for the integrity of family life and a respect for the orderly conduct of affairs, and all this served to strengthen the moral fibre of the people.

33. Summary Description of Italy. A survey of Italy in the early period shows us that the important peoples were the Etruscans, the Greeks, and of the Italic stock, the Latins, and the tribes which spoke Oscan. Etruria is of special interest to us because she introduced some elements of Greek civilization among the Latins. Later the Latins were greatly influenced by the Greek towns along the coast of southern Italy. The fact that Italy was occupied by different races, and has a variety of climates and products would tend to make her a land of many peoples, each under its own government, but the sea to the east, south, and west, and the Alps to the north ultimately ensured her unity. Rome on the west coast, where the plains and the harbors lie, was her natural capital. The Italians were mainly farmers and shepherds, had a compact family organization, and worshipped many gods.

CHAPTER III

(TO 509 B. C.)

How the city of Rome developed and was governed during the regal period —How the stories of the seven kings grew up.

34. What Determined the Location of Rome. The Romans were undoubtedly right in attributing the importance of their native city to the commercial advantages which its location gave it, but these advantages can hardly have counted for much in the minds of the first settlers on the Tiber, who had little to sell to others, and required little from abroad to satisfy their simple needs. They chose this spot on the left bank of the Tiber because it was easy to defend. The hills furnished them a natural stronghold. The surrounding plain was reasonably well adapted to tillage and pasturage.

SEPULCHRAL URN FOR ASHES (IN THE SHAPE OF AN ITALIAN HUT), WITH OTHER SMALL ARTICLES LATELY DUG UP IN THE FORUM; PROBABLY OF THE EIGHTH OR NINTH CENTURY BEFORE CHRIST

The Tiber afforded a protection to the north, and yet the island which lies in the river opposite the city made it comparatively easy for them to cross to the northern bank. Finally, the location chosen was fourteen miles from the mouth of the river, and, therefore, out of the reach of pirates.

35. The Growth of the Early City. The earliest settlement was on the Palatine hill, and portions of its encircling wall may still be seen, from which the compass of the primitive city may be fairly well inferred. As time went on, the population in the city and in the district immediately about it grew, for the advantages of the location attracted many, and new-comers were gladly received because of the fighting strength which they added to the community. Independent settlements had been made upon some of the neighboring hills, and in course of time they too cast in their lot with the Palatine community, and a great wall was built which made Rome the City of the Seven Hills, for it included within its limits the Palatine, the Capitoline, the Quirinal, the Esquiline, the Cælian, the Viminal, and the Aventine.

36. The Legendary Ancestors of the Romans. Greek and Roman writers, without any historical evidence on which to base their conclusions, date the founding of the city all the way from 753 to 747 B. C. The first of these dates, which Varro, a Roman antiquarian of Cicero's time, adopted, is perhaps the one most commonly accepted by the ancients. Scholars have established the fact that the people who founded Rome, like the other Italians, came from the same stock as the Greeks, and probably entered the peninsula from the north, but the account of their origin which Roman tradition preserved was a far different one. The story runs that when Troy had fallen, Aeneas fled across the sea and, after suffering much at the hands of gods and men, came to the west coast of Italy, where he was kindly received by King Latinus. Aeneas took Lavinia, the king's daughter, in marriage, and, after her father's death, ruled over the two peoples, who received the name of Latins from King Latinus. Ascanius succeeded his father Aeneas, and founded a new city called Alba Longa, where he and his descendants reigned for many years.

37. The Legend of Romulus and Remus. Now it came to pass that while Numitor was on the throne of Alba his younger brother, Amulius, formed a wicked plot against him, drove him into exile, slew his sons, and forced his daughter Rhea Silvia to become a Vestal Virgin. But Rhea Silvia was beloved of the god Mars, and she bore him twin sons. Whereupon Amulius was wroth and set the boys adrift in the Tiber, but the river carried the basket in which they had been placed to the foot of the Palatine, where they were found and suckled by a she-wolf. The king's shepherd, Faustulus, came upon them, took them with him to his own house, brought them up in his household, and named them Romulus and Remus. When they had reached man's estate they slew the usurper, Amulius, and restored their

THE CAPITOLINE WOLF SUCKLING ROMULUS AND REMUS

grandfather, Numitor, to the throne. In the fullness of time the two young men went forth from Alba Longa with other men of their own town to found a new city at the point where the Tiber had cast them up, and when they came thither, Remus took his stand on the Aventine to learn the will of the gods from the flight of the birds; Romulus on the Palatine. As the morning dawned, six vultures appeared before Remus, but twelve were vouchsafed to Romulus. So Romulus founded the city on the Palatine, and Remus, who scoffed at the weakness of his brother's wall, he slew. Then he gathered the whole people into three tribes, the Ramnes, the Tities, and the Luceres, and each tribe he divided into ten *curiae*, and from each *curia* he took one hundred men to serve on foot and ten horsemen. He chose also from among the people one hundred *senes*, or old men, to form a senate, which should counsel him upon matters touching the good of the whole people.

38. Numa Pompilius, Tullus Hostilius, and Ancus Martius. And when Romulus had been gathered to his fathers, the senate chose Numa Pompilius, a Sabine, to reign in his stead. Now Numa loved peace and turned the people from war to working with their hands and to tilling the soil. King Tullus Hostilius was a man of war. He conquered and destroyed the city of Alba Longa, and brought the Albans to Rome, settling them upon the Cælian hill. Ancus Martius, the fourth king, followed·in the footsteps of his grandfather, Numa.

39. Tarquinius Priscus. While Ancus still sat on the throne, a Greek, Lucumo by name, from Tarquinii in Etruria, came to Rome with his wife Tanaquil, and as they drew near to the city an eagle came from on high, plucked off the cap of Lucumo, and then, descending, placed it again upon his head. From this omen Tanaquil knew that the gods planned great things for her husband. At Rome he found favor with the king and with the people, and when Ancus Martius died, he was raised to the throne with the title of Tarquinius Priscus, from the city whence he came. He waged war against the Sabines and Latins and overcame them. He built a circus for the people in which races might be held, drew off the water from between the hills by a great drain, and did many things to make the city beautiful.

40. Servius Tullius. In the household of King Tarquin was a slave boy, Servius Tullius by name, and one day as this boy slept, those near him beheld a flame burning about his head, and yet he suffered no harm therefrom. Thereupon the queen knew that he had been chosen for some high place, and she married him to one of her daughters, and when Tarquinius had been slain by men whom the sons of Ancus Martius had chosen to that end, Servius Tullius was made king in his stead. During his reign the Quirinal, Viminal, and Esquiline hills were added to the city, and he built a great wall about Rome, and divided the people into classes according to their wealth, and each class into centuries, or companies of one hundred, to serve under him as fighting men, some as horsemen and some on foot, and these companies of warriors met, when the king called them together, to decide upon war or peace, and certain other great matters.

41. The Myth of Tarquin the Proud. But Servius Tullius was slain by the son of Tarquinius Priscus, to whom he had given his daughter, Tullia, in marriage. When Tullia heard of her father's death she drove to the senate house to greet her husband. In the way lay the dead body of her father, yet she turned not her chariot aside and her chariot wheels were stained with her father's blood. Tarquin the Proud, as the new king was called, forced the people to labor at the great works which his father had begun, until they murmured. Now, it chanced that the king was besieging Ardea, in the country of the Rutulians, and his son Sextus, leaving the camp secretly by night, betook himself to the house of his cousin Tarquinius Collatinus and dishonored Lucretia, the wife of Collatinus; and Lucretia told Collatinus and her father Lucretius of what had befallen her, and when she had told them all, she thrust a knife into her heart. Thereupon Lucretius and Collatinus, with their friends Publius Valerius and Junius Brutus, called the people together, and the king with his whole household was driven into exile.

42. Analysis of the Regal History. This is the story, with variations at certain points, of the founding of Rome and of the seven kings, which is recounted in prose by Cicero and Livy, and in verse by Vergil. It is manifestly fictitious. It is reasonably certain that the Romans kept no records during the regal period, and even if records had been kept, they would have been destroyed in the fourth century B. C. when the city was taken and burned by the Gauls. There were no documents, then, upon which this account could rest, and if it is based on oral tradition, absolutely no reliance can be placed upon it, because in the centuries which elapsed before this tradition was reduced to a written form, the true course of events must have been hopelessly

lost and distorted. If there were no other reason, the similarity
which many of the Roman tales bear to stories told in Greek
literature would show that they do not belong to Roman history.
Several cities of Greece and of southern Italy, for example, according to the mythical accounts of their early history, were
founded by twins, who were cast out by their natural protectors,
and suckled by animals. The story which attributed the founding of the city to twin brothers was adopted, because it furnished
a ready-made explanation of the later system of government by
two consuls. The name Romulus was derived from Roma, and
Remus comes from the same source with a slight modification.
Mars was made the father of Romulus and Remus because of
the warlike character of the Romans, and the two boys are reared
by a wolf, because the wolf was a sacred animal among the
Latins. In a word, a large part of the traditional narrative of
events at Rome during the regal period is made up of Greek
stories; and more or less cleverly dovetailed into these productions of the Greek fancy, or into the tales borrowed from Greek
history, are folklore stories, explanations invented at a comparatively late date to account for the existence of ancient
monuments, of old customs and of long established institutions,
and some remnant of authentic tradition.

43. The Growth of the Narrative. The process of selecting suitable elements for the story of Rome from this constantly
growing mass of myths, and of welding them into a continuous
narrative extended without doubt over many generations. In
all probability the story of the early period first became coher-
ent and took on a permanent form when it was set down in
writing in the third century B. C. by the poets Naevius' and
Ennius and the prose writer Fabius Pictor.

44. What our Sources of Information Are. Notwithstanding the fictitious character of the story of the seven kings,
we can get some light upon the life and institutions of the early
city. Tradition helps us a little, when it is supported by other
evidence. The remains which exist of the period, like the

"Wall of Servius" and articles of pottery, teach us something of the size of the city and of the progress which the Romans in early times had made in the arts.

THE SERVIAN CITY

45. The Appearance of the City. From some of these sources of information we get an idea how the city of Rome must have looked in early times. The houses were built of wood and thatched with straw. The roofs were pointed and had openings in the centre which let out the smoke and admitted the light to the single square room within, which was the living room for the entire family. Some houses doubtless had small sleeping rooms or store rooms adjoining, but there was no second story. Within the wall of the city we must think of buildings of this sort grouped together in little villages on the tops of the several hills, while between these small communities lay fields and valleys. Each of these hill-settlements had its characteristic life, which found expression especially in the worship of its tutelary deity or deities at the turf altars to be seen here and there.

46. Improvements made by the Tarquins. The valleys between the hills were subject to inundations from the Tiber, and one of the earliest improvements of the city consisted in constructing a huge sewer known as the Cloaca Maxima, which drained the market place or Forum, and protected the city in times of high water. This structure is attributed by tradition to the Tarquins, who are also said to have erected temples and other public buildings, the most notable of which was the temple of Jupiter on the Capitoline. To this period of the last three kings, tradition also assigned the construction of the great encircling wall. The assignment of these great public works to

A PORTION OF THE SERVIAN WALL

the Tarquins harmonizes well with the tradition that the first Tarquin came from Etruria, because the art of building was developed at an earlier period in Etruria than in Latium, and certain features of early Latin architecture—the use of the arch, for instance—were apparently borrowed from the Etruscans.

47. Agriculture the Main Industry. The main industry of the people was agriculture, and for generations, or centuries even, it was regarded as the freeman's natural occupation. This fact was of immense importance in determining the character of the individual Roman and of the state which he built up. A nation of independent farmers is almost sure to show more steadfastness and conservatism than a people made up of traders and handicrafts-men. This characteristic bent of the Romans toward farming accounts in part also for the permanency of their subsequent conquests. Having conquered a people, they invariably took from them a part of their land, settled their colonists on the newly acquired fields, and made the territory Roman in the strictest sense of the word. Membership in the military organization of the regal period, as we shall presently see, was practically restricted to freeholders, so that before the close of the period clan ownership of arable land must have given place to individual ownership. There were probably few slaves, and the small farms were tilled by the *paterfamilias* and his sons. Larger properties were held by the knights, as those who served as horsemen in the army were called, who probably granted small holdings to the landless on condition of receiving a share of the produce. In this way a relation of dependence, or clientship as it was called, grew up.

48. State-ownership of Pasture-lands. The pasture-lands were not acquired by individuals when the arable land was divided, but passed over from the clan to the state. Upon these lands citizens, on the payment of a small sum, were allowed to pasture their cattle. One can readily see that the rich man, through the large political influence which his wealth gave him, might crowd the poor man out of this land and out of the rest of the state land, and it is not surprising that the control of state land was one of the earliest questions at issue between the rich and the poor.

49. The Industrial Arts and Trade. The natural bent of the Romans for agriculture and the premium put on the ownership of land by the military system of the early period tended to depress the industrial arts, but in the city itself such crafts as those of the coppersmith, goldsmith, carpenter, and potter, flourished. The existence of the goldsmith's art indicates that some trade was carried on, for no gold is found within the limits of Latium, but the trade must have been insignificant, since the Romans had no coined money for several centuries, but depended upon crude copper and cattle, as media of exchange.

50. The King. The establishment of a monarchy meant the transfer of the supreme power from the elders of the clans to the king, who was the chief executive, the chief priest, and the judge of the people. He alone could levy and organize troops, choose leaders and conduct a campaign. The property of the state was under his control and he was the representative of the community in its relations with the gods, as well as in its dealings with other communities.

51. His Attendants, Insignia, and Assistants. He was attended by twelve lictors, who bore over the left shoulder a bundle of rods, called the *fasces*, within which was an axe to typify the king's power to inflict corporal punishment or to impose the death penalty. In time of war he wore the *trabea*, a purple cloak, in time of peace a purple *toga*. He was assisted by quaestors, or detective officers, by the *duumviri perduellionis*, or board of two men who investigated charges of treason, and by a tribune who commanded the cavalry.

52. The Senate. Custom made it incumbent on the king to seek the advice of the senate in important matters, but it was left for him to decide whether to bring a particular subject before it or not, and he was free to adopt or reject its advice, as he saw fit. The *patres*, or members of the senate, were chosen by the king, but, in accordance with principles handed down by tradition, the size of its membership increased as the community grew, until the number three hundred was fixed as a maximum.

53. Patricians, Plebeians, and Clients. The *patres* were chosen from the rich, prominent families, and membership in the senate became the hereditary privilege of the families thus distinguished. It is probably for this reason that those who belonged to these families were called patricians. The rest of the freemen in the city constituted the *plebs* or multitude, as the word means. The great majority of those who lived outside the city were tenants and farm laborers, who lacked the full rights of

freemen, but gained certain privileges by attaching themselves
as clients to the head of a prominent family. Their protector
was known as a *patronus*, who represented them before the law.
In return for protection they followed their patron to war, and
gave him such a part of the return from the land which they
held, or from the profits of their labor, if they were artisans, as
custom determined.

54. The Curia. The unit in the division of the people for
political purposes was the *curia*, whose organization resembled
that of the family in that it had common religious rites, common
festivals, and a common hearth. The *curia* was originally
composed of those who dwelt within a certain area, *i. e.*, it was
a local subdivision, but since kinsmen settled near one another,
both the element of kinship and of neighborhood entered into
its organization. There were ten *curiae* in each one of the great
tribes—the Ramnes, Tities, and Luceres—into which the population was divided.

55. The Comitia Curiata. These thirty *curiae* constituted
the *populus Romanus Quiritium* and the *comitia curiata*, the
organization based on them, was the only popular assembly of a
political or semi-political character during the regal period.
This body met to consider the advisability of declaring war, to
approve or disapprove of a newly elected king, and to take up
certain other general matters, especially those affecting the
clans. The place of meeting was the Comitium, at the corner
of the Forum. The action of the assembly was not determined
by a majority vote of all the people, but each *curia* had one vote;
a majority of the members of a *curia* determined the vote of a
curia, and a majority of the *curiae* settled the vote of the whole
assembly.

56. The Servian Reorganization of the Army. The early
army was also based on the *curia*, but under the Servian reorganization, which is so called because tradition attributes it to
Servius Tullius, freemen were divided into classes on the basis of
the land which they held, and were required to furnish horses or
a more or less expensive equipment of armor according to their

wealth. Each class was divided into a certain number of groups of men, and the entire army contained one hundred and ninety-three of these groups, or centuries, as they were called.

57. Summary of Events During the Regal Period. The city of Rome, first established on the Palatine, soon came to occupy the Seven Hills. The stories of the seven kings are legendary. Trustworthy information is very scanty. The city, which was made up of little villages of wooden houses on the tops of the hills, was much improved by the Tarquins. It was governed by a king, who sought advice from the senate and on very important matters from the people.

CHAPTER IV

THE CONQUEST OF ITALY

(509 – 264 B. C.)

How Rome conquered the Italians and Etruscans of Central Italy, the Greeks of Southern Italy, and thus made herself mistress of the whole peninsula.

58. Early Republican History. The traditional story of the kings is in large measure a transparent fiction. The history of Rome after the downfall of the monarchy seems possible and credible, but we should be mistaken in accepting the early part of it as trustworthy. The Romans had no written records for the period, and consequently we cannot rely upon the accounts which Latin writers give us of the causes of the early wars, nor can we accept their stories of the careers of great generals abroad and of distinguished political leaders at home, but we can understand how Rome succeeded in subduing the peoples about her; we can follow her step by step in her career of conquest, and reasoning back from the political and social institutions of the historical period, we can trace in outline at least the internal history also of the first two centuries after the expulsion of the kings.

59. Rome's Loss of Prestige. When Tarquin the Proud had been driven out, the people chose two magistrates, to be elected annually, called consuls, to rule over them. This change brought with it a great loss of prestige and power abroad. A single ruler, whose reign extended over a long period of years, could conduct the military operations of the state and direct its policy more effectively and more consistently than could two magistrates chosen for a year only.

60. Relations with Southern Etruria. Whether the story that the Tarquins came from Etruria really points to the control of Rome by Etruria, as some writers think, we shall probably never know. However that may have been, their expulsion involved Rome in a series of wars with the cities of southern Etruria, which raged at intervals for a century, and were brought to an end only by the capture and complete destruction of Veii, Rome's most persistent Etruscan enemy, in 396 B. C. It was in one of these wars that Horatius and his two comrades are said to have held the bridge over the Tiber against the entire host of the enemy.

61. The Latin League. But the Romans were not obliged to face their enemies single-handed. The language, religion, form of government, as well as the enemies, which the Romans and the Latins had in common, led to an alliance between the Romans and their kinsmen. The treaty with the Latins was primarily for defense, but probably also guaranteed to the citizens of one community special privileges in their dealings with those of another. Under it Rome was allowed to enter into an alliance with the league as a unit, and not with the separate Latin towns. Accordingly the spoils and conquered territory were divided equally between her and the league, and in alternate years the commanding general was a Roman. In 486, according to Livy and Dionysius, the alliance was strengthened by the adhesion of the Hernici, a people living in the valley of the Trerus. Both these treaties were most fortunate for the Romans. Between Rome and the Aequians and Volscians, lay the towns of the Latin league, and upon these towns fell the task of defending the plain against the forays of the men of the mountains. She could rest in comparative safety behind this bulwark. She might look forward, in fact, to the time when her allies, weakened by constant attacks, would be willing or could be forced, to accept her sovereignty. The land of the Hernici lay between the territories of the Aequians and Volscians. It prevented a union of the forces of the two communities, and furnished a convenient base of operations in an attack upon either people. For these reasons the support of the Hernici was of great value to the other two members of the league.

62. The Wars of the Early Republic. In spite of the protection which her allies gave her, for sixty years after the establishment of the republic, Rome fought for her life. The people of Veii harried her territory on the north, the Volscians swept the coast in their forays, and the raids of the Aequians brought them not infrequently to the very gates of the city. The mountaineers were no match for the allies in pitched battle, but

THE WARS WITH THE ETRUSCANS, AEQUIANS, VOLSCIANS, AND SAMNITES

they rarely staked their fortunes on such a contest. The Aequians, descending to the plains like a whirlwind, seized their booty and were back in their mountain fastnesses before the troops of the allies could intercept them, and once in their native hills it was dangerous to follow them. It would hardly be profitable for us to follow out in detail the stubborn struggle with these two peoples. Their power was broken in 425, and by the middle of the next century Rome had established colonies at Satricum, Setia, Antium, and Tarracina, and against the Volscians had made good her claim to the plain as far south as the last mentioned town. The territory of the Aequians was annexed in 304, and we hear no more of them as an independent people.

63. Why the Romans Succeeded. The comparative success, which, as we have noticed, attended the Roman armies from the middle of the fifth century on, may have been due partly to the improvement of conditions at home, which had brought about a better feeling between the patricians and the plebeians, and made these two elements of the population join more harmoniously in the common defense. It may be traced in part also to the fact that the enemies of Rome were being attacked by foes behind them. The Aequians and Volscians were weakened by the constant assaults of the fierce tribes beyond them, and the strength which they might otherwise have used against the Romans was exhausted in repelling the attacks of the enemy in their rear. The Etruscans, whose power Rome would have

AN ANCIENT INSCRIBED STONE LATELY
FOUND IN THE FORUM

had still greater reason to dread, and whose hostility was evident in the early part of the fifth century, had suffered serious reverses both on sea and land. Except for the enmity of Veii, Rome had little to fear from them. The Syracusans inflicted a disastrous defeat upon them in a naval battle off Cumæ in 474, and ravaged the coast of Etruria; the Samnites captured Capua in 423 and robbed them of their territory in Campania, and throughout this century the Etruscans were engaged in a fierce struggle with the Celts, or the Gauls as the Romans called them, on their northern frontier.

64. The Invasion of the Gauls, 387-382 B. C. These people came into northern Italy, perhaps from the valley of the

Danube, and swept everything before them. They entered Italy in 387, drove back the Ligurians, robbed the Umbrians of their territory on the Adriatic, and seized the possessions of the Etruscans on the banks of the Po. In 382 the Senones, a branch of the Celtic people, having crossed the Apennines, laid siege to Clusium in Etruria. A Roman embassy at Clusium, it is said, aided the people of the town, and so angered the Celts that they advanced upon Rome. The Roman army which met them on the banks of the Allia a few miles from Rome was annihilated. The city was panic-stricken. The fire of the Vestals and the utensils sacred to the gods were carried to Caere; some of the citizens fled to the neighboring towns, and others took refuge in the citadel. For seven months, we are told, the barbarians laid siege to the citadel, but without success, although one night, according to a fanciful popular tale, they had nearly succeeded in scaling the heights and entering the fortress when its Roman defendants were roused by the cackling of the sacred geese of Juno, and the Capitol was saved.

65. Withdrawal of the Gauls in 382 B. C. Wearied by the long siege, or alarmed by the report that their possessions in the North were threatened by the Veneti, they accepted a ransom of one thousand pounds of gold, or about $225,000, as the price of their withdrawal and returned to the North, making no effort to hold permanently what they had overrun in central Italy. Twice in subsequent years the raids of the Celts brought them within striking distance of Rome, viz., in 360 and 348. On the first occasion the Romans did not venture to give them battle; in 348, however, the Romans and their allies met them boldly, and the Celts retreated in disorder.

66. Events Following the Gallic Invasion. Strange as it may seem, the invasion of the Celts was probably of permanent advantage to Rome. The losses which Etruria suffered at their hands, following closely, as these disasters did, on the fall of Veii, made it easy for Rome to extend her control over southern Etruria. Four new tribes were established in the territory of Veii, Capena, and Falerii, and within twenty years after the withdrawal of the Celts, Latin colonies were founded at Sutrium and Nepete on the borders of the Ciminian forest in Etruria. About the same time Latin colonies were established in Volscian territory at Satricum and Setia, and before the middle of the century Roman citizens had been sent into this section and two new tribes organized there. The rapid growth of Rome's power, or the change which her attitude probably underwent in consequence of it, stirred up wars with some of her Latin allies, but peace was restored in the year 358, although probably the position of Rome's allies was less favorable than it had been before.

67. Growth of the Samnites. While the Romans were pushing their boundaries north into Etruria and south into the Volscian territory, another people of central Italy was following a career of conquest equally brilliant if less permanent in its character. We have already had occasion to notice that the Samnites, issuing from their mountain fastnesses, overran and occupied the territory of Campania and Lucania. In the latter half of the fourth century the Etruscan city of Capua, and the Greek city of Cumæ fell before them. The facility with which the conquerors accepted the civilization of the conquered is incredible. In their native hills they had supported themselves by rearing flocks and herds, and had lived the simple life of the mountaineer. On the fertile plains of Campania they collected in cities and adopted the luxurious mode of living of their Greek neighbors. They seemed to retain little of their past, except the Oscan language and the loose form of government which was characteristic of the Samnites. The tie of blood which bound them to their kinsmen in the hills was soon forgotten, or at least disregarded, by the latter, who plundered and pillaged them as they had plundered and pillaged the Greeks and Etruscans before them.

68. Their Relations with the Romans. At this point the Romans enter the story. Harried by the Samnites of the hills, the people of Campania, according to tradition, appealed to Rome for aid. The Romans came to their help, made an alliance with them, declared war against the Samnites in 343, and after a successful campaign of two years, forced them to retire from the lowlands. This is the story of the first Samnite war, as Roman historians tell it. The truth of the matter probably is that Rome, instead of supporting the Campanians in resisting the encroachments of the Samnites, joined with Samnium in a peaceful division of certain territory belonging to their weaker neighbors.

69. End of the Latin League, 338 B. C. The ambitious spirit of expansion which Rome showed in dealing with smaller states, supported as she was now by Samnium, suggests also a sufficient explanation of the desperate struggle which the Latin communities at once made to break her power. The explanation which has been given above of Rome's policy in Campania, accounts for the fact also that the Campanians allied themselves with the Latins against Rome, which they would scarcely have done had Rome so lately and so generously lent them her aid, as Roman tradition says she did. The war lasted for two years, from 340 to 338. It was brought to an end by the battle of Sinuessa, where the Latins and their allies suffered a disastrous defeat. With this war the Latin League came to an end. Rome made a separate treaty with each one of the Latin communities, with the express purpose of preventing confederations between them in the future, and they lost many of the rights which they had enjoyed. The terms adopted varied from state to state, but almost all the members of the old league were apparently restricted in their right to trade with one another. This continued to be the position of these towns down to the first century B. C., when they acquired Roman citizenship.

70. Military Reforms. The long wars which the Romans were now carrying on had led to many improvements in the equipment and organization of the army. These reforms are attributed to the dictator Camillus who brought the long siege of Veii to a successful termination. In the early days the Roman soldier had been called out for short summer campaigns only, and gave his services to the government without charge. Now that his term of service extended through the year, and sometimes

through several years, it became necessary for the state to pay
him. The money which was paid him made it possible for any
Roman, no matter how poor he might be, to provide his own
equipment, and it also allowed a reorganization of the army on
a new basis. Under the old system, when the individual provided his own armor, only the rich men could afford to buy a
full equipment. They, therefore, were placed in the front ranks,
while the light-armed poor men fought in the rear. Now that
the payment of the troops made it possible for each soldier to
provide himself with the sort of armor which he could use to the
best advantage, length of service was made the basis of classifi-
cation, the younger men being placed in the front ranks, and
the veterans in the rear, each line with its characteristic and
appropriate weapons. The new system promoted the efficiency
of the army, because under it each soldier performed the particular service for which his natural ability and his experience best
qualified him. The extension of the term of service led also to
a better training of the individual soldier, and to better discipline in the army as a whole. The change carries us a long
way forward from the old militia system toward that of a regular
army, and the Roman who left his home for a long term of service in Etruria or Campania stands midway in the line of development between the citizen of the early days who, to defend
his city from attack, left his fields after the sowing and returned
before the harvest, and the professional soldier of the late republic who gave his life to the pursuit of arms.

71. Second Samnite War, 326 - 304 B.C. The conclusion
of the war with the Latins left the Romans free to carry out their
ambitious designs in Campanian and Volscian territory. Samnium had fixed her eyes on the same districts, and a conflict
between the two peoples broke out. No trustworthy account
of the early years of the war has come down to us. The narrative
is hopelessly altered to suit Roman national pride, but even the
patriotic chronicler could not gloss over the overwhelming disaster which the Roman cause suffered at the Caudine Forks in
321. Decoyed into an ambush in a narrow defile in the Apen-

nines, the entire army was forced to surrender, and the Romans were obliged to give up the territory which they had captured. But in 314 fortune returned to Rome. The Samnites in Campania were driven back, the cities which had rebelled returned to their alliance with Rome, and a colony was established at Interamna on the Liris to protect the great military road which was built down to Capua in 312. The following year the Romans carried on their military operations in Apulia, and with success, but they were recalled in 310 by danger in a new quarter. This time it was the Etruscans, who were besieging the Colony of Sutrium, but the brilliant campaign of the consul Quintus Fabius in Etruria relieved Sutrium and forced the Etruscans to give up their warlike designs. For five years more the war dragged on, but the Samnites lost ground steadily, and in 304 were forced to sue for peace.

72. Some Reasons for the Success of the Romans. In numbers, courage, and skill in fighting, the Romans and Samnites had been well matched. With the Romans, however, lay the advantage which a united people always has in fighting a confederation of independent states. Both peoples showed remarkable powers of endurance, but the Romans surpassed their foes in the persistence with which they held what they had acquired, and in the care and wisdom which they displayed in making their acquisitions secure by building roads and founding colonies in the newly acquired territory. The Romans showed more diplomatic skill also than their opponents, for they succeeded in winning the support or in securing the neutrality of the people of Apulia and Lucania, as well as of some of the mountain tribes in central Italy. Perhaps the dread which the smaller states had of the Celts and Etruscans, and the feeling which they cherished that Rome could protect them against the encroachments of these peoples of the North better than Samnium could, made them incline to her side.

73. Some Results of the War. The war with Samnium served to knit the Romans and Latins together. The bitterness which the Latins must have felt after their defeat and loss of prestige in 338 was forgotten in the long struggle in which they fought side by side with the Romans, as men of a common stock, and representing the civilization of the plain against an alien people of the mountains.

74. Third Samnite War, 298 - 290 B. C. The peace with the Samnites proved to be only a suspension of hostilities, for when tidings reached them that the Celts were again moving southward, they joined the invaders against their old enemies at Rome, but the allies were overwhelmed at the battle of Sentinum in 295. Five years later Samnium was forced to sue for peace, and Roman interests in the north were protected against the Celts by the founding of a Roman colony in their country at Sena Gallica on the Adriatic.

75. The New Conquests are made Permanent. The conquest of central Italy was now complete. On the east side of the peninsula from Sena Gallica in the territory of the Senones to the Roman outposts at Venusia and Canusium in Apulia, and on the west coast from Sutrium to Cumæ, the overlordship of Rome was recognized. The newly acquired territory was secured by the establishment of strong fortresses, and the first step was taken toward the introduction of Roman ideas and Roman institutions by sending out Roman and Latin colonists. In the century which comes to an end with the battle of Sentinum fifteen or twenty colonies were established by the home government. Strategic considerations determined their location, and the choice was made with great wisdom. Fregellae and Interamna commanded the passage of the Liris, and kept a line of communication open to Capua along the great highway which Appius Claudius constructed in 312; Alba Fucens and Carsioli held the Aequians in subjection, and guarded the new military road, later known as the Valerian road, which had been built through their country; Narnia in southern Umbria protected the valley of the Tiber and the Flaminian Road, and on the borders of the Ciminian forest stood Sutrium and Nepete, "the gates of Etruria." The establishment of strong military outposts of twenty-five hundred and twenty thousand colonists at

Luceria and Venusia respectively brought the Romans within the Greek sphere of influence, and is the first step toward the conquest of Magna Græcia.

76. Samnium Encircled by Fortresses and Roads. These fortresses and military roads shut Samnium in upon all sides, and took from her the hope of joining her forces to those of any other people in central Italy. Rome was in this respect carrying out in military matters the same policy of isolating her rivals which she had adopted for political reasons in dealing with the members of the Latin league. Alba Fucens and Carsioli, and the Valerian and Flaminian roads, would prevent the Samnites from again entering Etruria; Saticula and the frontier fortresses to the south would protect Campania, and the strong outposts in Apulia hemmed Samnium in to the southeast.

77. Maritime Colonies and Foreign Trade. The maritime colonies which were founded during the century under consideration are of peculiar interest. The earliest of these was Antium, which was established in 338. Then follow the colony on the island of Pontia in 313, Minturnæ and Sinuessa in 296, Hatria in 289, Sena Gallica and Castrum Novum in 283. This new development of the national life points to the existence of a seagoing trade, or foreshadows its early growth. A commercial treaty which was made with Carthage in 348, and renewed in 306, is also an indication that foreign trade was developing, and that Roman interests were extending beyond the limits of Italy.

78. The Roman Fleet. The establishment of these towns on the coast, and the simultaneous appointment (311 B. C.) for the first time of naval officers, bearing the title of *duoviri navales*, make it reasonably certain also that within this period fall the beginnings of an organized fleet of war vessels, and probably the operations of the Roman forces on land were supplemented, now and then, by piratical enterprises along the coast. The establishment of garrisons at Hatria, Sena Gallica, and Castrum Novum on the Adriatic, which would furnish excellent naval stations in the future, is especially significant in this connection.

79. The Lucanians and the Greek Coast Towns. It was the possession of a fleet and the opening of naval stations on the Adriatic, as we shall presently see, which first brought the Romans into conflict with the Greeks of southern Italy, and led to the conquest of that part of the peninsula. For many years the Lucanians, Bruttians, and Apulians had been engaged in intermittent warfare with the thriving Greek towns along their coasts. Many of these towns had fallen before their attacks, and the Lucanians apparently made it a part of the bargain, under which they allied themselves with Rome during the Samnite wars, that they should be given a free hand in dealing with those which still maintained their independence. Thurii and Tarentum were among the coast cities which still held out. Accordingly, no sooner was the great struggle in central Italy at an end than the Lucanians and Bruttians renewed their attacks on the Greek cities by laying siege to Thurii.

80. The Incident at Thurii, 285 - 282 B.C. The people of this town applied to Rome for help, and the Romans, forgetting their compact with the Lucanians, or anxious to get a foothold in southern Italy, forbade their allies to carry out their hostile designs. This was in 285, but the Romans were prevented from enforcing their prohibition at once by the uprising of the Celts in northern Italy. The settlement of affairs in that quarter left Rome free to take a hand in matters in the South. In 282 the consul Gaius Fabricius Luscinus raised the siege of Thurii, and established a Roman garrison there, as well as at Croton, Locri, and Rhegium.

81. The Quarrel with Tarentum. At this point Tarentum was drawn into the quarrel. She must have watched with hatred and jealousy the gradual approach of Roman power along the coast, and when a Roman fleet of ten vessels on its way from the west coast put into the harbor of Tarentum, the passion of the people burst into flame. The action of the Roman admiral in entering the port was in violation of an old treaty between Rome and Tarentum under which Roman vessels were not to sail beyond the Lacinian promontory. The people were in their theatre, overlooking the harbor, when the Roman fleet appeared. In a transport of fury they rushed to the harbor, put out in their galleys, sunk or captured several of the vessels, and sold or put to death the members of the crews. Then they sent an expedition to Thurii which expelled the Roman garrison, and punished her citizens for soliciting aid from Rome.

82. Pyrrhus Aids Tarentum. In spite of these outrages the Romans adopted a very temperate course, but the people of Tarentum were bent upon war, and sent for aid across the Adriatic to Pyrrhus, the king of Epirus, whose long experience in the field and whose knowledge of the military art made him one of the greatest leaders of his time.

83. His Ambitious Designs. The ambition and the abilities of such a man could not be satisfied in the little kingdom of Epirus. Fortunately for him, at the very moment when his dream of building up a great power in Greece had been rudely shattered, came the call for aid from Tarentum. He responded, not with the expectation of merely driving back the rude enemies of the Italian Greeks, but in the hope of making himself master of southern Italy and of Sicily, and of building up an empire in the West, as Alexander had done in the East. Since Sicily was included within the scope of his plan, his ambitious designs threatened both the great powers of the West—Carthage as well as Rome. In fact, Carthage, in view of her Sicilian holdings, was more intimately concerned than Rome, whose possessions in southern Italy were not yet important.

84. His Campaign against the Romans, 280-275 B. C. Pyrrhus landed in Italy in the year 280 with some twenty thousand foot soldiers and three thousand cavalrymen. The Roman legions could not make a stand against the Thessalian cavalry and the elephants which the king had brought with him. They were routed at Heraclea and in the following year at Asculum. After the battle of Asculum negotiations were opened with Pyrrhus. Cineas, the king's minister, was sent to Rome to arrange the terms of the treaty, but the senate refused to make peace so long as Pyrrhus was on Italian soil. Tradition attrib-

utes its refusal to the indomitable spirit and the eloquence of
the blind old senator Appius Claudius, who had himself carried
to the senate-house to oppose the negotiations, but probably
the appearance in the harbor of Ostia of a Carthaginian fleet

THE WAR WITH PYRRHUS

offering aid had more effect than even the speech of Appius.
At all events the Romans rejected the proffers of peace. The
complete victory of the Romans in 275 proved the wisdom of
their decision, and Pyrrhus was forced to withdraw from Italy
and give up forever his dreams of a Western Empire.

85. The New Acquisitions of Territory. Tarentum, Rhegium, and the other Greek cities surrendered one after another,
and were made allies of Rome; colonies were planted at Pæstum,
Beneventum, and Æsernia, and the Adriatic coast-line was
strengthened by outposts at Ariminum and Firmum; and, thanks
to the party strife which broke out in Volsinii soon after the withdrawal of Pyrrhus, and to the appeal which one faction made to
the Romans for help against its opponent, this stronghold and

sacred centre of the Etruscan league fell into the hands of the Romans, and Rome was now mistress of all Italy as far north as the Arnus.

86. Relations of the Italian Communities to Rome. New territory had been brought under the control of Rome in a variety of ways—by the incorporation of new communities into the state, by colonization, by the annexation of conquered lands, and by the formation of alliances in which a certain degree of subordination to Rome was recognized. In dealing with the territory acquired in these different ways it was a part of Rome's policy to make differences in the rights and privileges granted to neighboring communities, in order that, not being subject to the same limitations, and so not having the same grievances, they might not have a common basis for joint action against her. In this way she hoped to prevent conspiracies against her power. Furthermore, little attempt was made to introduce the Roman system into local administrative affairs, but communities were allowed to retain in large measure their own local executive officers and courts. For these reasons Italian communities in their internal organization had little in common.

87. All Inferior to the Capital. Notwithstanding this diversity, all the communities outside of Rome had one common characteristic—a position inferior to that of Rome. Even the inhabitants of those towns to which the full right of Roman citizenship was granted, were at a disadvantage, when compared with people living in the capital. To exercise their political rights they had to go to Rome, for the Romans had no representative system, and yet they were so far away that it was rarely possible for them to go. They, as well as the people of other Italian communities which did not have the full rights of citizenship, followed the leadership of Rome. Rome alone had the right to declare war against foreign nations, and to make peace with them, and Roman coins were used throughout the peninsula.

88. Classes of Citizens. All the peoples of Italy fell into two classes, *cives*, or citizens, and *socii*, or allies. Citizens were of two sorts, those who had both private and political rights, and those who had private but lacked political rights. The latter were called *cives sine suffragio*. Private rights included the right to hold and exchange property and be protected in its possession, the right of appealing to the people in case a magistrate imposed certain severe penalties, and the right of contracting a marriage valid under Roman law. Those who had both private and political rights had the privileges just mentioned, and could also vote for magistrates at Rome, and were eligible to office in the Capital.

89. Additions to the Citizen Body. In the early period while Rome was struggling with states which were her rivals in point of strength and size, she freely admitted certain communities to the rights of citizenship. In fact, she forced certain conquered peoples to accept these rights. It has been calculated that at the close of the war with Pyrrhus the district occupied by Roman citizens "extended northward as far as the neighborhood of Caere, eastward to the Apennines, and southward as far as, or beyond, Formiæ." Within these limits there were, to be sure, certain towns which did not have these rights, and beyond them were a few cities to which they had been given, but, speaking with sufficient exactness, the district indicated above is the territory within whose limits the inhabitants enjoyed the privileges of Roman citizens. Besides incorporating communities Rome also sent out colonies of Roman citizens. Almost all of these settlements were located on the coast.

90. Cives Sine Suffragio. Communities with private rights only were subject to all the burdens of state, such as furnishing troops and paying taxes in time of war. Their local governments varied in independence according to the privileges allowed them by Rome. Caere was forced to accept citizenship without political rights in 351, and Capua and some other towns were put in the same category later. The total number of citizens, including both those who had full rights and those who had private rights only, has been estimated at two hundred and eighty thousand for the period immediately after the conquest of Italy.

91. The Latins and Other Allies. Of the allies, or the *socii* as the Romans called them, the Latins had the most advantageous position. These were not citizens of the Latin towns which in early days had made up the Latin league, for the members of that organization had either been destroyed or incorporated directly into the Roman state, but they were colonists living in towns founded in newly acquired territory to whom Rome gave private rights, an independent local government, and the privilege of voting at Rome under certain circumstances. This was the status of almost all the colonies planted in the interior. The other allies had their own courts and local magistrates, as the Latins had, but the citizens of these communities could not vote at Rome. The one duty which all the allies had to perform was to furnish Rome with their prescribed quota of troops, which was fixed from year to year by the senate. The relations which these states bore to Rome were established by charters or treaties.

92. Preparations for Conquest beyond the Sea. A new turn was given to the development of the Roman state by the conquest of the Greek coast towns in southern Italy and by the establishment of maritime colonies on both the east and the west coasts of Italy. In the earlier period the Romans had been so absorbed by their struggles on the mainland that they had been able to give little attention to the development of a navy, and their maritime interests had suffered in consequence. A treaty with Carthage which limited their right to trade in the Mediterranean, and the treaty with Tarentum which forbade their ships to sail beyond the Lacinian promontory, furnish proof of this fact. But the control of all the important harbors in Italy, and the power which the Romans now had to call upon the Greek towns for requisitions in ships gave promise of the development of a strong navy and a merchant marine, and indicated that Rome would soon be in a position to gratify beyond the sea that appetite for conquest which successes in Italy had developed. The troops were now paid, and had become accustomed to the long periods of service which wars in foreign lands require, and

Roman commanding officers had acquired the ability to conduct serious campaigns, and to control large bodies of men.

93. The Proconsulship Established, 327 B. C. The establishment of the proconsulship, like the building up of sea power and the development of a veteran army, helped also to put the Romans in a position to carry on foreign wars with success. The consul who commanded the army, held office for a year only, and at the end of the year became a private citizen again. If a nation is carrying on a long war at a distance from home, it cannot imperil its success by a frequent change of commanding officers. This the Romans felt in 327, when the term of office of the consul, Publilius Philo, their successful general, came to an end just at the outbreak of the second Samnite war. To meet the emergency he was authorized to remain in charge of his army *pro consule, i. e.,* with the power of a consul, until the campaign was finished. The innovation was a dangerous device from a political point of view, for such an extension of the term of a general's command, necessary as it was in long wars of conquest, established a dangerous precedent, and the frequent adoption of the device accustomed the Romans to the protracted exercise of supreme power by an individual, and thus prepared the way for the empire.

94. Summary Account of the Conquest of Italy, 509 - 264 B. C. An examination of the history of the early Republic shows us that Rome, aided by the Latin League, carried on a long series of wars with southern Etruria, with the Aequians, Volscians, Gauls, and Samnites, in all of which, thanks to her geographical position, her government, and the character of her people, she was in the end victorious. The successful completion of these wars made central Italy subject to her, while the war with Pyrrhus led to the conquest of southern Italy, so that at last the whole peninsula was brought under her control

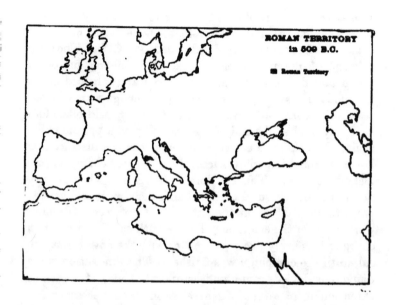

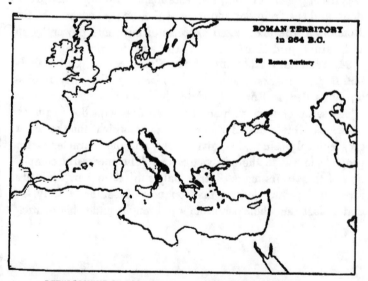

DEVELOPMENT OF ROMAN TERRITORY FROM 509 TO 264 B. C.

CHAPTER V

THE SUCCESSFUL STRUGGLES OF THE PLEBEIANS

(509 – 264 B. C.)

How the plebeians won their rights—How the nobility rose into power—How an advance in civilisation followed the conquest of Southern Italy.

95. The Consul. The most important result of the revolution of 509 consisted in the changes which the chief magistracy underwent. In place of a single magistrate, the king, who was selected by the senate, and held office for life, two chief executives, called consuls, were chosen each year by the whole body of citizens. The new system differed in three essential points from the old one. It involved a change in the number of magistrates, in their term of office, and in the method of choice. The change in the method of choice was of small importance at first, since the popular assembly, in which the consul was chosen, was controlled by the patricians, just as was the senate which had chosen the king. But the other two points of difference were far-reaching. A chief executive who holds office for a limited period only, as the consul did, can be held accountable for his conduct at the close of his term of office. This, of course, had been impossible in the case of the king. Furthermore, there were two executive officers henceforth, and to each of them was given the right to prevent his colleague from taking any action of which he disapproved; and this veto power, as the Romans called it, would naturally prevent a magistrate from becoming tyrannical. It is surprising that this dual system of government was workable. The political theorist would have been justified in saying that a scheme under which one magistrate could block the action of the other and stop the wheels of government at will could never last. That it did serve the purposes of the Romans admirably for centuries is one of the many proofs which history offers of the eminently practical character of the Romans and their skill in avoiding difficulties. The consuls—and a similar statement may be made of colleagues in the other official boards established later—avoided conflicts by alternating in the active exercise of their authority or by assigning specific duties on the basis of seniority or by lot. Thus, for instance, one consul took precedence over his colleague in the first month, and then relinquished his priority during the second month, or one consul commanded the army one day and his colleague the next day.

96. The Dictator. Now and then, however, in moments of peril the Romans found it desirable to place the fortunes of the state in the hands of a single magistrate, unhampered by a colleague. Not long after the establishment of the consulship such an emergency arose, the consuls chose a dictator to meet it, and subordinated themselves to him until the danger was passed. At intervals during the first three centuries of republican rule, especially when the consuls seemed unable to cope with wars abroad or insurrections at home, such an official was appointed, and all the powers of the state were placed in his hands.

MONUMENT SHOWING CURULE CHAIR AND FASCES

97. The Consul's Insignia and Attendants. The consul inherited all the powers of the king except the king's religious functions, which were delegated to priests. His dignity was indicated to the eye by the purple-bordered toga praetexta, which he wore in the city, by a short red cloak, which he used when abroad, and by the curule chair upon which he sat on formal occasions.

98. The Centuriate Organization. We have already had occasion to notice that the new chief magistrate was chosen not by the senate but by the people. His most important duty would consist in leading the army, and it was very natural that he should be chosen by the fighting men of the community assembled in centuries. The organization became, therefore, in the matter of choosing the consul, a political body. It is known in history as the centuriate comitia. The fact that, from this time on, appeals in a case of life and death were referred to it contributed also to its importance. This assembly was controlled by the rich, because they made up a majority of the centuries, and, since most of the rich landholders were probably patricians, the body had a pronounced aristocratic character also.

99. The Plebeians Oppressed. The king had held his position for life. Class prejudice, therefore, would not count for much in his case, but the consul, who was chosen from the ranks of the patricians, held office for a year only, and then returned to their number. Consequently his action must have been largely influenced by prejudice in favor of the patricians. We are not surprised, therefore, that the plebeians found their position intolerable under the new chief magistrates.

100. The Tribunate Established, 493 B.C. The condition of foreign affairs, however, helped them to wrest from the aristocracy some protection against the patrician consuls. In 494, when Rome was engaged in a fierce struggle with the Aequians and Volscians, the plebeian soldiers refused to march against the enemy, and, taking up their position on a hill a few miles from the city, returned only on condition that they should be allowed to elect five, or possibly two, annual officials, called tribunes, with power to protect them against the tyrannical action of the consuls. In a few years the number was increased to ten. Provision was also made for the election of two new plebeian officials, known as aediles, to assist the tribunes in the performance of their duties.

101. Meaning and Importance of the Office. This solution of the question at issue between the patricians and plebeians seems a strange one. Instead of protecting the plebeians by laws which limited the power of the patrician magistrates, the plebeians are given officials of their own who can step in and prevent a magistrate from arresting or punishing a citizen or from taking any action against him of which the plebeian official disapproves. If the magistrate persists in his course, he can be punished, even with death, while the person of the tribune is inviolable. But the tribune not only protected the individual plebeian, he also became a leader of all the plebeians in the great struggle with the patricians for political equality which begins with the establishment of the tribunate.

102. Three Great Questions. For a period of fifty years this struggle centres successively about three points. These three points were: the improvement of the plebeian organization, the more equitable division of the public land, and the setting down in a written form of the customary law.

103. The Concilium Plebis. The first object was accomplished without serious difficulty. At the outset the tribunes and their assistants, the aediles, had been chosen in a plebeian assembly made up of *curiae,* but in 471 the plebeian assembly was organized by tribes, and all the plebeian landowners were enrolled in it. This body was known as the *concilium plebis.*

104. The Land Question. A reform in the method of partitioning the public land was not brought about so easily as this political change had been. State land was made up of the pasture-ground which had never been assigned to individual owners, and of the territory which was seized in time of war. Newly acquired territory was divided into allotments and given outright to poor citizens, or it was leased, or it was held as common pasture-ground. Now the middle and lower classes complained that the rich and influential patricians got land at a nominal rental, secured control of the best and most accessible property, and pastured too large a number of sheep and cattle on the public domain. Here again the position of the plebeians was worse under the republic than it had been under the monarchy, because under the latter the king controlled the public land, while now the patrician senate and consuls disposed of it. An unfair division of the state land affected not only the pockets of the plebeians but their political standing also. Membership in the classes on which the centuriate organization was based, depended on the ownership of land. Now, if no new land was thrown open to the plebeians, as they increased in number from generation to generation, the average holdings of each of them would decrease, and plebeians would drop into lower classes, or become landless. This state of things led to the agitation which begins in the early part of the fifth century before Christ, and continues down to the end of the republic.

105. The People had no Written Law. Justice was still administered in accordance with the custom of the fathers which was handed down by word of mouth, and known to the patricians only. The plebeian neither knew what his rights were, nor did he know whether or not he secured justice under the law from the patrician magistrate who heard his case. This wrong could be righted only by codifying and publishing the law of the land so that every citizen might know what his rights were and how to secure them.

106. The Decemvirs, 451 – 449 B.C. The first proposition looking to this end is said to have been made by the tribune C. Terentilius Harsa in 462, and in 451 a compromise was arranged between the two parties, to the effect that the consuls and tribunes should both give place to a commission of ten men, who should not only act as chief magistrates, but should be empowered to publish a code of laws binding on the whole community. The commission of the first year drew up ten tables of laws, but left their task unfinished at the end of their term of office.

107. The Commission of the Second Year. To complete their work a new board of ten men was selected. Exactly what happened in the second year cannot be made out, but probably the new commission, which was partly composed of plebeians, and was largely influenced in its action by Appius Claudius, a man of great ability and far-sightedness, tried to incorporate in the tables certain changes which the patricians would not accept, and was driven out of office by them.

108. Secession of the Plebeians, 449 B.C. The plebeians were naturally angry at this unfair action on the part of the patricians, and besides they were probably left without adequate protection, since the tribunate had been suspended or abolished when the decemvirs were chosen. Accordingly they withdrew a second time to the Sacred Mount, as the hill was called whither they had seceded just before the tribunate was established, and exacted, as the price of their return, an acknowledgment of the validity of the last two tables, the restoration of the tribunate, and a promise of further concessions.

109. Character of the Laws of the Twelve Tables. Livy characterizes the twelve tables which the decemvirs prepared as "the source of all public and private law." Strangely enough, to our way of thinking, although they were the outcome of this long struggle between the two orders, they do not form in any sense a great document, like our Anglo-Saxon "Bill of Rights," in which fundamental principles of justice were set down, but they contained simply methods of procedure in bringing a legal action, and a specification of offenses against the law, with their penalties. The primary importance of the incident lies in the fact that henceforth the body of the law was known to all and was the same for all. Although these laws were not of great constitutional importance, and do not in this respect justify Livy's characterization of them, they form the earliest Roman code, the progenitor, so to speak, of that body of law which is perhaps the most valuable legacy left us by Rome.

110. Indicative of the Roman Character. The fragments of the twelve tables which have come down to us, unpolished and awkward as they undoubtedly are, in their directness, simplicity, and practical bearing are characteristic of the genius of the early Romans. They stand at the beginning also of Roman literature, before it came under the controlling influence of the Greeks, for, although the story may be true that an embassy was sent to Greece to examine Greek laws before the Roman code was drawn up, the spirit and form of the twelve tables are without doubt purely Roman.

111. Their Influence upon the Romans. Their influence upon Roman life and character must have been very great. For full three centuries and a half after their enactment, as we can infer from a statement made by Cicero, boys were obliged to learn them by heart. In fact, they probably formed the first schoolbook used by Roman children in learning to read and write, and the quotations from them which appear in the comedies of Plautus show that these laws must have been familiar to the average playgoer.

112. The Valerio-Horatian Laws of 449 B. C. The consuls Valerius and Horatius, who had represented the patricians in their negotiations with the plebeians, carried out faithfully the promises made by the patricians. In 449 they secured the passage of laws establishing the tribunate on a firm basis, and guaranteeing to citizens the right of appealing to the centuriate assembly when they had been condemned to death by a magistrate. A still more important piece of legislation made enactments of the plebeian tribal assembly valid when they had received in advance the approval of the patrician members of the senate. This law changed essentially the character of the plebeian assembly and of the tribunate. Up to this time the assembly of the plebs had done nothing more than to elect tribunes, and perhaps to meet for the discussion of matters of interest to the common people. Henceforth, under the limitation mentioned above, it was a law-making body, and the tribune, its presiding officer, had the right to introduce measures, and became, therefore, an effective leader of the plebeians in their efforts to secure their rights.

113. Why the Plebeians Succeeded. The great constitutional gains which the plebeians made during these first fifty years of the republic bear a close relation to the fact that Rome was harassed throughout this period by the fierce raids of the Etruscans, the Aequians, and the Volscians. The patrician state needed the support of the plebeians, and that could be had only in return for certain political concessions.

114. The Comitia Tributa Established, 447 B.C. The

tribal assembly of which we have just been speaking was made up of plebeians only, but from statements made by Cicero and Livy it seems reasonably certain that in this period a tribal assembly including both patricians and plebeians, and known as the *comitia tributa*, was established. By this assembly, which probably dates from the year 447, the quaestors, who had formerly been appointed by the king or consul, were henceforth elected. In this body one man's vote counted for as much as another's. It was, therefore, a much more democratic organization than the centuriate comitia. For this reason, and on the score of convenience, because it met in the centre of the city, while the centuriate comitia held its meetings in the Campus Martius, it acquired in time great importance as a legislative body, and ultimately in large measure supplanted its rival in making laws.

115. The Canuleian Law of 445 B. C. A great social change with important political results was effected in 445 by the passage of the Canuleian law which removed all legal hindrances to the intermarriage of patricians and plebeians. This enactment aided the plebeian cause and helped to unite the patricians and plebeians into a harmonious community.

116. The Plebeians Aspire to the Consulship. The great majority of the measures whose passage the plebeians had secured since 509 had for their avowed object the protection of the plebeians against the class prejudice of the patrician consul and against unfair treatment at his hands. Hitherto the common people had tried to accomplish their object by indirect methods. Now they felt themselves in a position to make a direct assault on the patrician stronghold by demanding a representative in the consulship. The patricians had always claimed the exclusive right to this office, and made good their claim to it.

117. The Military Tribunate, 445 – 367 B. C. They opposed vigorously, therefore, the proposal which the tribune Canuleius submitted in 445, that the plebeians should be represented in the consulship, but in the following year they granted a compromise by providing that each year the senate should decide whether the chief magistrates were to be consuls or military tribunes with consular powers.   The military tribunate was open to plebeians as well as to patricians, so that by this concession the demands of the plebeians were nominally recognized. It was a nominal and not a real concession, however, because the patricians managed to prevent plebeians from being elected to the office.

118. The Censorship Established, 443 B.C. In their anxiety to concede as little as possible to the plebeians, the patricians, when they allowed the substitution of the consular tribunate for the consulship, detached certain functions from the office of the chief magistrate, and assigned them to the incumbents of a new magistracy. At least this seems to be the natural explanation of the establishment in 443 (or possibly in 435) of the censorship, to which only patricians were eligible. The new office was really needed in carrying on public business in the city, because the consuls were absent so much of the time in conducting military campaigns that they could not properly attend to their civil duties, which were rapidly increasing with the growth of the city. The censor's duties consisted in assessing the property of citizens, and arranging them in tribes, classes, and centuries, and in managing the finances of the state. Later, as we shall see, the duty of revising the lists of senators and knights was entrusted to him. This meant, for instance, that he supervised the collection of the taxes and the expenditure of public money, and determined the class and the century in which a citizen should vote, and we can readily appreciate how important his office was. The censors, two in number, were elected every five years, and held office for a year and a half. New business which came up during the remaining three and a half years of the five year period was performed by the consul.

119. Quaestorship opened to Plebeians, 421 B.C. Although they failed to get all that they had hoped to get from the consular tribunate, the plebeians won an advantage in 421 in gaining admission to the quaestorship, the first permanent magistracy thrown open to them. About the same time the number of quaestors was increased from two to four.

120. The Distress of the Poor. The bitterness of the political struggles between the patricians and the plebeians was aggravated by the development of the land question. We have noticed elsewhere the unfair division of land, and the economic and political hardships which the plebeians suffered from it. The long series of wars with the Gauls, the Aequians, the Volscians, and the people of Veii made the situation worse by keeping them under arms and leaving their farms without tillage.

121. The Licinian Laws of 367 B. C. This was the condition of the plebs which the two tribunes of the year 377, Gaius Licinius Stolo and Lucius Sextius, endeavored to relieve. The fiercest passions were aroused in the struggle which followed, and the patricians fought vigorously to retain their privileges, but in 367 the two plebeian leaders secured the passage of a law covering the various matters in dispute. The contents of this law are somewhat in doubt, but, if we may follow Livy and Appian, it included the following points:

(1) Abandonment of the military tribunate and the restoration of the earlier system of government under which consuls were elected every year, with the provision that one of the two consuls should always be a plebeian;

(2) A provision forbidding an individual to occupy more than five hundred *iugera* of arable land belonging to the state, and to pasture more than one hundred head of cattle and five hundred sheep on the common pasture-land;

(3) An article fixing the proportional number of free laborers and slaves to be employed on any estate;

(4) A clause providing that interest already paid on a debt should be deducted from the principal, and that three years should be allowed for the payment of the rest of the debt;

(5) A provision that the number of priests in charge of the Sibylline books should be increased to ten, and that five of them should be plebeians.

122. Admission of the Plebeians to the Consulship. The first article in these laws which gave the plebeians a consul marks the beginning of the end of the struggle between them

and the patricians.   When the plebeians carried this stronghold
of patrician exclusiveness, the other positions of patrician privilege could not hope to hold out long.   That this victory was
not a nominal one, as had been in some degree the plebeian
success in the case of the consular tribunate, is shown by the fact
that in the year following the passage of these laws one of the
plebeians who proposed them, Lucius Sextius, was elected to
the consulship.

123. Other Articles of the Law.   The second law was a general measure applicable to any time and to any place, whereas the
agrarian bills which had preceded and which followed it applied
to a particular district, and ceased to be of effect when the allot-
ment in that territory had been made.   If the third provision,
which the Greek historian Appian tells us was a part of these
laws, really belongs to this period, its appearance shows us that
even at this early date free laborers were beginning to suffer from
competition with the slaves, who we know were captured and
brought into Italy in such large numbers in the next century.
The fourth article too points to an evil of which we hear a great
deal more in the next century, and it foreshadows a redivision
of the people into the rich and the poor as soon as the plebeians
have secured political equality.   The admission of the plebeians
to the exclusive college of priests which had charge of the Sibylline books indicated the early admission of the plebeians to all
the important priesthoods, to which hitherto patricians alone
had been eligible.

124. The Praetorship and Curule Aedileship, 366 B. C.
In 366 two new offices were established, those of praetor and curule aedile, and certain judicial duties which the consul had performed were transferred to the praetor.   In this way, when the
consulship was thrown open to the plebeians by the Licinian
laws, the patricians reserved for officials of their own order certain magisterial powers, because plebeians were not eligible to
the praetorship.   The curule aedileship also was open only to
members of the favored order, and apparently the establishment

of these two magistracies was part of the bargain on the basis
of which the patricians admitted the plebeians to the consulship. In this case, however, as in that of the censorship, there
was probably also a real need of more officials to attend to
the public business.

**125. Compromise Arranged between the Senate and
the Tribunes.** The tendency of the patricians and plebeians to
work together more harmoniously is shown in the development
of more friendly relations between the tribune and the senate.
The improvement in their relations came about in this way. The
senate might pass a bill, but as soon as the magistrate tried to
apply it to the citizens concerned, the tribune could interpose
his veto and stop all action. When this happened, the working
of the machinery of government would be completely suspended,
and the Romans felt that it would be far better to get the opinion
of the tribunes with reference to a measure before action was
taken on it. With this purpose in mind the tribunes were given
seats in the senate, and were allowed to interpose their objections
formally at any point in the proceedings, and if they objected
to a bill, no attempt was made by the magistrates to carry it out.
Probably in this period too the tribunes acquired the right, which
they exercised freely in later times, of calling meetings of the
senate and laying matters before it for consideration. This
was another step—and a very natural one—toward the amalga-
mation of the two elements in the community.

126. Further Successes of the Plebeians. When the integrity of the patrician system had been successfully assailed at
one point, we are not surprised to find that it soon yielded at others also. In 339 a law was passed providing that one of the two
censors should be a plebeian; in 337 the great plebeian leader
Quintus Publilius Philo was elected to the praetorship, and even
the curule aedileship was thrown open to the plebeians in alternate years. Consequently, before the close of the fourth century,
the plebeians had gained one of the important political rights
for which they were struggling, viz., the right to hold any one of
the magistracies—the consulship, praetorship, censorship, quaes-

torship, and curule aedileship.   A plebeian was even appointed
dictator in 356.   •

127. The New Nobility. By these measures a profound
change was effected in the organization of the ruling class.   The
first result of them, of course, was the actual election of plebeians
to the magistracies.   A second, and perhaps more important,
outcome of this legislation was unexpected.   One would naturally have supposed that, since elevation to a magistracy came
through free election in the popular assemblies, of two plebeian
candidates, the abler man would always be chosen; and this
was probably the way things went at first, but in a short time the
comparatively few plebeian families with ancestors who had
held a curule office and distinguished themselves in the service
of the state, acquired such prestige, that "new men," as those
were called who could point to no ancestral consul or praetor,
had little chance of securing political honors.   With his deeply
rooted respect for the past the Roman preferred for the consulship a man whose father or grandfather had been consul.   He
seemed to feel that political ability descended from one generation to another, and the family name seemed to him a guaran-
tee of competence.   Then, too, those who belonged to this priv-
ileged class exerted themselves vigorously to keep all new aspirants out of it.   In this way a new nobility grew up, composed
of those in whose families there had been curule magistrates, and
the new nobility became hereditary, and was well-nigh as exclusive as the patriciate had been.   The privileges of the new
aristocracy depended, as we see, not on the law, but on the organization of society.   Consequently nothing but a revolution could
take them away.

128. The Nobility Acquires Control of the Senate. A
measure, known as the Ovinian law, and passed toward the
close of the fourth century, made the influence of the new order
still greater and its position still more exalted.   This empowered
the censors to draw up the list of senators, and instructed them
in making it out to give a preference to ex-magistrates.   Consequently, membership in the senate also became practically the

hereditary privilege of the new aristocracy, and the control of both the executive and the legislative branches of the government passed into its hands.

129. The Consul Becomes the Senate's Minister. All of the senators were now men of experience in government. They often had a more intimate knowledge of the technical matters which came before them than their presiding officer, the consul, had. Some of them were ex-consuls, and had filled with distinction the position which he held at the moment. They were bound together by mutual interests in defending one another and in advancing the prestige of the body to which they all belonged. Their *esprit de corps* was not unlike that of our own Senate. In many ways, also, they could thwart the consul's political plans and personal ambition. The result was inevitable. The consul was forced to yield to the senate, and became its minister in executing its wishes, and the senate became the real source of authority in all matters of state.

130. The Publilian and Hortensian Laws. Two important pieces of legislation in the period under discussion remain for consideration—the Publilian law of 339 and the Hortensian law of 287. Taken together they theoretically made the popular assemblies independent of the senate. After 287 the action of the plebeian tribal assembly, and probably of the patricio-plebeian tribal assembly, no longer needed the confirmation of the patrician members of the senate to make it valid, as had been hitherto necessary, and in the case of the centuriate comitia the patrician element in the senate was obliged to approve a bill before the centuries had acted upon it, instead of afterwards. But we must not suppose that these two laws gave the assemblies of the people practical control of legislation, or that the passage of the Hortensian law marked the final triumph of democracy over aristocracy. In point of fact, only a magistrate could bring a bill before one of the popular assemblies, and the senate found means to control the magistrates, as we have already noticed, so that, with rare exceptions, only those measures of which the senate approved were submitted to the assemblies.

131. The Senate Usurps the Power of the Assemblies.
The reasons why the people allowed the senate to rule them are
not far to seek. The citizens who had the right to vote numbered
in this period from two hundred and fifty thousand to three
hundred thousand. Many of them lived at a distance from
Rome. It was obviously impossible in such circumstances, to
call the popular assemblies for the transaction of ordinary public business. Probably the people, too, tacitly recognized the
fact that the members of the senate—ex-magistrates as most
of them now were—were far better qualified than the average
citizen to legislate for a society which was becoming every day
more complex, and for a state which was no longer bounded
by the walls of the city or the frontiers of Latium, but extended
from one end of the peninsula to the other. The superior quali-
fications of the senate must have been especially apparent
during the series of long wars which begin in the middle of the
third century. These wars were for the most part carried on at
a great distance from Rome, and the average Roman could
scarcely form an intelligent opinion in regard to the difficult
military and diplomatic questions at issue. For the good of the
state he was willing to leave such matters to the senate, even
though his doing so involved a failure to exercise the very power
for the possession of which he had so long fought.

132. Summary of the Political Changes, 509 – 264 B.C.
If we stop to ask ourselves what political changes the first two
centuries and a half of the republic have brought about, we shall
find them very radical. The senate, which has lost its exclusively patrician character and has been strengthened by the
infusion of plebeian blood, controls all legislation, and has made
the magistrates its ministers. Administrative affairs are no
longer left to a single college of magistrates, but the original
functions of the consul have been divided between the consulship and several newly created offices, and administration has
been made more efficient thereby, for the praetor, the censor, the
tribune, the plebeian and the curule aedile, and the quaestor now

relieve the consul of many of the duties which had fallen to him
at the outset.   Citizens who own land, meeting in their popular
assemblies, have the unrestricted power of legislating on any
subject whatever.   The common law is published, so that every
man may know it, and no citizen can be condemned to death
without the consent of the centuriate assembly.   The plebeian
has the same right as the patrician to stand for political office,
and is even eligible to those priesthoods which have a political
influence.   Even the freedmen and the landless freemen have
some share in the government.   All these changes are over-
shadowed, however, by the growth of a new nobility, which is
made up of patricians and plebeians, perpetuated from generation to generation by its own efforts and by the conservative
habits of the Roman freeman.

133. Improvement of the Currency.   The economic and
social development of the people from 509 to 264 was as marked
as the political.   The practice of bartering commodities, for
instance, had long been given up, and the use of copper money,
which succeeded that, gave way in 268 to a currency made up
of silver and copper coins.   At the same time a common mone-
tary standard was adopted for the whole peninsula, and the right
to coin money, with one or two unimportant exceptions, was reserved by Rome as her exclusive prerogative.   These changes,
it will be noticed, followed closely on the conclusion of the war
with Pyrrhus and the subjugation of Magna Græcia.   They
point clearly to the development of commercial relations between the different parts of Italy, to the increase of wealth, and
to an intention on the part of Rome of making herself the commercial centre of the peninsula.

134. The Italian Yeomanry.   The Licinian laws, by re-
stricting the amount of arable state land which an individual
could acquire, must have helped to increase the number of small
farmers.   The policy of sending out colonies of needy citizens
to newly acquired territory tended in the same direction.   Upon
the population of Italian yeomen thus developed depended in
large measure the sturdy resistance which Rome made in the next

few generations under the crushing weight of the wars with Carthage.

135. Great Estates and Slaves. The increase of wealth, however, which we have already noticed, threatened the peasant proprietor. The rich acquired great estates in Italy, had them cultivated by slaves, and, carrying on the cultivation of the land on a large scale with cheap labor, could undersell the free owner of a small farm. It was this state of things which the Licinian laws vainly sought to remedy through the provision which limited the number of slaves to be employed on a given estate. The number of slaves and freedmen too in the city was increasing. They absorbed the manual arts, so that there must have been very few free artisans.

136. Improvement of the City. The increase in the wealth and importance of Rome was reflected in the growth and improvement of the city. At the beginning of this period it had been a village; it was now a city. Toward the close of the fourth century the great censor Appius Claudius constructed the Appian Aqueduct, the first of the great aqueducts upon which even modern Rome depends for its generous supply of pure water, and within a half century a new aqueduct, known as the Anio Vetus, was added, which brought the pure water of the river Anio to the city by a conduit whose length, if its windings be counted in, was more than forty miles. Private houses were larger, and were built of better material. Many temples had been constructed, and the city was adorned with monuments and with statues of the gods and of illustrious Romans.

137. The Construction of Roads. The construction of the great system of military and commercial roads begins in this period with the building of the Via Appia from Rome to Capua in 312 B. C. by Appius Claudius. Within a short time this road was extended to Brundisium. Before the close of the next two centuries four other great thoroughfares, and numerous connecting roads, had been constructed in the peninsula. The Via Flaminia, which was begun in 299 B. C., ran almost due north to Ariminum, and under the name of the Via Aemilia was

continued to Placentia.　The Via Cassia passing through central
Italy was built as far as Luna in Cisalpine Gaul about 171 B. C.
The Via Aurelia was the coast road to the same point, and was
prolonged to Genoa in 109 B. C.　The fourth great road, the
Via Popillia, took its name from Popillius, the consul of 132 B. C.
It branched off from the Via Appia at Capua, and ran to Rhegium.　The provinces also were provided with an excellent
system of roads.　So, for instance, in the middle of the second
century B. C., immediately after the acquisition of Macedonia,
a road was built to connect Dyrrachium, the port of entry from

THE APPIAN WAY NEAR ROME, WITH TOMBS

Brundisium, with Thessalonica, and the Via Aurelia, in course
of time, was extended through southern Gaul and along the
eastern coast of Spain to the straits of Gibraltar, with branches
running to all the important towns in the interior.　These roads,
like the Trans-Siberian railway in Russia, first of all served the
purposes of the government in sending communications, supplies,
and troops to points in Italy and the provinces, but in a greater
degree they facilitated trade throughout the empire, and formed

a powerful agency in introducing Roman civilization, in making the empire a unit, and in developing a common life and common institutions throughout the world. Portions of these roads which are still in existence show the care with which they were built. Some of them were constructed of as many as five layers of rubble and thick flat stones, with a top layer of hard paving blocks. Under the empire a regular postal system was instituted along the public roads, inns were built, and relays of horses and vehicles were obtainable.

138. Influence of Magna Græcia upon Rome. That Rome came into contact with the Greek civilization of southern Italy at the moment when her wealth was increasing rapidly had a marked effect on social conditions and on the state of the arts among the Romans. They acquired a taste for luxuries and for the refinements of life and at the same time the means to gratify it. The Roman soldiers serving in Magna Græcia came to know something of Greek styles of architecture and ornamentation in private and public buildings, of the appliances which make life more comfortable, of the use of more beautiful materials to please the eye, or of delicacies to tempt the appetite, or of pleasures, like the theatre, to divert.

139. Religious Changes. Upon the character of the Roman religion the Greeks exerted a profound influence. All of the Greek gods had forms and qualities not unlike those of men and women, so that when they were brought to Rome they were represented by statues and had temples built for them in which they were thought of as living. The tendency to personify the gods naturally extended to the national Roman deities. So, for instance, at an early period we hear of a statue of Jove and a temple of Jove on the Capitol. This change in the conception of the gods brought men into closer relations with them, and made people take a more active part in public worship. We have noticed a few of the points at which the contact of the Romans with the Greek civilization of southern Italy made itself felt. How profoundly Greek influence developed or moulded Roman religion and literature, and how it affected the daily

life and way of thinking of the Romans as time went on, we shall
see more clearly, as we trace the course of affairs in subsequent
periods.

140. Summary of Events at Home from 509 to 264 B. C.
At the beginning of this period, as we have seen, a revolution
leads to the substitution of the consulship for the kingship.   The
plebeians obtain the tribunate, a better political organization,
the publication of the common law, and the right to intermarry
with the patricians.   After a long struggle they secure the passage
of the Licinian laws, admission to the consulship and to the newly
established offices.   These victories bring to a successful completion the long struggle of the plebeians for political equality
with the patricians.   The nobility gains control of the senate,
and through the senate controls the magistrates.   The Publilian
and Hortensian laws make the popular assemblies nominally,
but not really, independent of the senate.   Aqueducts and roads
are built; the money is improved, and the condition of the
farmers in Italy is temporarily relieved.

CHAPTER VI

(264–133 B. C.)

How Rome wrested from Carthage the control of the Western, from Macedonia and Syria, of the Eastern Mediterranean countries.

141. Rome's Preparation for Wars Abroad. With the fall of Tarentum and the subjugation of the other cities of Magna Græcia the conquest of Italy is complete. The next stage in the development of Rome is one of territorial expansion outside the limits of Italy. It is a period of struggle with a great Mediterranean power for foreign commerce and for the control of

THE ISLAND IN THE TIBER

the western Mediterranean. The changes which her military system have undergone during the Italian wars have prepared Rome in no small measure for the task which she now takes up. Her generals have gained experience in the management of large bodies of troops. The adoption of the proconsular system has made it possible to carry out consistently a plan of campaign running through several years. Her soldiers are well trained and efficient.

142. Reorganization of her Army. She has reorganized her army, as we have observed, and improved her tactics. The soldiers are better armed, and the solid phalanx, which had been thrown into disorder if broken at any point, has given way to a more flexible formation, which allows the soldiers of the front rank to retire between those of the rank immediately behind. This change makes it possible to oppose fresh men to the enemy constantly, and to use the weapons and method of fighting most suited to the needs of the moment.

143. Its Size. The Roman army has also been greatly enlarged by the addition of troops furnished by the Italian allies. Just before the second great war of the period which we are now taking up, the Roman annalist Fabius drew from the records of the time the official estimate of seven hundred and seventy thousand as the number of troops at Rome's disposal. Of these Rome furnished three hundred and twenty-five thousand and the allies the remainder. The infantry numbered seven hundred thousand, the cavalry seventy thousand. In actual service at any one time toward the close of the third century there were from eighteen to twenty-three legions. This would indicate an army running from one hundred and eighty thousand to two hundred and thirty thousand men actually in the field.

144. The Navy. On the sea the Romans were lamentably weak. We see ships of war represented on early Roman coins, and the commercial treaties which she had made with Carthage and Tarentum, as well as the appointment of naval officers, point to the development in some measure of Rome's seagoing power, but her navy was small, and her sailors inexperienced, in comparison with those of the great Mediterranean states, Carthage and Greece.

145. The Situation of Carthage. We have already noticed that Italy faces the west. This fact made her commerce develop in that direction and brought her into conflict with Carthage, the great commercial power of the western Mediterranean. The city of Carthage lay on the shore of northern Africa where it juts out toward Sicily and Italy, at the bottom of a deep bay whose

sides extend out to form the promontories of Apollo and of
Hermes. It was built on a peninsula which projects into the
open bay, was provided with a citadel, or Byrsa, considered impregnable, two artificial harbors, as well as an open roadstead,
and was said to contain over seven hundred thousand inhabitants.

146. Her Colonial Empire. The leadership of Carthage
was acknowledged by the coast towns of northern Africa as far
west as the Pillars of Hercules, by certain colonies on the opposite
coast of Spain, and by important commercial centres in Sicily and
Sardinia. Her ambitions were purely commercial. Wherever
the natural advantages seemed tempting, her enterprising merchants established a trading-post, or founded a manufacturing
colony, or developed the mineral wealth of the country.

147. Her Government, Army, and Navy. The government of Carthage was conducted by a "committee of one hundred," membership in which became hereditary in the families of
the mercantile aristocracy, but the effective administration of public affairs by this oligarchy was seriously hampered by the great
influence which the army acquired in political matters. When
Rome was brought into conflict with her, the armies of Carthage
were made up of mercenaries of Numidian cavalry, of slingers
from the Balearic Isles, of trained Greeks and undisciplined
Gauls. Her men-of-war, on the other hand, were manned by
citizens who had spent their lives at sea, and the number and
size of her vessels made her the foremost naval power in the
world.

148. Elements of Weakness : Her Extended Territory.
The points in which Carthage was weak when compared with
Rome are apparent. Her territory was made up of a narrow
strip of land stretching for hundreds of miles along the northern
shore of Africa. Her possessions in Spain and Sicily were also
confined to the coast. To protect so straggling a domain, and
to secure prompt, concerted action from peoples so widely scattered was well-nigh impossible. The territory of Rome on the
other hand was compact, and Italy was a geographical unit.

149. Her Loose Organization. This element of difference was increased by the fact that the colonial empire of Carthage was an organization whose parts were very loosely held together, while the several Italian states were welded into a strong confederation which had come to recognize the comparative liberality of Rome's policy toward them and the wisdom of accepting her leadership. The war against the foreign king, Pyrrhus, had even developed in them a sentiment of regard for United Italy.

150. Her People Less Hardy. Then, too, the Romans were a race of soldiers, and had been trained for generations in the school of war. Their new territory had been gained and held by force of arms. The primary purpose of the Carthaginians, on the other hand, was the extension of their commerce, and their outposts were held rather by the trader than the man-at-arms. Furthermore, as Polybius, the Greek historian says, in comparing the two peoples, "the Italians as a nation are by nature superior to Phoenicians and Libyans, both in physical strength and courage."

151. Her Home Government Narrow. Both governments were controlled by an aristocracy, but the Carthaginian nobility perhaps showed more class selfishness and more jealousy of its successful commanders than did the Roman aristocracy. This very fact often deprived it of the loyal support both of the general in the field and the citizens at home. In this connection, however, we may notice one important military advantage which the Carthaginians had. Their army was intrusted to a single leader, who was often allowed to conduct military operations for several years in succession, while the Roman army was ordinarily in charge of two consuls, and a change of leaders was usually made each year.

152. Her Army Inefficient. The difference in the composition of the two armies had an important bearing upon the outcome of the struggle between the two peoples. The Carthaginians hired mercenaries to do their fighting for them, so that the great body of the citizens continued to carry on their occupations as usual during a war. A campaign meant to them, therefore, merely a temporary increase in taxation. When Rome engaged in a war her active, able-bodied citizens were drafted for service, and the very strength of the state was sapped. This is, however, only one side of the case. The other side has been clearly seen ·by Polybius: "The Carthaginians have their hopes of freedom ever resting on the courage of mercenary troops; the Romans on the valor of their own citizens and the aid of their allies. The result is that even if the Romans have suffered a defeat at first, they renew the war with undiminished forces, which the Carthaginians cannot do. For, as the Romans are fighting for country and children, it is impossible for them to relax the fury of their struggle; but they persist with obstinate resolution until they have overcome their enemies, and they are never so dangerous as when they seem reduced to desperation."

153. Carthage and Syracuse. The interests of the Carthaginians in Sicily brought them into rivalry with the Greek towns of that island. The most powerful of these towns was the city of Syracuse, and some of the ablest rulers of that city had succeeded in confining Carthage to the western end of the island. But the Syracusans found it impossible to check permanently the advance of their enemies, and in the early part of the third century the Carthaginians controlled two-thirds of the island, that is to say, the portion which lies between Camarina and the western coast.

154. The First Punic War Begins in 264 B.C. The situation had now become ominous for Rome and Italy. If the Carthaginians should reach the eastern coast of Sicily, the safety and freedom of southern Italy would be imperilled. A sudden turn of fortune gave them a foothold there. A band of Campanian mercenaries had occupied the town of Messana on the Strait of Messina, and were besieged by Hiero, king of Syracuse. One party appealed to Carthage, the other to Rome, for help. The Carthaginians granted the request for aid, and after much hesitation the Romans, too, sent a relief expedition, which succeeded in landing in Sicily, in spite of the efforts made by the

Carthaginian fleet to prevent their crossing the Straits, and defeated first the Syracusan, then the Carthaginian forces.

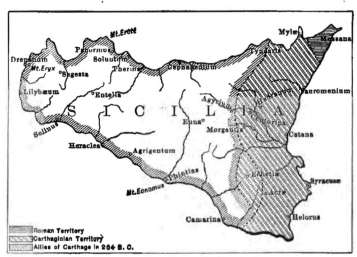

SICILY: THE FIRST PUNIC WAR

155. Progress of the War in Sicily. Fortunately the Romans came to an understanding with Hiero, and, profiting by their alliance with him, they found no serious difficulty in making themselves masters of those Carthaginian towns in Sicily which lay at a distance from the coast. They even captured Agrigentum, which the enemy had made its headquarters, but they could not take the seaports, because they could not blockade them by sea, and the Carthaginian fleet constantly relieved them with supplies and reinforcements of men. To make matters worse, the coast towns of Italy were exposed to naval attacks against which they had no adequate means of defense. To quote a comparison often applied to the contest, it was "a battle between a whale and an elephant."

156. Construction of a Fleet in 260 B.C. The needs of the situation were brought home to the Romans so forcibly that they determined to build ships capable of meeting the enemy at sea on equal terms. The audacity of this move and its success impressed the Roman imagination in later days very deeply, and marvelous stories grew up of the way in which the vessels were constructed and the seamen trained. While the Romans were being taken across the Strait of Messina to relieve the town of Messana, we are told, a great Carthaginian vessel put to sea to intercept them, and charged so furiously that it ran aground and fell into their hands. Modelling their vessels on this ship of the enemy, so the Roman historians say, they built a fleet of a hundred quinquiremes, or vessels with five banks of oars, and twenty triremes, which set out for the scene of hostilities in 260. The oarsmen were trained on land, it is said, by being placed on rowers' benches, and they learned in this improvised way how to propel and direct a vessel at sea.

157. The Invention of the Corvus. Such amateur training would not have been very effective probably, had it not been for the invention of a device which prevented the Carthaginians from profiting by their experienced seamanship. Each Roman ship was provided with a gangway thirty-six feet long and four feet wide, which swung on a pivot about the lower end of a stout pole firmly fixed in the prow. When not in use it was raised, but when the enemy came near enough it was suddenly dropped across his deck. The impact drove a curved iron spike, which was let into the lower side of the drawbridge, into the deck of the enemy's vessel and held the two ships together. The spike was shaped like a crow's beak, and from this fact the whole device was called a *corvus* or crow. Across the gangway, thus held firmly, the Romans rushed, boarded the enemy's ship, and converted the contest into what was essentially a land fight. In such a battle they felt no anxiety about the result.

158. The Battles of Mylæ in 260 and Ecnomus in 256 B. C. Armed with this device, of which the Carthaginians knew nothing, the Romans set sail, and met the enemy's fleet off Mylæ, on the north coast of Sicily. "No sooner did the Carthaginians sight their opponents," as Polybius tells us, "than with joy and alacrity they put to sea with a hundred and thirty sail, feeling supreme contempt for the Roman ignorance of seamanship.

When they neared the enemy, and saw the 'crows' raised aloft
on the prows of the several ships, they were for a time in a state
of perplexity. Feeling, however, great disdain for their opponents, those on board the ships that were in the van of the
squadron charged without flinching. But as soon as they came
to close quarters their ships were invariably tightly grappled by
these machines; the enemy boarded by means of the 'crows',
and engaged them on their decks. The result was that they
lost the first thirty ships engaged, crews and all, and eventually
turned and fled, bewildered at the novelty of the occurrence, and
with a loss of fifty ships." On the return of the Roman commander, Gaius Duilius, to the city, a monument adorned with
the *rostra* or brazen beaks of the enemy's captured ships, and so
known as the *columna rostrata*, with a long inscription reciting
the achievements of the fleet, was set up to commemorate this
first great victory at sea. This memorial, in a restored form, has
come down to us, and constitutes one of the most ancient and
interesting records of Roman history. Four years later the
Romans won another great naval victory off the south coast of
Sicily, near the promontory of Ecnomus.

159. The Carthaginians Make Xanthippus their Leader.
Rome followed up her success at Ecnomus by landing troops on
the coast of Africa, and Carthage seemed at the point of falling
into the hands of the Roman leader Regulus, but it chanced
that at this moment her recruiting agent brought back with him
from Greece a Lacedaemonian named Xanthippus, who was
trained in the Spartan discipline, and was an experienced soldier.
His skill in handling troops and his success in enforcing discipline and in inspiring enthusiasm in the army was so apparent
that the Carthaginians entrusted the defense of the city to him.

160. The Defeat of Regulus and the Loss of the Fleet.
The essential point in his method of fighting lay in the choice of
level ground where the cavalry, in which the Carthaginians out-
numbered and surpassed their opponents, and the elephants
could be used to the best advantage. The elephants were placed
in a single line in front of the whole army, and the cavalry was

stationed on the wings.   When the two forces met, the elephants
broke through the centre of the Roman line and crushed the Romans by their mere weight, while the cavalry swept around the
enemy's flanks and threw the rear into confusion.   This plan
worked well, for Regulus was taken prisoner, and barely two
thousand of his army escaped from the battle-field and were
rescued by a Roman fleet.   As if misfortunes would never cease,
this fleet encountered a fearful storm on its return voyage to Italy
and out of three hundred and sixty-four vessels only eighty
escaped.

161. The First Punic War Ends in 241 B.C.   The scene of
active operations was now transferred to Sicily, where war raged
for nearly fifteen years.   At last Hamilcar Barcas ("the Thunder-
bolt"), the brilliant leader of the Carthaginians, was hemmed
in by land and sea and forced to surrender.   A treaty was made
in 241 under which the Carthaginians were obliged to give up
their Roman prisoners, to surrender their holdings in Sicily,
and to pay the Romans in ten years the sum of three thousand
two hundred Attic talents, or about $3,800,000.

162. The Results of the War for Carthage.   The loss of
Sicily and the payment of an indemnity constituted but a small
part of the damage done to Carthage.   Her resources had been
exhausted by the demands of the war; her trade had dropped
away; she had lost control of the sea and of the commerce of the
western Mediterranean, and her colonial empire was thrown
into confusion.   To crown her misfortunes, no sooner was the
war over, than an insurrection broke out among her soldiers, and
when Hamilcar set out with a fleet to quell the mutinous troops
in Sardinia, which still belonged to Carthage, the Romans
claimed that the expedition was really directed against Rome,
and the poor Carthaginians found no other way to satisfy them
than by giving up Sardinia to Rome and paying an indemnity of
twelve hundred talents more.   Corsica was occupied by the
Romans at the same time.

163. The Results of the War for Rome.   The material
gains which Rome made lay in the acquisition of Sicily, Sar-

dinia, and Corsica, in her growth as a naval and commercial power, and in the greater sense of security which Italy felt with the two neighboring islands under Roman control. Sicily is so much nearer to Italy than to any other part of the mainland that it is natural to think of it as belonging politically to the peninsula. At all events, to see it in the hands of another strong and ambitious power might well be a source of great anxiety to Italy. Consequently the First Punic War was not in its primary purpose a simple war of conquest for the sake of acquiring more territory, nor was it a conscious step toward expansion. The desire to extend trade, and an ambition to make Rome one of the world-powers were among the motives for the first expedition to Sicily, it is true, but the war was primarily waged for the defense of Italy against an ambitious rival who seemed steadily creeping nearer and nearer. It was a war to prevent the town of Messana, and the consequent control of navigation in the Strait of Messina, from passing into the hands of Carthage. But with the winning of Sicily and Sardinia, the appetite for conquest sprang up at Rome, and the commercial ambitions of the people developed. Henceforth the merchant is constantly sending the soldier forth to open up new avenues for commerce, and to protect his commercial enterprises in fields which have already been occupied.

164. The Government of Sicily. How to govern territory outside of Italy was a new problem for the Romans, and it was fourteen years after the acquisition of Sicily before a permanent system was adopted for the island. The Italian policy of isolating communities, and of varying the relations which they bore to Rome, was applied to Sicily also, but in most other respects she was put on a different basis from the conquered states in the peninsula. The Romans probably thought that loyalty to the home government could not develop so easily, and that Roman institutions could not be introduced so readily in Sicily as in the communities of Italy, on account of her position outside of Italy, and because of the allegiance which her people had lately borne to another government. So in place of the military service

required of the Italian states they substituted tribute, in the form
of tithes, and governed the province, as the new territory was
called, by a praetor sent out from Rome.

**165. The Illyrian War, 229 - 228, and the Gallic Wars,
238 - 222 B.C.**   Roman energy had been so absorbed during
the war with Carthage by the struggle to the south, in Sicily and
Africa and in the adjacent waters, that trade in the Adriatic had
been left to the mercy of the Illyrian pirates.   A campaign of two
years drove them from the sea, however, and led many of the
towns on the Greek coast across the Adriatic to join the Roman
alliance.   An uprising among the Gauls in northern Italy was
also checked after a hard struggle, and their territory was occupied.   The road to the north, known as the via Flaminia, was
extended to Ariminum, and Latin colonies were planted at
Placentia and Cremona.   This conquest brought the district
of Cisalpine Gaul within the confines of Italy, and extended the
Roman frontier to the Alps.   Rome was henceforth mistress
of all Italy from the Alps to the Strait of Messina, and now
that the pirates had been swept from the Adriatic and northern
Italy protected by the barrier of the Alps, she could look forward to the impending struggle with Carthage with a reasonable
hope that she would not be harassed by enemies in the rear.

166. Carthage Develops her Power in Spain.   While the
Romans were engaged in strengthening themselves in the North,
Carthage had built up a new empire in the West.   Shut out of
her old trading posts in Sicily and Sardinia, she allowed her brave
and capable leader, Hamilcar Barcas, to cross over to Spain, and
develop her interests there.   He found the country fertile and
rich in minerals, and, thanks to the vigor and wisdom which he
showed in dealing with the natives, the territory within which the
authority of Carthage was recognized grew with extraordinary
rapidity.   When Hamilcar died in 228, his son-in-law Hasdrubal,
who succeeded him, carried on the same policy of developing
the country and with equal success.   The Romans were too
much occupied with the Gallic wars at the time to watch closely
the course of events in Spain, and contented themselves with

binding Hasdrubal in 226 by a treaty not to advance beyond the Ebro, while giving him a free hand to the south of that river.

167. The Character of Hannibal. On Hasdrubal's death in 221 the command of the army passed to Hannibal, the eldest son of Hamilcar, who was at this time in his twenty-seventh year. Even his enemies recognized in him a born soldier and leader. As Livy says of him, "Never was a genius better qualified for two most contrary duties—obeying and commanding. . . . He combined the greatest fearlessness in facing perils with the greatest wisdom when surrounded by them. By no hardships could his body be wearied or his courage broken. With equal indifference he bore heat and cold. The amount which he ate or drank was determined by the needs of nature and not by the cravings of the palate. He had no fixed periods by day or by night for working or sleeping. The time which was left him after finishing his work, he gave to sleep. Sleep he did not woo on a soft couch, nor in a quiet spot, but often you would see him with his soldier's cloak over him lying on the ground among the guards and outposts of his forces. He was the first to enter battle and the last man to leave, when battle had been joined."

168. Immediate Cause of the Second Punic War. One city to the south of the Ebro had not accepted the rule of Hannibal—the town of Saguntum. This city was under the protection of Rome and in case of war, Roman troops might at any moment enter Carthaginian territory through this gateway. Hannibal saw that he must take it. He found a pretext, attacked Saguntum, and, after a hard siege of eight months, took it. Carthage ratified his course, and Rome declared war against her.

169. Hannibal's March into Italy in 218 B.C. The Roman plan of campaign was comprehensive. It included the simultaneous invasion of Spain and Africa. But Hannibal did not give the Romans time to put it into execution. Assembling an army at his capital, New Carthage, in the spring of 218, he boldly set out to invade Italy by land. It was a plan which **only**

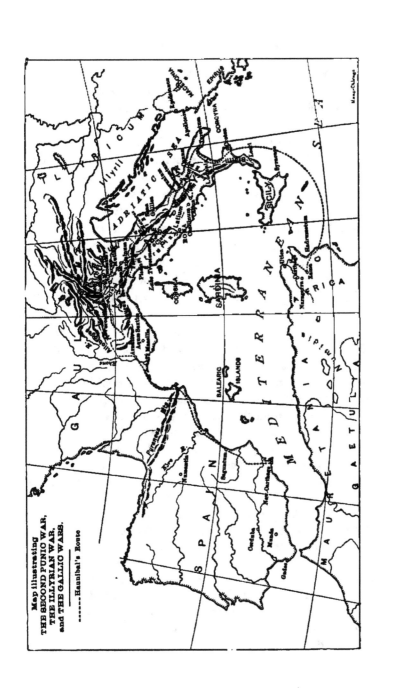

Map illustrating
THE SECOND PUNIC WAR,
THE ILLYRIAN WAR,
and THE GALLIC WARS.

------ Hannibal's Route

a Hannibal, a Caesar, or a Napoleon could have conceived or carried out. It involved taking a large army with all its supplies, its equipment, and beasts of burden along almost the entire eastern coast of Spain and through southern Gaul. It involved the crossing of the swift Rhone in little boats, and the passage of the Alps in the late autumn. As soon as he crossed the Ebro, Hannibal was in hostile territory, and from that point on he had to make his way by persuasion or by force of arms until he entered northern Italy. At the Rhone he found a large force of the natives collected on the eastern bank to prevent his passage, but he sent a detachment of his troops across at a point higher up the stream, where the water was shallower, took the enemy by surprise in the rear, and brought his soldiers over in canoes and his elephants on huge rafts. After having received this salutary lesson the barbarians did not molest him again until he reached the mountains. The passage of the Alps was attended by untold difficulties. "The paths were narrow and rough, and flanked with precipices, and at every movement which tended to throw the line into disorder, large numbers of the beasts of burden were hurled down the steeps with their loads on their backs. Meanwhile the Gauls from their vantage-ground above moved along the slopes parallel with the army below, and by rolling down boulders, or throwing stones, reduced the troops to a state of utmost confusion and danger." At one point the path was too narrow for the elephants and beasts of burden, and with infinite toil his troops constructed a road along the face of the precipice. They found the summit covered with snow and bare of trees and vegetation. Battling their way down the southern slopes against heavy snowstorms, exhausted by cold, fatigue, and hunger, the troops at last reached the plains of northern Italy. The passage of the Alps had occupied fifteen days; the entire march from New Carthage five months, and on the way the army had been cut down from fifty thousand infantry and nine thousand cavalry to twenty thousand infantry and six thousand cavalry.

170. Battles on the Ticinus 218, on the Trebia 218, and near Lake Trasimene 217 B. C. The Romans were taken by surprise; their cavalry was routed on the banks of the Ticinus; twenty thousand of their soldiers were caught in a trap and fell in the battle on the Trebia; and the army of Flaminius, enticed into a narrow valley near Lake Trasimene, and enveloped in a mist so thick that the Roman soldiers could not tell friend from foe, was completely annihilated.

171. Q. Fabius Maximus. The news of the battle of Lake Trasimene made a deep impression at Rome, and the people chose a dictator, Q. Fabius Maximus, who adopted an entirely new policy. Without offering Hannibal battle, he hovered in his neighborhood, occupied the points of vantage, and cut off his foraging parties. This plan of campaign was little to the taste of the Roman populace, who nicknamed Fabius "Cunctator," or "the Laggard," and insisted that more vigorous measures should be taken against the enemy.

172. Cannæ, 216 B. C. Accordingly, in the spring of 216 the new consuls, L. Aemilius Paulus and C. Terentius Varro, set out with an army of eighty thousand infantry and six thousand cavalry, almost double the force of Hannibal, to crush the invader once for all. They found him at Gerunium, near the northern border of Apulia. Their experience at the Trebia and Lake Trasimene had led them to dread his ruses, and, when the Carthaginians, not long after their arrival, broke camp, the Romans, fearing another trap, made no move, until, to their astonishment, they found that Hannibal had marched to Cannæ and seized their supplies. They were forced to fight or to retire in the face of the enemy. They chose the former alternative and joined battle with Hannibal at Cannæ, on the banks of the Aufidus. On each side the cavalry was placed on the wings and the infantry in the centre, but the Carthaginian centre was weak and gave way, as Hannibal intended it to do, before the onslaught of the heavy Roman formation. The very success of the Romans proved to be their undoing, for in pursuing its opponents the Roman infantry lost its formation,

and advanced so far as to expose its right flank to the Libyan
infantry, while in the meantime the heavy-armed Carthaginian
cavalry circled about the Roman army and attacked it in the
rear. The legions were now exposed to attack on three sides;
a strong south wind drove the dust in the faces of the soldiers,

the sun shone in their eyes, and their close formation prevented
them from using their weapons effectively. Of the seventy-five
thousand Romans who took part in the battle a bare three
thousand escaped by flight, with their leader Varro. Hannibal
lost about six thousand men.

173. The War in Italy from 216 to 211 B.C. The victory of the Carthaginians did not turn northern and central Italy, nor even the Greek coast towns in southern Italy, from their loyal support of Rome, but many of the Italian communities in the South went over to the side of Hannibal after the battle of Cannæ, and for the next five years it was the first object of the Romans to recover these rebellious towns and to carry out the Fabian policy of weakening the force of Hannibal and of cutting off his supplies. In spite of some serious reverses, these tactics were in the main successful. Casilinum and Arpi were retaken and in 212 the siege of Capua began. Hannibal came to its relief, but he could not raise the blockade. He marched north to the very gates of Rome, hoping in this way to draw the besieging forces away from Capua, but recruits flocked into Rome. Hannibal's army was not well provided with machines for a siege, his cavalry—the strongest part of his force—was of little use in such an enterprise, and he was forced to withdraw, without either taking Rome or relieving his allies in Campania. Weakened by the long siege, and reduced to the direst straits by hunger, Capua fell in 211. The Romans inflicted such a punishment upon her as might well serve to deter other Italian cities from allying themselves with Hannibal. Her nobles were put to death; the common people were sold as slaves; the city was deprived of her constitution, and her public buildings and land were appropriated by Rome.

174. The War in Sicily from 216 to 210 B.C. But the fate of Hannibal was really decided outside of Italy—in Sicily, Macedonia, and Spain. The death in 216 of Hiero of Syracuse, the faithful friend and ally of Rome, was a severe blow to the Romans. He had loyally helped them in fair weather and in foul. After his death Syracuse hesitated for a time, but ultimately threw in her lot with Carthage. Her example was followed by Agrigentum and many other Sicilian towns. In 214, Marcellus, the Roman commander, appeared before Syracuse, and began the siege of the city by land and sea. Forts and walls afforded it admirable protection; a Carthaginian army and fleet came to its support, but the city found its most effective defense in the ingenuity of Archimedes, the great mathematician of Syracuse. He invented catapults which hurled great stones upon the decks of the Roman ships and sunk them, huge cranes with grappling hooks which seized the enemy's vessels by the bows and overturned them, and he even set their ships on fire, if we

STORMING A TOWN; RELIEF FROM TRAJAN'S COLUMN

may believe the story, with immense burning glasses. For two years the siege was carried on without avail, but in 212 Marcellus, taking advantage of the festival of Artemis, caught the defenders of the city off their guard, and took it. The conquest of the rest of Sicily quickly followed, and in 210 the Carthaginians had been entirely driven from the island.

175. Philip of Macedon Allies himself with Hannibal in 215 B.C. Hannibal's success at Cannæ, which had brought so many towns in southern Italy over to his side, also led Philip V of Macedon to listen favorably to the proposals of the Carthaginians. He agreed to support them in Italy, provided Corcyra and the Roman towns on the coast of Illyria should be turned over to him in case of success, but the danger of an invasion of Italy by the Macedonians the Romans cleverly averted by forming an alliance with the Greek states which were hostile to Macedonia. This coalition kept Philip out of Italy, and took his undivided attention for ten years.

176. The Battle on the Metaurus in 207 B. C. In Spain the struggle between the Romans and the Carthaginians was a bitter one. Hasdrubal, the brother of Hannibal, attacked sepaıately and defeated the two Roman armies under Publius and Gnaeus Scipio, and eluding young Publius Cornelius Scipio, who had been sent to Spain at the head of new levies, set out on the long overland march toward Italy to relieve his brother. He crossed the Alps in the spring of 207 and descended into Italy with an army of over fifty thousand men. The fortunes of Rome seemed at their lowest ebb. Her own population was nearly exhausted; her allies were none too loyal; her land had almost passed out of cultivation, and famine stared her in the face. But the Roman steadiness in a crisis, a piece of good fortune, and the brilliant move of the consul, Gaius Claudius, saved the day. He had been sent south to watch Hannibal, and fortunately the messengers whom Hasdrubal had despatched posthaste to apprise his brother of his approach fell into the hands of Claudius. Withdrawing the greater part of his force without exciting the suspicion of Hannibal, he sent it with all speed to reinforce his colleague Livius in the North. The two armies effected a junction, fell upon Hasdrubal on the banks of the Metaurus near Sena Gallica, routed his army completely, and killed Hasdrubal. His head severed from the body, carried off by the victorious Roman army, and cast into Hannibal's camp, informed the Carthaginian commander of his brother's fate and of his own desperate situation.

177. Publius Cornelius Scipio. Meanwhile Publius Cornelius Scipio had made up for his blunder in allowing Hasdrubal to slip past him by bringing the campaign in Spain to a brilliant end. In 206 he returned to Rome and claimed without boasting that he had fought against four generals and four victorious armies, and had not left a single Carthaginian soldier in Spain. His success in Spain, his popularity with the masses, and his family connection won him an election to the consulship for the following year. Rome had at last found in him a worthy leader to pit against the great Carthaginian captain who for thirteen years had worsted every Roman general sent against him, from the impetuous Flaminius to the cautious Fabius. Polybius, who lived not long after Scipio, might well say of him that "he was perhaps the most illustrious man of those born before the present generation."

178. He Proposes to Invade Africa. Upon taking up his office he showed his daring and originality by proposing, not that the Romans should bend their energies to crush Hannibal in Italy, but that they should invade Africa and force the home government to recall Hannibal. His proposal was bitterly opposed by the timid, who feared the presence of Hannibal in Italy, by the conservative leaders, like Fabius, who were naturally distrustful of so bold an enterprise, and by the senate, which dreaded the ascendency of one man.

179. Preliminary Movements in Africa in 204-203 B.C. He received from the government, therefore, only a half-hearted support for his enterprise, but supplementing the insufficient force which the state allowed him with the recruits who flocked to his standard, Scipio crossed over from Sicily in 204 and effected a landing at Utica. The Carthaginian army under Hasdrubal Gisgo and the Numidians under their king Syphax were defeated in turn, and the Carthaginians were forced to sue for peace. One of the conditions insisted on by Scipio was the recall of Hannibal. To this the Carthaginian senate agreed, and Hannibal with his troops landed at Leptis.

180. Battle of Zama in 202 B.C. But the return of Hannibal inspired the Carthaginians with courage again, and they reopened hostilities. Scipio thereupon advanced farther into Carthaginian territory. His army had been meanwhile greatly strengthened by the adhesion of Masinissa, the rival of Syphax for the throne of Numidia. The combined forces met Hannibal near Zama, and about five days' march from Carthage. Hannibal's elephants charged harmlessly through the wide alleys which Scipio had left between his columns for their passage, or were turned by the Romans against the Punic cavalry; the Roman veterans broke the enemy's line; the cavalry of Masinissa encircled the enemy, and the rout of the Carthaginians was complete. Hannibal escaped to Hadrumetum.

181. The Treaty of Peace in 201 B. C. After this defeat Carthage gave up the struggle. She agreed to relinquish Spain, and not to make war at all outside of Africa and in Africa only with Rome's consent, and to surrender her fleet. She bound herself also to pay within fifty years a sum of ten thousand talents, or about $12,000,000. To ensure the observance of these conditions, hostages were exacted of her, and Numidia, under Masinissa, Rome's efficient ally, was made an independent state to watch all her movements.

182. How Rome Acquired Supremacy in the West. The unification of Italy was the first step in the development of the Roman empire. The second stage came to an end with the defeat of Carthage. The control of the western Mediterranean, to which Rome's geographical position and the fact that her harbors faced the west predestined her, was now assured. Toward this end she had been driven more by the force of circumstances than by the political and commercial ambitions of her people. To protect the southern coast of Italy she opposed the growth of Carthaginian power in Sicily, and finally drove the Carthaginians out of the island. The same instinct of self-preservation led her later to expel them from Sardinia also. At this point both peoples opened their eyes to the fact that the combat was a life-and-death struggle for supremacy in the West. The feverish eagerness with which Carthage sought to build up a new colonial empire in Spain seems to indicate that she first saw that the conflict was inevitable and that defeat meant ruin. Thus, starting with the sole object of ensuring the integrity of Italy, with no large schemes of conquest beyond the sea, Rome drifted into the struggle for supremacy, and the outcome left her mistress of the West.

183. The Relations of Rome with the East. Now that the power of her only rival was broken, and her authority recognized in this quarter of the world, the problem before her was to pacify, to consolidate, and to civilize her newly acquired territory;

but the situation in the East claimed her immediate attention, and diverted her from this work before it was actually begun. With the development of the Eastern question begins the third stage in Rome's career of expansion. In the political drama which comes to an end with the defeat of Carthage the action is comparatively simple. The minor rôle which Syracuse or Capua plays never really distracts our attention from the two leading characters, Rome and Carthage. In the East the movement is much more complex. Rome, Macedonia, Syria, Egypt and a host of small states are all concerned, and for the simple motives of self-preservation or commercial and political ambition which actuated Rome and Carthage we find substituted a large number of political, personal, and even sentimental considerations.

184. Macedonia, Egypt, and Syria. The far-reaching empire of the East which Alexander left at his death in 322 B. C. broke up into the three great kingdoms of Macedonia, Egypt, and Syria. Macedonia controlled the greater part of the Balkan peninsula, Thessaly and some of the smaller states of Greece. Egypt, besides her territory in northern Africa, controlled Judæa and Phoenicia, a strip of land along the coast of Asia Minor, and Thrace, and most of the islands in the eastern Mediterranean. The authority of Syria was recognized in the interior of southern Asia Minor, along the eastern Mediterranean coast from Tyre to Seleucia, and in the country to the east through the valley of the Euphrates and Tigris as far as the borders of Media.

185. Ambitious Designs of Macedonia and Syria. The trouble in the East began in 205, on the death of Ptolemy Philopator of Egypt, who left the throne to his infant son. Thereupon Philip of Macedon and Antiochus III of Syria seized the opportunity to extend their territory at the expense of Egypt. Philip directed his efforts against the Egyptian dependencies on the Aegean coast, and against the coast towns in southern Thrace and on the Hellespont. Rhodes, which was a most flourishing and independent commercial state, was unwilling that this great thoroughfare should fall into his hands, and made war upon him, and both Egypt and Rhodes asked Rome to intervene. Rome

was only too willing to do so, because of the alliance which
Macedonia had a few years before made with Hannibal, and on
account of the threatening growth of Macedonian power.

GREECE AND ASIA MINOR : THE WARS WITH THE MACEDONIANS AND ANTIOCHUS

186. Second Macedonian War, 200 - 196 B.C. Macedonia
refused to make the concessions to Egypt and Rhodes which
Rome proposed, and Rome declared war upon Philip. Antiochus was induced to sever his connection with Philip, and the
successes of the Romans during the first year of the war brought
the Aetolians, the Achaian league, the Boeotians, and the Spar-
tans over to their side; and it was largely due to the support of
the Aetolian cavalry that they gained a decisive victory over
Philip in 197 B. C. at Cynoscephalæ, a range of round-topped
hills in Thessaly.

187. Treaty of Peace, 196 B. C. The treaty which the
Roman leader, Flamininus, and a senatorial commission forced
Philip to sign imposed hard conditions upon him. He agreed to
relinquish all conquered territory, to grant the Greeks their
freedom, to surrender his fleet, to pay a war indemnity, and to

direct his foreign policy in accordance with the wishes of the Romans. Rome annexed no territory, established no garrisons in the country of her late enemy, and left Macedonia and the Greek states free to manage their own internal affairs. Polybius gives us a graphic account of the way in which the proclamation of independence was received by the Greeks at the Isthmian Games in July, 196 B. C. "While people were still in a state of uncertainty, all the world being assembled on the stadium to watch the games, the herald came forward, and having proclaimed silence by the sound of a trumpet, delivered the following proclamation: 'The senate of Rome and Titus Quinctius [Flamininus], proconsul and imperator, having conquered King Philip and the Macedonians in war, declare the following peoples free, without garrison, or tribute, in full enjoyment of the laws of their respective countries; namely, Corinthians, Phocians, Locrians, Euboeans, Achaians of Phiotis, Magnesians, Thessalians, Perrhæbians.' Now, as the first words of the proclamation were the signal for a tremendous outburst of clapping, some of the people could not hear it at all, and some wanted to hear it again; but the majority, feeling incredulous, and thinking that they heard the words in a kind of dream, so utterly unexpected was it, another impulse induced every one to shout to the herald and trumpeter to come into the middle of the stadium and repeat the words. . . . But when the herald, having advanced into the middle of the crowd, once more, by his trumpeter, hushed the clamor and repeated exactly the same proclamation as before, there was such an outbreak of clapping as is difficult to convey to the imagination of my readers at this time,—and after the games were over, in the extravagance of their joy, they nearly killed Flamininus by the exhibition of their gratitude. Some wanted to look him in the face and call him their preserver; others were eager to touch his hand; most threw garlands and fillets upon him; until between them they nearly crushed him to death."

188. The Reasons for Rome's Generous Policy. The self-restraint which Rome showed in her arrangements with

Macedonia and her generous treatment of the Greek states may be traced partly to sentimental, partly to practical, considerations. The Romans admired the Greeks; they believed in their capacity for self-government, and they had repeatedly promised to give the Greek states their freedom. Flamininus, in particular, who led the Roman peace commission, showed marked sympathy with the Greek passion for independence. The hostility to an Eastern war which the great mass of the common people at Rome had shown at the outset also probably prevented the government, at the close of the war, from occupying territory which might involve it in complications in the future. In fact, the constant quarrels between the several Greek states and leagues might well deter Rome from assuming any authority and responsibility in that quarter. Finally, if the integrity of Macedonia was respected she could protect Roman interests against the Gauls and Thracians, while the Greek leagues would hold in check Macedonia's ambitious designs. These various considerations probably explain Rome's generous treatment of her Greek enemies and allies.

189. War with Antiochus III, 192 - 189 B.C. To separate as much as possible the interests of Antiochus and Philip, and in that way to prevent Syria from coming to the help of Macedonia, the Romans had allowed Antiochus a free hand in his campaigns against the Egyptian dependencies on the shore of the Aegean Sea; but when the Aetolians and their allies, discontented with Rome's considerate treatment of Macedonia, invited him into Greece, and made him their commander-in-chief, a force was promptly sent into Thessaly under M'. Acilius Glabrio. The Syrian king made a stand at the historic pass of Thermopylæ, was defeated, and forced to retire from Europe.

190. Hannibal and Africanus once more Brought Face to Face. The Romans had now made up their minds to humble Antiochus. They may have been led to follow up their advantage at once by the fact that their old enemy Hannibal was one of the advisers of the Syrian king. Driven out of his own country by the hostility and the jealousy of the Carthaginians, he had taken refuge at the court of Syria, perhaps hoping that through her he might gratify his unwavering hatred of Rome; and it was one of the strange decrees of fate that this war brought face to face once more the two great leaders of the Second Punic War. The leader of the Romans in the Asiatic campaign chanced to be L. Cornelius Scipio, but he was allowed to assume command only on condition that he should be governed by the advice of his brother Africanus, who accompanied him. Unfortunately for Syria, Antiochus could not grasp the comprehensive plans of Hannibal, or would not follow his advice, and with a fatuity which is almost incredible, gave up the strongly fortified Chersonese, so that the Roman army, after executing safely a long march through Macedonia and Thrace, entered Asia Minor without difficulty, and coming up with the king near Mt. Sipylus, utterly destroyed his forces at the battle of Magnesia in the year 190.

191. Treaty of Peace, 189 B.C. When the ambassadors of Antiochus came after the battle to learn the terms which the Romans would allow them, Publius Scipio replied: "He must abandon Europe altogether and all of Asia this side of the Taurus, the boundaries to be fixed hereafter; he must surrender all the elephants he has, and such number of ships as we may prescribe . . . he must give twenty hostages . . . and pay for the cost of the present war, incurred on his account, five hundred Euboic talents down and twenty-five hundred more when the Senate ratifies the treaty; and twelve thousand more within twelve years."

192. Death of Hannibal and Scipio, 183 B.C. These demands, which were ultimately somewhat increased, Antiochus accepted. Hannibal, who the Romans had expected would fall into their hands, fled to the court of Bithynia, but six years later took his own life, to escape murder at the hands of his enemies. Strangely enough, P. Cornelius Scipio died in the same year at Liternum in Campania, having withdrawn from Rome on account of the bitter attacks made upon him by his fellow-citizens.

193. Roman Policy in Asia. Even at the close of the war with Antiochus the Romans took no territory for themselves and established no garrisons in Asia. They followed there the same policy which they had adopted in Africa and in Greece, of weakening the strong states and strengthening the weak ones. Syria was robbed of so large a part of her territory that she lost completely her importance as a Mediterranean power. While on the other hand the faithful little kingdom of Pergamum, in northwestern Asia Minor, strengthened by the addition of Lydia, Phrygia, Caria, and a part of Pamphylia, was set up as a counterpoise to Syria, just as the kingdom of Numidia had been created to hold Carthage in check.

194. Third Macedonian War, 171 - 168 B.C., and its Results. Macedonia made one more effort under her king Perseus to recover her position, but was beaten at the battle of Pydna, and lost her integrity as a result of the war. The country was divided into four districts, which were allowed to manage their own internal affairs but not to make war or peace. Illyria, too, which had sided with Perseus, was divided into three separate states. The other states and the individuals who had espoused the cause of Perseus were treated with the utmost severity. A thousand Achaians, suspected of sympathy with him, were transported to Italy and held in confinement without trial for many years. Among them was the historian Polybius, to whose enforced stay in Italy we probably owe his account—the most detailed and accurate one we have— of the events of this period.

195 Macedonia Made a Province in 146 B. C. The plan of isolating but leaving independent the newly created Macedonian states did not work as well as a similar policy had done in Italy. The situation inevitably tempted ambitious Macedonian leaders to try to bring about a reunion of the four districts. After an attempt of this sort had been made by a certain Andriscus, the senate gave up the plan, and made Macedonia a province like Sicily and Spain.

196. Greece Subdued in 146 B. C. The arrangement in Greece proved as unsatisfactory as had that in Macedonia. The jealousy which the different states felt toward one another broke out in 148 into open war between the Achaian league and

Sparta, and the Achaians tried to make Sparta yield to their confederation. When Rome intervened, the league, forgetting the severe lesson which the Greeks had been taught after the third Macedonian war, boldly challenged her. The struggle was short and decisive. All the towns which had taken part in the movement were razed to the ground. Corinth, the principal town of the league, and one of the most beautiful cities of antiquity, suffered with the rest. Polybius, who was an eyewitness of its destruction, tells us that "the incidents of the capture of Corinth were melancholy. The soldiers cared nothing for the works of art and the consecrated statues. I saw with my own eyes pictures thrown on the ground and soldiers playing dice on them." Many of the statues and pictures were taken to Rome to grace the triumph of the commander L. Mummius, and Roman ignorance in matters of art is well illustrated by Mummius's stipulation that, if any of the works of art should be lost in transit, "they were to be replaced by others of equal value." The people of Greece were left nominally free, but they were subject to Roman taxation and were under the central authority of the Roman governor of Macedonia.

197. The Fate of Egypt. Egypt, the third of the great Oriental powers mentioned above, was essentially a commercial state, and had not assumed the aggressive in any of the quarrels which embroiled the East. In fact, she found it hard to keep her possessions out of the hands of the rapacious Antiochus. In 198 when Rome was occupied with Philip he seized and held for a time some Egyptian territory in Asia, and later, when Rome was at war with Perseus, the Syrian king again tried to add to his empire at the expense of Egypt. Rome saved her from spoliation, however, and assumed a protectorate over the country in 168.

198. The Government of Sicily. As we have already noticed, the difficulties in Macedonia and Syria prevented Rome from giving her undivided attention to the development of the territory which she had acquired from Carthage as a result of the Punic wars. The two countries, Sicily and Spain, which fell to her as the heir of Carthage, presented very different problems. Sicily had a well-established civilization, was peaceful, and accepted Roman rule without question. A few cohorts sufficed to enforce the authority of the praetor who governed the island.

199. Spain and the Lusitanians under Viriathus, 149 - 139 B.C. But four legions had to be stationed in Spain, and for seventy years the peninsula was the scene of revolt after revolt. These wars were due partly to the natural desire of the Spaniards to throw off the Roman yoke, but more to the bad faith of the Romans, to their defective administrative system, and to the incapacity of their commanders and governors. The principal leader of the Spaniards was the brilliant, chivalrous Viriathus. His undying hostility to the Romans was aroused by the perfidy of the praetor, Servius Sulpicius Galba. In 160 B. C. this officer had massacred seven thousand unarmed Lusitanians who had surrendered to him. Viriathus, one of the prisoners, escaped, and being chosen as their leader by his countrymen, lured into the mountains the Roman commander Vetilius, who was sent to pursue him, and cut his army to pieces. A little later an army of four thousand men which had just arrived from Rome was destroyed by a similar strategy. For three years the Lusitanian leader overran the country without check, defeating legion after legion, and constantly pushing back the Roman forces. Servilianus, who commanded the Romans in 141, was signally defeated, and concluded a treaty recognizing Lusitania as an independent state, and Viriathus as its chief magistrate. But Caepio, the newly appointed Roman general, though he was the brother of Servilianus, treacherously broke the treaty, and reopened hostilities against the Lusitanian chief.

200. The Murder of Viriathus, 139 B.C. Finding himself unable to cope with the enemy he brought the war to an end in a way which harmonized well with the treacherous methods which the Romans had adopted in all their dealings with the Lusitanians. His object was accomplished during an interval between the campaigns, when peace negotiations were going on. The story is told by Appian in *The Wars in Spain*: "Viriathus sent his most trusted friends, Audax, Ditalco, and Minurus, to Caepio to arrange terms of peace. Caepio bribed them, by large gifts and promises, to assassinate Viriathus, which they did in this way. Viriathus, on account of his excessive cares and labors, slept but little, and for the most part took rest in his armor so that when aroused he should be prepared for every emergency. For this reason it was permitted to his friends to visit him by night; taking advantage of this custom, those who were associated with Audax in guarding him entered his tent as if on pressing business, just as he had fallen asleep, and killed him by stabbing him in the throat, which was the only part of his body not protected by armor." Thus passed away the leader against whom the Romans had sent legion after legion without avail for nearly ten years. After his death the rebellion collapsed. All this took place in Farther Spain.

201. The War with Numantia, 143 - 133 B.C. In the province of Hither Spain, war was going on at the same time. Its story is a similar one of broken pledges, incapable commanders, and undisciplined armies. At last the Romans found an able leader in Scipio Aemilianus, who had already distinguished himself in Africa, and the last opposition to Roman rule disappeared when Numantia was blockaded by him and reduced after an heroic resistance.

202. Carthage Recovers her Prosperity. We have traced the history of the two provinces which Rome exacted from Carthage as the spoils of war. We must turn now for a moment to follow the career of Carthage herself. The restoration of peace in 201 brought her prosperity again. Her commerce sprang up; the city grew, and the wealth of her citizens increased. This very development, although Carthage faithfully observed her treaty obligations both in letter and spirit, excited anxiety, jealousy, and the old animosity at Rome. In the quarrels which arose between her and her neighbor Masinissa, king of Numidia, Rome steadily abetted and favored Masinissa, watching for some pretext to declare war upon Carthage. At last the Carthaginians, driven to desperation by the encroachments of Masinissa, opened hostilities against him.

203. The Third Punic War, 149 - 146 B.C. To wage war in Africa without Rome's consent was in violation of the treaty of 201, and the war party in Rome, led by M. Porcius Cato, eagerly seized this pretext to invade Africa, and demand the immediate submission of Carthage. The Carthaginians hastened to yield. They condemned to death the leaders in the war against Numidia; they gave hostages, and surrendered all their arms and munitions. When the Carthaginian ambassadors had satisfied all these requirements, Censorinus, the consul, stated Rome's final demand: "Your ready obedience up to this point, Carthaginians," he said, "in the matter of the hostages and the arms, is worthy of all praise. In cases of necessity we must not multiply words. Bear bravely the remaining commands of the senate. Yield Carthage to us, and betake yourselves where you like within your own territory to a distance of at least ten miles from the sea, for we are resolved to raze your city to the ground."

204. The Destruction of Carthage, 146 B.C. The Carthaginians were fired with the courage of despair. They made Hasdrubal their leader. "All the sacred places, the temples, and every other unoccupied space, were turned into workshops, where men and women worked together day and night without pause. Each day they made one hundred shields, three hundred swords, one thousand missiles for catapults, five hundred darts and javelins, and as many catapults as they could. For strings to bend them the women cut off their hair for want of other fibres," and, when the Romans appeared before the city, they found it prepared for a desperate defense. The bravery and skill of the Carthaginians coöperated with hunger and disease in the Roman camp to thwart all attempts at capturing the city for two years. The Romans were even put on the defensive. One Roman leader, a mere military tribune, P. Cornelius Scipio Aemilianus, son of L. Aemilius Paulus, who defeated Perseus, and the adopted grandson of the victor at Zama, distinguished himself in the siege. Although he was only thirty-seven years old, the Romans, contrary to all precedent, chose him consul for 147, and gave him command of the forces in Africa. He restored discipline in the army; inspired it with confidence

1 Harbor for merchant vessels
2 Fortified harbor
3 The Citadel
The encircling black line represents the city wall

NEW CITY

Scipio's Camp

OLD CITY

Scipio's Mole

LAKE OF

TUNIS

PLAN OF CARTHAGE

again, and cut Carthage off both by land and sea. By desperate assaults one part after another of the city was captured, until at last the whole town was taken. Carthage was burned to the ground by order of the senate. Its site was dedicated to the gods of the world below, and its territory became the province of Africa.

205. Asia Minor. Still more territory came to the Romans on the death of Attalus III, king of Pergamum, who bequeathed his kingdom to Rome. Such resistance as was offered to the assumption of this inheritance was overcome without serious difficulty, and the Romans took the opportunity to organize their possessions in this quarter into the province of Asia.

206. Roman Territory in 133 B.C. As a result of the Great Wars which began in 264, Rome had acquired seven provinces, Sicily, Sardinia and Corsica, Hither Spain, Farther Spain, Macedonia, Asia, and Africa, while Cisalpine Gaul and Illyricum, although not erected into provinces, were administered by the consuls.   Under her suzerainty were Numidia, Libya, Egypt, the islands of Cyprus and Crete, and the whole of Asia Minor to the west of the Taurus range of mountains, except the province of Asia, which was of course an integral part of the empire.

207. The Government of a Province.   Various forms of government were tried in the earliest provinces, but after 146 B. C., when new territory was acquired, the senate adopted the uniform practice of sending out a commission, made up of ten senators, which coöperated with the commanding general in drawing up the constitution of the province.   In two important particulars the government of the provinces differed from that of the Italian communities.   In the first place, Italy was under the direct supervision of the senate, while each province was governed by a praetor.   The second important difference consisted in the fact that the Italians were free from taxation, while most of the provincial towns were subject to certain imposts.   The provincial tax usually took the form of a fixed contribution, or *stipendium* laid upon a community, or else a certain proportion of the annual returns from the land, a *vectigal*, was required.   The method of managing local affairs varied in different provinces, and was adapted in some measure to the needs and traditional practices of the people, and the degree of independence allowed to a town depended upon the attitude which she took or had taken toward Rome.   Communities which were loyal to her sometimes became free states. Those which resisted her authority were made dependent, while towns, like Carthage and Numantia, which opposed her to the end, were destroyed.   Free states enjoyed the privilege of local self-government, but were not allowed to enter into negotiations with other states.   Dependent communities paid taxes, and conducted their local affairs under the supervision of Roman officials.

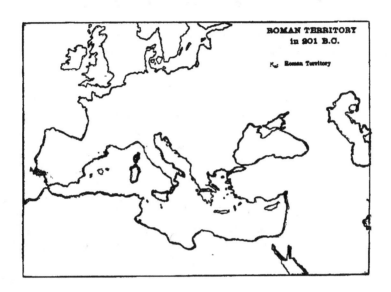

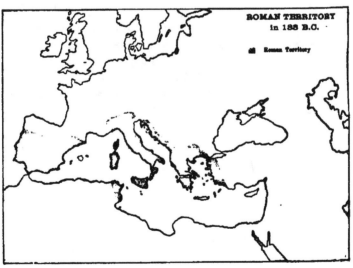

DEVELOPMENT OF ROMAN TERRITORY FROM 201 TO 133 B. C.
(For Roman Territory at the beginning of the Punic Wars, see Map facing page 92.)

**208. Summary Account of the Conquest of Mediterra-
nean Lands, 264-133 B. C.**   We have noticed that Rome's war
with Pyrrhus made her at last mistress of all Italy, gave her a
large, well-trained army, and so raised her to the position of a
Mediterranean power, and made her the rival of Carthage for
the trade and the political control of the western Mediterranean.
Rome had an advantage in the compactness of her territory
and in the composition of her army; Carthage in the excellence
of her navy.   The war was carried on mainly in Sicily and the
adjacent waters, and ended with the triumph of Rome.   She
won Sicily, Sardinia, and Corsica, and thus acquired her first
territory outside of Italy, and established her first province.
Both Rome and Carthage prepared for another struggle, Rome
by protecting herself in the rear, Carthage by establishing herself in Spain.   The Second Punic War began with a quarrel
over Saguntum.   Hannibal, after taking the city, marched overland into Italy, defeated the Romans in numerous battles, but
was ultimately forced to return to Africa, and was defeated at
Zama.   Carthage lost Spain.   The ambitious designs of Macedonia and Syria were thwarted, and the territory gained was
organized into the provinces of Macedonia and Asia.   A protectorate was established over Egypt.   With the fall of Carthage
Rome's old-time rival disappeared.   At the close of the period
Rome was in control of both the eastern and western Mediterranean.

CHAPTER VII

(264–133 B. C.)

How the senate controlled affairs at home and abroad—How the conquest of Mediterranean lands affected Italy.

209. Political Inactivity at Rome. The first two centuries of the Republic had been years of creative activity in political affairs. Offices had been established, principles of government adopted, and precedents set which were permanent and far-reaching in their application. But the passage of the Hortensian law marked the end of the struggle. The plebeians had secured political equality. In the period whose external history we have been following in the last chapter, the energies of the Romans are expended in struggles with their Mediterranean rivals, and in establishing an orderly government in the provinces. The scene of political activity is changed from Rome to the newly acquired territory outside of Italy. At home the Romans content themselves in the main with adapting the newly established institutions, like the magistracies and the popular assemblies, to the pressing needs of the community.

210. Reform of the Centuriate Assembly about 241 B.C. The most comprehensive political change in domestic affairs was the reform of the centuriate assembly. Under the old arrangement there were more centuries in the first class, made up of the rich, than there were in the lower classes, and consequently the rich controlled the assembly. In the reformed organization each one of the five classes, into which the citizens were divided according to their wealth, had the same number of centuries, and by the change the vote of a poor man counted for almost as much as that of the rich man.

211. Control of Affairs by the Senate. The composition of this body, however, was not a matter of much moment at

114

the time, partly because the tribal assemblies were preferred to the centuriate comitia on account of their simpler and more democratic organization, but mainly because the greater part of the legislation of the period emanates from no popular assembly whatsoever, but from the senate. Government by the senate had its advantages and its disadvantages. It gave a continuity to Roman policy, which chief magistrates, changing from year to year, could not have secured. It prevented the individual commander or magistrate from subordinating the public good to his personal ambition. On the other hand it hampered the commander in the field and the governor in a province, and in some measure took the management of distant affairs out of the hands of those who were on the spot, and, therefore, best qualified to reach a wise decision. But perhaps its greatest disadvantage was on the score of morals rather than of efficiency. A body of men will oftentimes instruct its executive to perform an act which an individual member of the body, with the full sense of responsibility resting upon him, would neither carry out of his own initiative, nor authorize another to carry out. Such an act, for instance, was the burning of Carthage, which Scipio Aemilianus carried out against his will under express orders from the senate.

212. How the Senate Maintained its Exclusive Character. The senate managed to make itself essentially a close corporation. Only a man like Cato, of exceptional ability and force of character, if he were outside the charmed circle of the *nobilitas*, could hope to secure office and thus enter the senate. Like every other oligarchy, this body had to protect itself at two points. It must keep outsiders from getting in, and it must prevent any citizen, whether one of its members or not, from acquiring great power, and from limiting its influence by exercising this power. The circumstances which gave to it its exclusive character we have already observed, and the new weapons which it forged against the knights, the rich men outside its number, we shall have occasion to notice shortly.

213. How It Held Popular Favorites in Check. To protect itself against ambitious individuals, the nobility in the year
180 secured the passage of a law fixing directly or indirectly
the age at which citizens might become candidates for the more
important offices. This law covered only two or three of the
principal magistracies, but the practices of many years had
fixed the position of the other offices also in a carefully graded
system, so that the *cursus honorum*, or fixed order in which
the magistracies were to be held, was established—an arrangement resting partly on law and partly on custom. In this
established order the military tribunate came first, then a position as one of the twenty-six commissioners who had charge
of the mint, of the streets, and other matters, followed by the
quaestorship, the tribunate of the plebs (required of plebeians only), the aedileship, the praetorship, and the consulship.
About the middle of the second century reëlection to the consulship was forbidden. By the first safeguard, that is, by the
establishment of the *cursus honorum*, the senate aimed to make
the political promotion of a popular favorite as slow and as
regular as possible, by obliging him to take the lower magistracies before he could be advanced to the higher. By the
second measure, which prohibited reëlection to the consulship,
it hoped to prevent an ambitious politician from holding office
too long.

214. Misgovernment in the Provinces. We already know
the general form of government which the senate after some
experiments worked out for the provinces. Affairs were at first
administered by praetors sent out each year from Rome, and
later by propraetors and proconsuls, that is, by ex-magistrates
holding the rank and powers of a praetor or consul. The
governor was assisted by a quaestor, or treasurer, and a board
of advisers, representing the senate. At first sight it would
seem as if the provinces might expect a reasonably just and
efficient government under this system, especially since each
province had a constitution, and since, after 149, governors
were liable to trial for misconduct before a permanent court.

But the management of the provinces was far from being either just or efficient. It was not just because the natives had no real protection against the unbridled avarice of the governor and the taxgatherer. It was inefficient because Roman officials had no acquaintance with the conditions of the provinces over which they were placed.

215. The Autocratic Power of Governors. When the magistrate passed beyond the bounds of Italy, all the constitutional limitations laid upon his action were suspended, and he became a ruler with arbitrary power. He had no colleagues; the provincial had no right to appeal from his decision, and no tribune interposed the shield of his protection between the autocrat and the subject. The quaestor had no independent authority, and the members of the provincial board of advisers were appointed by the governor himself, and could be trusted not to thwart his wishes. Even the constitution of the province afforded the native little protection. It was a costly matter to bring an action in Rome against a governor who had violated the constitution of a province; it was a dangerous thing to give evidence against him, and there was little hope of justice from a court whose members either openly sympathized with the culprit, or could be bought by his money, or who based their verdict on party considerations.

216. Their Rapacity. What the fate of the provinces was under this system, when they fell into the hands of men whose only objects in going abroad were to recoup themselves for the immense sums which they had spent in securing election to office at Rome, and to amass a fortune to meet their future needs at home, is shown clearly enough at a later date in Cicero's scathing arraignment of Verres, the governor of Sicily.

217. Their Ignorance of Local Conditions. Even if a governor were honest, the case was almost as bad. He would probably have little or no previous knowledge of his province or its people; his staff was composed of men as ignorant of the conditions as himself, and in the twelve months of his term of office, he could gain little information, correct few abuses, and establish no policy of his own. In such circumstances, to send off to Asia, among Orientals, a governor who knew nothing but Roman institutions and Roman ways of living and thinking could not fail to result in misgovernment. If one calls to mind England's method of governing India, for instance, one sees by contrast how fundamentally wrong the Roman system was. The governor-general of England's colony and his council hold office usually for five years, and the majority of the council must have been in the Indian service for ten years at least, before they are appointed councillors, while subordinate posts are filled by men who have specially prepared themselves for the work, and intend to spend a large part of their lives in India.

218. Economic Condition of the Provinces. In the train of the governor came the trader and the tax-farmer. Roman merchants and bankers absorbed the trade of the province, and loaned money at usurious rates to impoverished communities and individuals, enforcing their nefarious contracts with the connivance, and often with the direct support, of the governor. Taxes in the provinces were not collected by government officials, but the state sold at auction to the highest bidder the right to collect them. The profit of the tax-farmer lay in what he could collect over and above the amount which he had bid for the privilege, and he, like the banker and the merchant, relied upon the good offices of the governor, and woe betide the governor who attempted to defend the native against the extortionate demands of the taxgatherer and his rich and influential backers at Rome. Between the requisitions of the governor, the usurious practices of the money lender, and the insatiable demands of the *publicanus*, or taxgatherer, the poor provincial sunk into a hopeless state of debt and misery, or sought relief in a desperate attempt to throw off the yoke of his Roman master.

219. The Benefits which Rome Conferred on the Provinces. This is the dark side of the picture, but it has its bright side. Evil as the Roman administrative and financial system in the provinces was, in many cases it compared favorably with that which had preceded it. In most localities probably the tribute paid directly or indirectly to Rome was no greater than the provincial had in former days paid to the native ruler, and it was of the greatest advantage to him that Rome established order in each community, prevented the petty states from making war on one another, introduced a uniform system of laws, opened courts for the orderly settlement of cases under civilized methods of procedure, built roads and bridges, excavated harbors, and protected each province against the incursions of its less civilized neighbors. These were the permanent benefits which Rome conferred on her provinces, and one can readily see that if, in the course of time, a governor is chosen on the score of fitness, with a reasonably long term of office, and is made subject to proper limitations on his exercise of authority, and if the abuses of the tax system are removed, the territory which Rome has acquired will have gained in a material way, at least, by its transfer to Roman authority. And this happy result came in time, as we shall see.

220. Soldiers Unfitted for Peaceful Occupations. The political and social changes which war and the expansion of Roman territory effected in Italy were almost as marked as those which the conquered nations themselves experienced. The citizen-soldiers of earlier days returned at the end of a summer's campaign to resume their old vocations and to take their part again in the political life at home. But men who had served, perhaps for years, in Greece, Africa, or Spain, who had known the perils and the excitement of a soldier's life, and who had filled their purses from the booty of a captured town, were quite unfitted to settle down to the laborious, humdrum life of a farmer and an artisan. They were really soldiers by profession, and with the close of a campaign their occupation was gone. They had become accustomed to depend upon the state for their livelihood in time of war, and in time of peace they looked to the same source for their support. The restoration of peace, therefore, threw upon the community a great

body of men disinclined to any peaceful occupation, and unfitted
for it.

221. Unfitted for Political Life. In the sphere of politics
the result was almost as disastrous. The spirit of democracy
has little in common with military ideals. The freeman should
think and act and vote for himself. The soldier must surrender his own opinion and judgment to another. To put it
in another way, the successful prosecution of a campaign calls
for the complete submission of the individual soldier to the
will of his commander, while successful democratic government
depends upon the active, intelligent, and free participation of
the individual citizen in the conduct of affairs. Even if the
returned soldier had been inclined to take up his political duties
again, and capable of it, he would have found that the senate
had taken to itself the real functions of government, while to
him was left only participation in the rather meaningless meetings of the comitia.

222. Decline of Italy. The economic condition of Italy
outside of Rome was worse than that of the capital, because
the trade of the city developed, whereas the country districts
depended entirely on agriculture, and agriculture was ruined.
War had drafted off the vigorous young men, and much of the
land relapsed into its primitive state for lack of cultivation.
The campaigns of Hannibal in Italy also had laid waste a
great part of the peninsula. But the acquisition of Sicily, Sardinia, and Africa dealt the severest blow of all to Italian agriculture. These three fertile regions sent their grain to be sold
in Rome at prices with which the Italian farmer could not
compete, and, to make matters worse, in times of scarcity the
government itself sold grain at prices far below their natural
level. The condition of the Italian peasant went from bad to
worse. He struggled as long as he could to make a living in
these adverse circumstances, until finally, weighed down by debts
and mortgages, he was forced to sell his little farm to swell
the estate of some landed proprietor. In this way the peasant

proprietor was crowded out by the great landowner. The lot of the free agricultural laborer was equally unfortunate. Thousands of prisoners had been taken in war, brought as slaves to Italy, and set to work in the country. The free laborer could not and would not compete with them. There was nothing left for him to do but to betake himself to the capital along with the bankrupt farmer, and join the great army of the unemployed, in the hope of picking up a precarious living by honorable or dishonorable means, or of being supported by the government.

223. Accumulation of Large Fortunes. While the poor became poorer, the well-to-do and the rich amassed great fortunes. The destruction of Carthage and Corinth, and the decline of Rhodes made Rome the commercial and banking centre of the Mediterranean. Her ships absorbed the carrying trade, her merchants and money lenders penetrated to all parts of the world, and her citizens secured the contracts for the construction of roads and bridges and the collection of taxes.

224. Development of the Equites. Inasmuch as the senate was called upon to pass laws affecting the award of state contracts, the members of that body were not allowed to take contracts from the state. They were also forbidden to own vessels beyond a specified tonnage, and it was considered unseemly for them to speculate. For this reason they had to restrict their investments to landed property and the newly developed industries were left to the middle class, the *equites*, or knights, as they were called. This title henceforth comes to indicate practically the wealthy men who were not members of the senate, because, in the early period, when a man's property had reached a certain amount he was liable to service in the cavalry, and the title was still given to those whose fortunes amounted to a certain sum, even after they were no longer expected to serve as horsemen. The new opportunities for making money which the expansion of Roman territory offered, increased immensely the size and influence of this class of citizens, which became essentially, but not yet legally, a new order

of nobility, just below the senate in social and political importance.

225. They Aspire to Political Honors. The political
ambitions of its members brought it into sharp conflict with
the senate and the *nobilitas*. The senatorial nobility had
managed for generations to keep all the offices in its own hands.
The *equites* challenged this privilege, and they supported
their claims by the lavish use of money for political purposes
upon the needy farmers and farm laborers who had thronged
to the city and upon the veterans whom the return of peace
had left without employment. In such circumstances wide-
spread political corruption was inevitable. It was to prevent
the *equites* from buying the votes of these classes of people at
the elections that the senatorial nobility secured the passage,
in the second century, of laws against bribery, and of measures
which provided for a secret ballot at the meetings of the comitia.

226. Growth of Luxury. The evils which naturally follow
a sudden increase of wealth were aggravated by the fact that
the conquest of Magna Græcia and the East brought the Romans
into contact with a highly developed civilization to which their
previous simple life was in marked contrast. The development
of luxurious tastes and the means of gratifying them came simultaneously, and the rich Roman rushed into reckless expenditure
on his household and his retinue with the intemperance which
characterizes those who have become suddenly rich.

227. The Opposition Led by Cato. The advocates of
old-time simplicity, led by Cato, the Censor, set their faces like
flint against this tendency to luxurious living. They called in
the law to their assistance, and provided by statute that no
woman should wear more than half an ounce of gold and that
she should not use purple cloth. Laws were passed limiting
the number of guests whom a householder could entertain,
and the amount which he could spend upon a single dinner.
These laws accomplished little. Thus, for instance, twenty years
after its passage, the Oppian law, mentioned above, which had
been directed against display in dress, was repealed in spite

of the vigorous opposition of Cato, who was at the time consul. In the speech which the historian Livy puts into Cato's mouth the orator makes this gloomy forecast of the future: "You have often heard me lamenting the extravagance of women and of men, of magistrates as well as of private citizens, and maintaining that the state is burdened by two contradictory vices, greed and a taste for luxury, evils which have overthrown all great empires. As the lot of the state grows better and happier day by day, and as the empire develops—and at this moment we are passing over into Greece and Asia, which are filled with everything to tempt the desires of man, and are laying hands even upon the treasures of kings—as the empire grows, I say, I dread the more these vices of greed and luxury, for fear that these possessions have captured us and not that we have captured them. Hateful, I assure you, are the works of art brought to this city from Syracuse. Already I hear too many people expressing praise and admiration of the statues of the gods at Corinth and Athens, and laughing at the little clay images of Roman gods."

228. His Censorship. Cato represented in his person the protest of the old Rome against the new, and the peculiar mission of his life was to stem the tide of luxury, and to maintain the old-time simple standards of living. He preached frugality without ceasing; he supported measures intended to limit expenditures, and by its rigor, made his censorship long remembered by his countrymen. The senators who were excluded from the senate by the new censor on account of their lax mode of life, the rich who found articles of luxury rated for purposes of taxation at ten times their real value, and the tax-farmers who were held strictly to their contracts, all protested, but without avail, because Cato had the confidence of the people. He saw clearly that Greece and Asia were the source of the evils which he was attacking, and he opposed vigorously the introduction of Greek philosophy, culture, and modes of living; but it was beyond the power of any one man to stem the tide.

229. Thé Effect of Greek Influence on the Romans.
In fact, the conquest of Greece and of the countries in which
Greek civilization existed worked a complete transformation
in the life and character of the Romans.   As soon as Rome
became the capital of the world, throngs of Greeks flocked
there, or were brought there as slaves. Thousands of Romans
too engaged in trade with Greek lands, or went to the East
as soldiers or officials.   Greek literature and art, Greek modes
of living and ideas of life became known at Rome, and were
not unwillingly received by many.   The effect upon Roman
character was disastrous.   The Romans suffered in much the
same way as peoples on a lower plane of civilization suffer to-day
when brought by conquest under the influence of a more highly
civilized race.   They were hardly prepared to take what was
best in Greek civilization, but yielded to the vices and weaknesses of the more highly developed people.   Greek influence
gave a great stimulus, it is true, to the growth of literature
and art, but even this was not an unmixed blessing, because
it prevented Rome from developing a literature and art along
the lines of her own national genius.   The Roman writer or
the Roman artist tried to imitate his Greek models.   As a
result, he failed either to equal them or to bring out the best
of which he was himself capable.

230. Narrow-mindedness Disappears.   By coming into
contact with the outside world Rome in a large measure lost
her contempt for other peoples and her belief in the perfection
of her own institutions.   She went so far as to recognize the
fact that the individual freeman, whether a Roman or a foreigner, had certain rights, and when settling judicial questions,
even those in which foreigners were concerned, she did not
insist upon the application of Roman law in all its details, but
applied the customs of the civilized world, and thus developed
the *ius gentium*, an international private law.   Such concessions
as this show clearly enough that Rome was losing her narrow-
mindedness and was able to find something worth adopting
in the practices of others.

231. Changes in Roman Character. This tolerant attitude toward foreign ideas and practices had its drawbacks, however. In the everyday life of the citizens the *mores maiorum*, or practices of the fathers, lost much of their compelling power, and were no longer obeyed without question. Simplicity of life, the ability to endure hardship, upright conduct, and the maintenance of personal dignity and independence ceased to be the universal ideals which they had been in the past. Men developed a craving for the comforts and luxuries of life, and in order to get them were willing to sacrifice their honesty and self-respect. Those who possessed a large measure of the good things of the world were puffed up by their possessions, and were fawned upon or envied by their less fortunate fellow-men. The invectives of Cato, the prosecutions for extortion, the laws against bribery, all of which we have already noticed, and the struggle between the poor and the rich in the generation which follows bring out plainly these changes in Roman character.

232. Changes in Education. The influence of Greek culture both for good and for evil was the more effective because it was brought to bear directly upon the young. In early days a Roman boy received his training from his father. It was very simple. It consisted in the main of such physical exercises as swimming, running, riding, and the use of arms, and the acquisition of an ability to read, write, and make simple calculations. This was the sort of education which Cato gave his son. The girl was trained by her mother so that she might be able to manage a household when the time came for her to marry. From the beginning of the second century before our era the hardening physical exercises fell more into disuse, and in their stead there were substituted the study of Latin and Greek literature, rhetoric, and law, and what was a still more significant change, a boy's training was entrusted to a professional Greek teacher, who was often a slave in the household. No way more effective than this of grafting Greek qualities on the old Roman stock could have been devised.

233. The Integrity of the Family Weakened. The new influences threatened the unity of the family. Wives successfully asserted their freedom in certain matters from the control of their husbands. In some cases women on marrying even retained control of their own property. Divorce was not unknown. A son too acquired some measure of independence, and not infrequently slaves by their cleverness and ability gained a virtual control of the household. Such a state of affairs was far removed from that of the primitive days, when marriage was indissoluble and the right of the father over the life and property of every member of his household could not be questioned even by the state.

234. New Inventions. It was during this period that many of the conveniences of civilized life were introduced into Rome. From the Egyptians, for instance, came the water-clock and the hydraulic pump; from the Greeks various musical instruments; from the Gauls vehicles of different kinds, and tiles to be used in building.

235. New Industries. That life in Rome was becoming more complex is clearly shown also by the introduction of new industries and occupations. We hear, for instance, of inn-keepers and dealers in wine, of professional cooks and scribes, of physicians, actors, and gladiators, and of teachers of music and dancing. The city took on more of a metropolitan appearance from the fact that men engaged in the same trade showed a tendency to gather at a given point. For example, the butchers and oil-merchants had their stands in the Velabrum, as we know from Plautus.

236. Extravagance. The passion which the common people developed for theatrical and gladiatorial performances shows itself in a marked way in this period. Fights with wild beasts and contests between professional athletes were introduced in 186, and elaborate musical entertainments about twenty years later. As for the well-to-do, we have noticed that they spent their money with the lavishness characteristic of those who have become suddenly rich. They built fine houses and villas, laid out magnificent gardens, bought costly articles of furniture, made collections of works of art and bric-a-brac, and employed large numbers of house slaves. Trade with the

Orient responded quickly to the demands for articles of luxury by pouring into Rome purple stuffs from Miletus, glassware and garments of linen and cotton from Egypt, fine wines from Greece, and spices from Ethiopia and Syria.

237. Religious Changes. The crude conceptions which the Romans in the early days had of the gods would not harmonize with the wider knowledge which they had acquired from contact with the outside world. The old religion seemed cold, formal, and colorless, too, in comparison with

ROMAN GLADIATOR

the religions of Greece and Asia, and ceased to satisfy the aspirations of the people. The need for something more personal and more spiritual was supplied in part by investing certain Roman gods with the attributes of the Greek deities which were most like them, and by introducing bodily the worship of certain foreign gods. Thus the Roman Jupiter and the Greek Zeus were identified, Juno and Hera, Mercury and Hermes, Mars and Ares, the worship of Serapis was brought from Egypt, and that of Cybele from Asia Minor. Reverence was still paid to the Lares and Penates in the household, and the state still maintained the forms of the old faith for official purposes, but for the mass of the people the old religion was rapidly losing its meaning and its restraining force. The more intelligent had become skeptical, and the common people were lapsing into the lower forms of superstition.

238. Roman Poetry.   Perhaps in the long run Roman literature would have developed in a more healthy and characteristic way, if it had not been brought at the outset under Greek influence.   Whatever opinion we may hold upon this

CHAPEL IN HOUSE

point, it is undoubtedly true that the first impulse to literature came from Greece.   The father of Roman literature was Livius Andronicus, who was brought to Rome after the capture of Tarentum in 272.   He took up the teaching of Latin and Greek, and, finding no suitable book to use in teaching Latin, translated the Odyssey into Latin verse. Later, in 240, when the Romans wished to celebrate their success over the Carthaginians

A ROMAN THEATRE AT POMPEII

by a dramatic festival, Livius Andronicus produced Latin translations of a Greek tragedy and a Greek comedy, and sub-

SCENE FROM A COMEDY

sequently he composed hymns for another occasion. Epic, dramatic, and lyric poetry, therefore, begin with him. The

first native Latin poet was Gnaeus Naevius, who is best known
for his national epic, which Vergil has followed at many point:
in the *Aeneid*, but Naevius's work was surpassed by the *Annals*,
the great epic poem of Ennius, a citizen of Calabria.   In this
composition the story of the Romans was told from the arrival
of Aeneas in Italy down to the time of the writer.   Some six
hundred lines of the poem are extant, and they justify the admiration which the Romans had for it.   This is the flourishing period
of Roman tragedy, which reached its highest point of development in the dramas of Pacuvius and Accius.   Unfortunately
their writings have come down to us only in fragments, so that
we can form no adequate notion of the merit of the complete
works.   We are much more fortunate in the case of comedy.
Some twenty comedies of Plautus and six of Terence are extant.
They are translations or adaptations from the New Attic comedy
which flourished shortly after the death of Alexander.   Comedy,
like tragedy, really begins and ends in the years under consideration.   In this period satire also is cultivated by Ennius and
Lucilius.

239. Roman Prose.   The first important work in Latin
prose we owe to Marcus Porcius Cato.   His purpose was to
tell the history of his native land and to show that Latin as well
as Greek could be used in prose composition.   In his work
called the *Origines*, he traced the history of Rome from the
beginning down to the year 149.   This book is lost, but we
have his treatise *On Agriculture*, which was very likely intended
in part to check the growing tendency to give up agriculture
for commercial occupations.   We know from statements made
by writers in the first century before our era that the great
speech which Appius Claudius Caecus delivered in the senate
in 280 against the ratification of the treaty with Pyrrhus was
written out and handed down to succeeding generations, but
it was Cato who first made a collection of speeches.   One
hundred and fifty of his orations were known in Cicero's time,
and were held in high regard.   The natural bent of his mind
turned the Roman to the study of law, and in the early part

of the second century systematic works on legal subjects began to appear. The three forms of literature mentioned above—history, oratory, and jurisprudence—proved to be the most characteristic types of Roman prose, and it is interesting to bear the fact in mind that two of them originated with Cato, the sturdy and uncompromising representative of everything Roman.

240. Summary of Events at Home from 264 to 133 B. C. It is clear that throughout this period affairs at home and abroad were managed by the senate, which found means to control the magistrates and hold in check popular leaders. Abroad, the point of greatest political interest was the development of provincial government, which was inefficient, but gave the provincials law and order. At home, in the country districts slave labor, the sale of imported grain at low prices, and the growth of large estates were ruining the small farmer; in the city great fortunes were acquired in trade with the provinces, and the knights became influential. Contact with Greece and the East led to the introduction of new inventions and industries, to important changes in the Roman religion and character, and to the development of literature. Taken all in all, the conquest of Mediterranean lands brought about profound changes in the Roman character and civilization.

CHAPTER VIII

(133–49 B. C.)

How the conquest of Gaul by Caesar and of Asia Minor by Pompey changed political conditions, and brought monarchy nearer.

241. Gallia Narbonensis Organized as a Province about 118 B. C. The conquest of Cisalpine Gaul in the early part of the second century had carried the limits of Roman territory to the Alps. For a half century thereafter these mountains were accepted as a natural frontier, but, thanks to roads and colonies, in these fifty years the district to the south of the Alps, known as Cisalpine Gaul, had developed so rapidly that the great returns which capital and industry win in a new land were no longer to be had, and the eager merchant and capitalist were casting covetous glances across the Alps, and waiting impatiently for the time when Roman arms should open the country to trade. The need of better communications between Italy and the Spains was also apparent. An opportunity to accomplish both these objects was offered in 125 by the request which the city of Massilia made for help against the tribes to the north of her. An expedition was willingly sent to her relief, which brought the hostile tribes to submission without serious difficulty. In fact, the greater part of southern Gaul was subdued and organized into a province which took its name of Gallia Narbonensis from the Roman colony established at its capital, Narbo, on the reconstructed Via Domitia from the Rhone to Spain.

242. The First Province of a New Empire. With the occupation of southern Gaul a new chapter of expansion begins. Just as the passage of the Straits of Messina had led on step by

step to the acquisition of Sicily, Sardinia, northern Africa, and
Spain, so, when the tide of conquest had once passed beyond
the Alps, its progress was not stopped until it had swept across
Gaul, Germany, and even Britain. The petty successes of
Fulvius and Fabius over the Arverni and their neighbors were
the forerunners of the great conquests of Julius Caesar, of Tiberius, and of a long line of victorious leaders, and Gallia Narbonensis was the first province of the great empire which within
the next one hundred and fifty years the Romans created in
central Europe.

**243. Invasion by the Cimbri and Teutones, 113–101
B. C.** The immediate effect, however, of the policy of expand-
ing to the north was disastrous. Hitherto Roman territory
had been protected against the tribes of central Europe by barriers of mountains—Italy by the Alps, Spain by the Pyrenees.
Now Rome was called upon to maintain her authority in a
region which had no such bulwark behind it. The Gallic
tribes in the past had furnished an additional barrier against the
incursions of the northern people, but the conquest of their
country by the Romans had broken their spirit, so that when
in the second century B. C., a horde of German warriors advanced
southward from their homes on the Baltic Sea, they met little
effective resistance from the Gallic tribes on the frontiers of
the Roman territory. These German peoples, known as the
Cimbri and Teutones, were not making a simple incursion into
Roman territory for the sake of booty, but were accompanied
by their wives and children, and were planning to seize and
occupy any territory which seemed available. Their warriors, giants in stature, clad in heavy coats of mail, and armed
with powerful swords, were bound to one another in battle
with thongs, as it was said, so that their lines could not be
broken. They had already defeated the Romans in three
pitched battles, when Gaius Marius, the great popular leader
who had just brought a difficult war in Africa to a successful
termination, took the field against them.

244. Battles at Aquæ Sextiæ in 102 B. C., and on the Raudine Plains in 101 B. C. The enemy sought to enter Italy at two points. The Teutones with their allies advanced along the coast of southern Gaul, while the Cimbri were to force an entrance by way of Illyricum. Marius himself met the Teutones at Aquæ Sextiæ and destroyed their army, and in the following year hastened into Italy to relieve Catulus, who had been obliged to retire before the Cimbri. The two Roman forces engaged the enemy on the Raudine Plains near Vercellæ, and annihilated their entire force of one hundred thousand men.

245. Caesar's Conquest of Gaul, 58–50 B. C. Henceforth for several centuries Italy had no occasion to fear an inroad of the barbarians, and for nearly half a century peace along the northern frontier was broken only by the occasional uprisings of petty tribes. But in 58 B. C. the Roman province in southern Gaul and the peoples to the north of it were threatened by a movement not unlike that of the Cimbri and Teutones. In that year the Helvetii, to the number of three hundred and sixty-eight thousand, who had long been making preparations for the purpose, set out from their old home with their wives and children, to seek new lands to the west. To check this movement C. Julius Caesar, who had been consul the preceding year, was made governor of the three provinces of Cisalpine Gaul, Illyricum, and Transalpine Gaul, and commander of the troops assigned to the protection of these provinces, for a period of five years counting from March 1, 59 B. C. Marching rapidly to the north, Caesar forced the Helvetii to give up their intention of passing through the province, and ultimately defeated them near Bibracte and obliged them to return to their own country. Later in the year the Germans, who had crossed the Rhine into Gaul, were forced to return and to accept the Rhine as marking the limits of their territory. In the following year he reduced the confederated states of the Belgæ, which occupied the territory between the the Seine and the Rhine, and penetrated to the North Sea. He even made two

expeditions across the Channel into Britain. No more serious
movements occurred in Caesar's provinces until 52 B. C. In
that year the Gauls found an able commander in their chief
Vercingetorix. He gave strict orders to his own people and
their allies to burn all their towns and their stores, and with
his cavalry he swept through the country and laid it waste,
in order that the enemy might be starved into submission.
Never before had Caesar been reduced to such straits. His
soldiers were nearly famished; his assault upon the stronghold
of Gergovia was beaten back, and the Gallic cavalry harassed
his troops in their retreat to the north. But in spite of all these

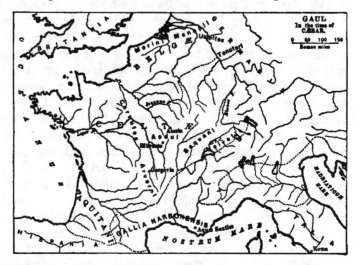

difficulties Caesar succeeded in shutting up Vercingetorix in
his fortified camp at Alesia. Emissaries sent throughout Gaul
by the beleaguered town brought to its succor a fresh army of
two hundred and fifty thousand men, but the legionaries not
only succeeded in repelling the relief party, but maintained so
effective a blockade of the town that Vercingetorix was finally
compelled to yield, and riding into Caesar's camp surrendered
to his conqueror. The Gallic chief was kept a prisoner, to
lend distinction to the triumph of Caesar, and to atone by death

at the hands of the public executioner for his brave resistance
to the Romans.

246. The New Empire in the North. The fall of Alesia
put an end to all serious resistance in Gaul, and, as a result
of the campaigns which had begun seventy-five years before
with the expedition to the relief of Massilia, Roman authority
was now recognized in Belgica, Gallia Narbonensis, and in the
districts known later as Aquitania and Gallia Lugdunensis,
i. e., throughout the territory now covered by France and the
Netherlands.

247. Conditions in the East. Almost as noteworthy
additions were made to the Roman empire in the East in the
period which we are studying, and the successful completion
of the wars of conquest in the West and in the East by Caesar
and Pompey respectively made these two men rivals for the
control of the Roman world, and put the republic in jeopardy.
One of the weakest of the states which Rome left in Asia Minor
after her defeat of Antiochus, king of Syria, was the little kingdom of Pontus on the southeastern coast of the Euxine. For
many years Pontus was the faithful ally of Rome, but, with
the accession of Mithridates the Great in 114, she changed her
policy. The new king was a man of indomitable energy, of
versatility, and of great political ability. Without serious
difficulty he made himself master of the Greek settlements
along the north shore of the Euxine, of the states in Asia Minor
which had been allied with Rome, and of the islands along
the coast.

**248. The Three Wars with Mithridates, 88-84, 83-81,
74-63 B. C.** But his attempt to occupy Greece was thwarted
by the Roman leader Sulla, and he was forced to give up his
conquests in Asia Minor. The irregular hostilities which
followed the conclusion of peace took the form of open war
in 74 when the kingdom of Bithynia, which had been a buffer
state between Pontus and the province of Asia, fell into the
hands of the Romans. Lucullus, who commanded the Roman

troops, drove Mithridates out of Pontus, defeated the army of his son-in-law Tigranes, the king of Armenia, with whom he had taken refuge, and seemed on the point of bringing the war to an end; but, before he could make his conquests permanent, his soldiers, who were clamoring for release from service, mutinied, and the senate at Rome, listening to the tax-contractors, whose exorbitant demands Lucullus had checked, transferred his command to another.

249. Pompey Subdues the Pirates in 67 B. C.   The recall of Lucullus and the diversion of Roman energy to the suppression of piracy in the eastern Mediterranean gave Mithridates and Tigranes an opportunity to recover their strength and to regain some of the territory taken from them by Lucullus. From the beginning of the war with Mithridates the pirates had taken advantage of the turmoil to ply their trade vigorously along the coast of Asia Minor. With the progress of the war their numbers and their boldness increased. "They fell upon unfortified towns," as Appian tells us. "They undermined or battered down the walls of others. They carried off the wealthier citizens to their haven of refuge and held them for ransom. . . . They had castles and towers and desert islands and retreats everywhere. . . . When the Romans could no longer endure the damage and disgrace they made Gnaeus Pompey, who was then their man of greatest reputation, commander by law for three years, with absolute power over the whole sea within the Pillars of Hercules, and of the land for a distance of four hundred stades from the coast. . . . Never did any man before Pompey set forth with so great authority conferred upon him by the Romans. . . . The terror of his name and the greatness of his preparations produced a panic among the robbers. . . . Within a few days he took seventy-one ships by capture and three hundred and six by surrender from the pirates, and one hundred and twenty of their towns, castles, and other places of rendezvous. About ten thousand of the pirates were slain in battle."

250. Pompey Brings to an End the Third Mithridatic War, 66-63 B. C.   Pompey was still in Cilicia, the country of the pirates, when the Manilian law added to his naval power the governorship of Bithynia and Cilicia, and the conduct of the war against Mithridates and Tigranes.   It was in support of this law, and as a representative of the great middle class, whose interests as merchants, bankers, and tax-contractors were imperilled by the situation in the East, that Marcus Tullius Cicero comes into prominence as a political leader.   After Pompey's assumption of the command in Asia events moved rapidly. He drove Mithridates out of Pontus and forced him to take refuge on the north shore of the Euxine.   He entered Armenia, and received the unconditional surrender of Tigranes.   All this was accomplished in the first year's campaign.   Within the next two years he annexed Syria, took Jerusalem, and restored order in Palestine.   While on his way toward Jerusalem in the spring of 63 he learned that Mithridates, deserted by his favorite son Pharnaces, and abandoned by his troops, had taken his own life.   With the death of Mithridates, and the voluntary submission of Pharnaces, resistance to Roman authority in Asia Minor came to an end.

251. Pompey's Triumph on returning to Rome.   Pompey's conquests in the East made a deeper impression on the imagination of the Romans than did Caesar's more noteworthy achievements in Gaul.   Plutarch gives us an enthusiastic description of the triumph which he celebrated after his return to the city.   "In it tables were carried, inscribed with the names and titles of the nations over which he triumphed. . . . There was set forth in these tables an account of all the tributes throughout the empire, and how that before these conquests the revenue amounted but to fifty millions, whereas from his acquisitions they had a revenue of eighty-five millions.   The prisoners of war that were led in triumph, besides the chief pirates, were the son of Tigranes, king of Armenia, with his wife and daughter; as also Zosime, wife of king Tigranes himself, and Aristobulus king of Judæa, the sister of King Mithridates and her five sons, and some Scythian women." At the head of the procession which entered by one of the city gates and passed through the Forum along the Sacred Way to the Capitol, were the senate and the magistrates. Behind the tablets, the trophies, the captives, and the white bulls intended for sacrifice, preceded by lictors with their *fasces* crowned with laurels, came Pompey standing in a chariot drawn by four horses. He wore a gold-embroidered robe and a flowered tunic. In his right hand he held a laurel bough; in his left a sceptre, and on his head rested a laurel wreath. The streets and squares were crowded with people; the shrines were decorated with flowers, and through the open doors of every temple could be seen the smoke of incense rising from the altars.

252. The Credit due to Pompey. Pompey well deserved the honors which his fellow-citizens paid him on his return. In three years he had brought to an end a state of hostility which had alternated between open war and armed truce for a quarter of a century. He established permanent peace where his predecessors, Sulla and Lucullus, had only secured a temporary cessation of hostilities. But it is only fair to Sulla, and to Lucullus especially, to remember that they broke the power of Mithridates and shattered his prestige. It was Pompey's good fortune to grasp the laurels which they had brought within his reach.

253. Political Reorganization of Asia Minor. In his political reorganization of Asia Minor his policy was so thorough and so wise that his arrangements were left without important change for many decades. Western Pontus and Bithynia were united and Syria was made a province, although certain principalities were still allowed to exist within its borders. Outside of these districts, and of the province of Asia, the rest of Asia Minor was left in the hands of princes whose fidelity to Rome was unquestioned.

254. The Financial Condition of Asia. The management of Asiatic finances shows a steady improvement from the time of Sulla to that of Pompey. When Mithridates in his early

campaigns had made himself master of Asia, he courted the
popularity of the provincials by releasing them altogether
from the payment of tribute.   The taxes were thus left unpaid
for five years, and one of Sulla's first measures, after reconquering the province, was to require these arrears of taxes,
as well as an indemnity for the war of twenty thousand talents.
To meet these demands, "the cities," as Appian tells us, "borrowed money at high rates of interest and mortgaged their
theatres, their gymnasiums, their walls, their harbors, and
every other scrap of public property."   From the financial
ruin which the exactions of Sulla brought upon the country

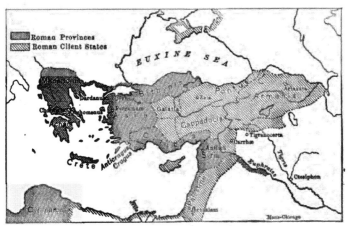

ASIA MINOR AT THE CLOSE OF POMPEY'S CONQUESTS

Lucullus relieved the people in a measure by checking the un-
just methods of the *publicani*, or taxgatherers, and by cutting
down the rate of interest to twelve per cent.   Pompey in his
turn suppressed the pirates who had preyed upon the ships
trading in the Mediterranean, and had plundered the coast
towns; he restored law and order; he guarded the frontiers, and
he gave a large measure of freedom to the commercial towns.

**255. Effect on the Home Government of the Policy
of Expansion.**   By the conquests of Caesar and Pompey the
frontiers of the empire were pushed on the eastern border to

the Euphrates, north to the Rhine, and westward to the Atlantic, while the entire Mediterranean coast, with the exception of Mauretania, was brought under Roman control. The acquisition of this great territory and the provisions made for its government had a reflex effect upon the character of the home government and the relative importance of the elements which made it up. Practices altogether out of harmony with tradition were adopted, and unwritten laws which had thwarted the projects of ambitious leaders in the past were violated. To put it briefly, the old machinery of government broke down under the strain put upon it by the demands of imperialism. The traditional prejudice against the reëlection of the chief magistrate was thrown to the winds when Marius was elected six times to the consulship. A similar precedent was violated when Caesar was made proconsul for five years, and when

TOMB OF A CENTURION.

Pompey was given charge of the forces acting against the pirates for a period of three years. The very length of their terms of office freed Pompey and Caesar in large measure from the danger of being held to account for their actions, and rendered impracticable any serious attempts which the senate might make to control the direction of campaigns. In the old days the senate limited the powers of its commanders and kept them in hand by holding back the appropriation bills. This policy was now given up. Indeed, it is remarkable that Rome carried on her long foreign wars successfully on the old plan. When Pompey assumed command against the pirates he was granted an unlimited *imperium;* he was authorized to collect all the troops and supplies he might need, and Roman officials and allied states were directed to render him all possible assistance. Such powers made him not the military representative of the senate, nor even of the state, but an independent Eastern

TOMB OF A STANDARD BEARER

monarch. The long terms which many of the soldiers served under Marius, Sulla, Pompey, and Caesar turned their feeling of allegiance away from the senate or the people to their military leader, while for the many foreigners who served in the Gallic army patriotism meant little more than loyalty to Caesar. In a word, the development of a colonial empire had transferred the real power from the senate to the commanders of the armies.

256. Summary Account of the Conquests of Gaul and Asia Minor, 133–49 B. C. In this period we have seen Rome extend her conquests in the West and in the East under her two great leaders Caesar and Pompey. The occupation of southern Gaul was necessary to give her direct communication with Spain by land, and to protect this territory from the tribes to the north the conquest of all Gaul by Caesar seemed necessary. In the East, piracy was suppressed, and Asia Minor reorganized under Roman authority. The result for the home government was to build up great armies of veterans under able leaders, and to make it possible for the army to control the state.

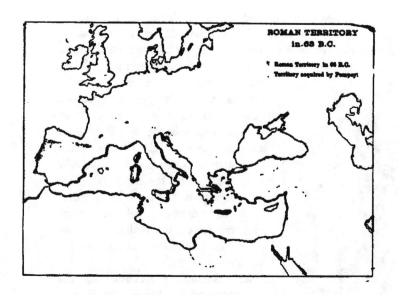

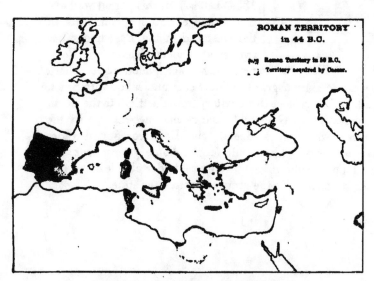

DEVELOPMENT OF ROMAN TERRITORY FROM 133 TO 44 B. C.

CHAPTER IX

(133–49 B. C.)

How the struggle against the senate and the rich, beginning under the Gracchi, was advanced by Marius, was checked by Sulla, and developed into a personal contest between Caesar and Pompey for the supreme power.

257. The Desire of Tiberius Gracchus to Relieve the Poor. We have already had occasion to notice that the long wars abroad, the acquisition of provinces, the accumulation of large fortunes, and the development of slavery had driven Italian farmers into bankruptcy, and left the farm laborer and the free artisan without employment. The middle class which in the past had given the social organization its strength and stability was thereby blotted out of existence, and the movement which Tiberius Gracchus led in the period now under consideration had for its object to build this class up again.

258. His Motives. He was a man of the people by sympathy rather than by birth, because his family and his family connections were all aristocratic. To the sympathy which they and other powerful personal friends felt for the movement the reforms of Tiberius and Gaius owed in some degree that measure of success which they won. Many of the more progressive Romans, like Tiberius's grandfather Africanus, had shown their hostility to the new aristocracy of wealth, or had dreamed of lightening the burdens of the common people, but they lacked the ability to formulate measures of relief, or the energy to carry them through. It was left to Tiberius and his brother to translate their passive sympathy into action.

259. His Agrarian Measure. Tiberius thought that he could relieve the distressed by assigning state lands to citizens. With this purpose in mind, he secured an election to the tribunate for the year 133, and at once proposed a reënactment of that

143

clause of the Licinian law which limited the amount of public
land to be held by an individual to five hundred *iugera,* with
the modification that for each of two grown sons two hundred
and fifty *iugera* in addition should be allowed. The land
which would in this way be brought again under the control
of the state was to be leased on the payment of an annual rental.
A standing commission of three, whose members were to be
chosen each year, was to carry out the provisions of the law.

260. Its Character and Effectiveness. This proposal
was essentially different from earlier colonizing projects. It
was clearly socialistic. Earlier colonies had been sent out to
points of danger to hold and to Romanize newly acquired territory. The protection which they gave the state was a sufficient
return for the land which the state gave them. The colonists
of Tiberius were to be settled in peaceful sections of Italy;
they were to receive land solely because of their poverty. It
is clear that his measures could not have removed the real evil
of the situation. That lay in the fact that the farmers and
free farm laborers were ruined, as we have already seen, by
the low price at which imported corn was sold and by the use
of slave labor. Tiberius's bill did not touch these difficulties.

261. It is Finally Adopted. It met with violent opposition from the rich who were in possession of the land of which
the state proposed to resume control, and they prevailed upon
Octavius, one of the tribunes, to interpose his veto. This
opposition drove Tiberius to adopt an extreme course. Declaring that a representative of the people ceases to be such when
he acts out of harmony with the popular wish, he summoned
the assembly and asked it to vote whether or not Octavius
should be deposed from office. The people voted in the affirm-
ative, and Octavius was deprived of the tribunate. The
action which Tiberius took in this case was even more revolutionary and more at variance with Roman tradition than his
agrarian measure had been. It was subversive of stable
government, and rested upon the theory that the permanent
institutions of the state were at the mercy of a temporary popular

majority—a theory which ultimately took practical form in the democratic empire of Julius Caesar. The agrarian law of Tiberius was adopted but he himself was killed while seeking reëlection to the tribunate.

262. Results of the Movement led by Tiberius. His efforts, however, were not fruitless. From 135 to 124 B. C., the number of citizens increased from three hundred and eighteen thousand to three hundred and ninety-five thousand, and a large majority of those whose names were added to the lists must have gained their right to be enrolled as citizens by becoming landowners under the new law. A less desirable outcome of the measure probably its author had not anticipated. By its operation the privileges which the Latins and other Italians had enjoyed in the public land were taken from them; they were made to feel more keenly than ever the drawbacks under which they suffered when compared with Roman citizens, and were soon driven, as we shall see, into open revolt against Rome. But the most important result of the agitation which Tiberius started was the development of a democratic opposition to the *nobilitas*. Economic conditions for a century or more had been putting wealth, social station, and political influence in the hands of the few at the expense of the many, and the ill-defined hostility which the poor felt against the rich in consequence of this state of affairs resulted in the struggle for agrarian rights. In this struggle the senate championed the cause of the wealthy landholder. This was only natural, because the senate was made up of rich men, but the turn which affairs thus took converted the economic into a political struggle, and arrayed the poor, with the comitia as their organ, against the rich nobles who were firmly entrenched in the senate.

263. The Policy of Gaius Gracchus. Gaius Gracchus, who succeeded his brother in the leadership of the democracy, and was elected to the tribunate in 123, saw clearly that the senate must be his point of attack. To succeed he must lessen its power, lower its prestige, and take from it its political and social privileges. But Gaius was not an idealist, as his brother had been. He was a practical politician of great constructive ability, and he knew that to secure from a powerful, compact body, like the senate, the political and economic rights of the people, it would not suffice to rely upon the justice of his cause—he must fight the senate with its own weapons. He must combine, too, all the elements in the state whose interests were opposed to those of the senate, and, to win the support of different classes of society, he must include in his political programme projects which would appeal to each of them. To this task he applied himself. The two classes upon whose backing he counted were the proletariat, or poor people, and the knights.

264. How He Won the Support of the Poor People. To win the adhesion of the former he secured the reënactment or reaffirmation of his brother's land law; he provided for the establishment of colonies for the needy in southern Italy and across the sea; he lightened the hardships of military service, and he had a *lex frumentaria*, or corn law, passed, which put grain at the disposal of the poor at a price lower than the market rate.

265. How He Won the Knights. To secure the support of the knights, or the rich men who were not members of senatorial families, Gaius turned over the control of the courts to them, and gave them a monopoly in collecting the taxes in Asia. From this time on they formed a recognized order of nobility, and it was probably he who first indicated their aristocratic standing to the eye by allowing them to wear gold finger rings, and tunics with a narrow border, and by giving them separate seats at the games.

266. His Direct Attacks upon the Senate. He secured the passage of a law prescribing the manner in which the senate should assign provinces to the consuls, and in this way lessened the senate's control of the chief magistrate. He also sought to give importance to the comitia, and to substitute their action for the decrees of the senate. In one important matter especially he secured a restatement of the principle that the senate was subordinate to the popular assemblies. After the death of

Tiberius, the senate established a judicial commission to investigate the action of some of his followers. They were tried and executed. To protect himself and future democratic leaders from such a fate, Gaius secured the passage of a new law reaffirming a citizen's right to appeal to the people from a capital sentence.

267. The Political Ability and Ideals of Gaius. To weld together into one political party two classes whose interests and sympathies were so opposed to each other as were those of the Roman populace and the knights was a problem requiring a clear insight into political and social conditions, extraordinary tact, and remarkable executive ability. That Gaius conceived the plan and carried it out successfully shows how able a politician he was. The democratic party was inspired by Tiberius, but was made an accomplished fact by Gaius. The movement to which he gave meaning and direction brought about in the end a complete change in the form of government. The system toward which he seemed to aim was a democracy expressing its will through the comitia, and carrying out its purpose through the tribunate. In such a form of government there was no place left for the senate and the nobles, and it is clear that the success of his cause meant a political revolution. The next century saw the natural development of his policy in the decline of the senate's power and the establishment of the democratic empire of Julius Caesar. This is not to say that Gaius aimed at a tyranny for himself or for his successors in the tribunate, but the circumstances, the forces which he set in motion could lead only to the humbling of the senate and the ascendency of one man.

268. His Motives. The motives of Gaius were mixed. He sought to build up a democratic party, to reduce the senate to its constitutional position, to relieve the distress of the common people, and to avenge his brother. Some of his measures, therefore, like his land laws, his law of appeal, and his colonizing projects, were intended to promote the best interests of the people; other reforms, like the reorganization of the juries and the change made in the method of selecting provincial governors, Gaius perhaps thought would be salutary, but they were proposed mainly for political reasons, while still other bills, like the corn law, were either sincere, but unwise, attempts to relieve the poor, or were inspired solely by political motives, and were wholly pernicious.

269. Effects of the Corn Law. This last measure, the corn law, accomplished its main purpose of detaching clients from the patrons upon whom they had relied for largesses in the past, and of attaching them to the democratic party, but its ultimate effects were disastrous. By providing for the sale of grain at prices lower than it could be grown in Italy, the law neutralized the efforts which were making to build up the farming industry; by giving the idle a chance to get food at unnaturally low prices it kept them in the city, attracted hordes of needy Italians to Rome, and so more than offset the attempt which was being made to draw the unemployed into the country by the establishment of colonies. Worst of all, it accustomed the great mass of the Roman people to depend upon the state rather than on their own efforts for a livelihood.

270. The Downfall and Death of Gaius Gracchus in 121 B. C. It was this debased populace which deserted Gaius when he proposed the second part of his great scheme of reform—the bestowal of Roman citizenship upon the Latins, and Latin rights upon the other Italian allies. Selfishly unwilling to share their privileges with others, the people failed to elect him to the tribunate for the third time; an attack was made upon his laws; an armed conflict followed; Gaius was killed, and three thousand of his followers were condemned to death by a judicial commission—the very weapon which, by his law of appeal, he had tried to strike from the hands of the senate.

271. Jugurtha and the African Scandal. The senate had triumphed again, but it failed to heed the warning which the movements led by Tiberius and Gaius Gracchus should have given it. It adhered to its selfish policy of governing in the interests of the *nobilitas*. Its venality, selfishness, and incapacity were painfully apparent during the war with Jugurtha, and lost it the prestige which its victory over the Gracchi had won. Jugurtha, an African prince, had inherited the kingdom of Numidia conjointly with two of his cousins in 118 B. C. He soon found means, however, of murdering both his rivals and of making himself master of all Numidia. One of the claimants to the throne, before his death, appealed to Rome for help, and the scandal which followed scarcely finds a parallel in Roman history. Two commissions, headed by distinguished members of the aristocracy, were sent to Africa, but Jugurtha had a long purse, the Roman envoys were amenable to reason, and the commissions returned to Rome, leaving a free hand to the African king. But the massacres which followed the return of the second embassy forced the senate to declare war, and the consul L. Calpurnius Bestia was despatched to Africa with an army. To the surprise even of the senate, Bestia made a disgraceful treaty with Jugurtha, and left him in undisputed control in Africa.

272. The War with Jugurtha, 112-105 B. C. Ultimately the senate was forced to declare war upon him, but it proved to be as incapable in carrying on military operations against him, as it had been venal in conducting negotiations with him. The series of disgraceful negotiations and disastrous defeats which had extended through eleven years gave the popular party its opportunity, and the democrats and middle classes uniting upon Gaius Marius, who had served with distinction in a subordinate capacity in Africa in the year 107, secured his election to the consulship by a large majority, and entrusted to him the conduct of the campaign against Jugurtha. In two years' time Marius brought the king of Numidia in chains to Rome.

273. Marius and Sulla Become Known. This war is interesting in that it brought to the front two men, Marius and Sulla, one belonging to the commons, the other to the aristocracy, whose personal rivalry and political animosity plunged Rome into a fierce civil struggle, and drew more rigidly than ever the line between the senate and the democracy. The part which Marius played in the campaign we have just noticed. His future rival, Sulla, won a name for himself in the war by his brilliant leadership of a cavalry force. In fact no small share of the success of the campaign was due to his skill and daring.

274. Their Character. The two men were as far removed as possible from each other in antecedents, character, and methods. Marius was the son of a laborer; Sulla was a member of a noble family. Marius passed his youth in the village of Arpinum. On the drudgery of farm labor followed the hardships of a private soldier's life. His world was the camp. Of politics, society, or the refinements of life he had no knowledge. Serious-minded to the point of being obstinate, or even stolid, he fought his way upward with a grim determination over all the obstacles which the jealous and contemptuous nobility always threw in the way of a "new man." Sulla, on the other hand, belonged to a noble family. He was brought up at Rome, and plunged with abandon into every form of pleasure which the society of the metropolis offered. Familiar with the refinements of life, of an emotional temperament, and yet touched with the cynicism of a man of the world, he ruled men because of his inborn genius to rule and not because, as with Marius, years of hardship had taught him the importance of discipline, and how to enforce it on others. To him the path of preferment was easy, for he was the chosen champion of the senate.

275. Marius Allies Himself with the Democracy in 100 B. C. The democrats were quick to take advantage of the brilliant success which their champion won in Africa, and later over the Cimbri, and formed a political alliance with him. In accordance with its terms they elected him to the consulship for the sixth time in 100 B. C., assigned lands to his veterans, and, by these concessions, secured his support of the agrarian measures of their tribune. But the violent means

which the democratic leaders used to secure the passage of
their land bills obliged Marius, as consul, to take active measures
to restore order. By this action he disappointed the democrats,
and was forced into retirement at the end of his year of office.

**276. M. Livius Drusus Proposes to Give the Italians
Roman Citizenship.** The measure which had led to the defeat of Gaius Gracchus was his proposition to grant citizenship
to the Italians. The agent whom the senate had used in encom-
passing his downfall was a tribune named Livius Drusus. It
is a strange illustration of the irony of fate that the son of this
man, holding the same office of tribune, should have revived
the agitation in favor of the Italians, and should thereby have
lost his life. The political aim of the younger Drusus differed
essentially, however, from that of Gaius Gracchus. The tribune
of 123 had tried to overthrow the senate by combining all the
other forces in the state against it. Drusus, on the other hand,
sought to strengthen the conservative position by removing
the principal causes of discontent, not only in Rome but in all
Italy. But the same selfish unwillingness to share their privileges with others, which the Romans had shown before, and
which had thwarted his predecessor, brought the efforts of
Drusus also to naught, and he became a victim of popular
passion, as Gaius Gracchus had been.

277. The Defeat of his Bill Leads to War. The bill
which Drusus submitted in the year 91 was the last of many
attempts to better the condition of the Italians by constitutional
methods. When, like its predecessors, it resulted in failure
and was followed by severe repressive measures directed against
them, the discontent of the Italians broke out into an open
revolt, in which all except the Latins and the aristocratic states
of Umbria and Etruria joined.

278. The Grounds of Italian Discontent. The grievances
of the Italians were partly economic and partly political. The
well-to-do citizens of one state were galled by the restriction
which prevented them from trading directly with citizens of
another state, and which gave Roman citizens a monopoly of

this lucrative business.   They were indignant at being obliged to meet a large part of the expense of foreign wars, while they had little share in the distribution of land or booty.   The poorer Italians envied the Roman populace its privilege of getting free grain and of selling its votes at a remunerative figure.   Politically the ambitious Italian was also at a great disadvantage, because he was not eligible to any of the important civil or military positions.   As the empire increased in size and wealth, the importance of the governing city of Rome grew, and made the value of Roman citizenship greater and more apparent.   Consequently, when the Romans refused to give them Roman citizenship freely, the Italians demanded it as a right, and, failing to gain their demand, they set up an independent government with its capital at Corfinium.

279. The Italians Win Citizenship in the Social War, 90-88 B. C.   The advantage in the early part of the war rested with the Italians, and within a year and a half of its outbreak Rome was forced to grant the right of acquiring Roman citizenship to the citizens of allied states who should register their names with a Roman praetor within sixty days.   This concession satisfied a majority of the Italians, and before the close of the year 88 the disaffected, who still held out among the Bruttii, in Samnium, and in Lucania, were forced to submit by Sulla.

280. But it had Little Political Value for Them.   The extension of Roman citizenship to the Italians brought about a complete transformation in the relation of the Italian cities to one another.   They were no longer communities vested with the right of self-government in varying measure, carefully isolated from one another, and acting under the leadership of Rome, but they were on a plane of political equality with one another and with Rome, and their citizens were Roman citizens.   But in practice this did not mean that the people of the small towns throughout Italy exercised all the political rights of Roman citizens.   Just so long as they were obliged to go to Rome to vote that was impossible.   Had the Romans, when they granted citizenship to the Italians, adopted the method of electing magistrates which we follow to-day, and provided that elections should be held in all the Italian towns simultaneously with the elections in Rome, and that the candidates receiving the majority of all the votes thus cast should be declared consuls, or praetors, or tribunes; or if they had even admitted representatives of Italian cities to the senate, then the Italians would have actually enjoyed the political rights of Roman citizens. But the old plan was adhered to, of keeping the senate a close corporation, and of holding the comitia in Rome only. Now only those living near Rome could come to the city to vote, and consequently magistrates were still elected, and laws were still enacted, as they had been in the past, by the populace of Rome. Rome was still a city-state, and the equalization of political privileges throughout Italy which the Social War brought about was one in form rather than in reality.

281. The War Brings Monarchy Nearer. Had some adequate system of representation for Italy been adopted, it is conceivable that the republic might have been given a new lease of life thereby. But under the new settlement all the weaknesses and evils of the old system persisted, and the drift toward autocracy was the more rapid, for it was intolerable that Italy and the world should be ruled either by a selfish Roman aristocracy or an ignorant, fickle city mob. A question of internal politics, which it seemed impossible to settle by peaceful means, had been settled by the arbitrament of arms. Why might not other domestic questions be disposed of in the same way? The war had raised up a great leader in Sulla, supported by a well-trained and devoted army and enthusiastically welcomed as the champion of the conservative cause. Over against him stood Marius, late ally of the democrats, whose veterans, already impatient of a farmer's humdrum life, were waiting for his call to arms. Neither of these men succeeded in substituting the will of one man for that of the many, but they prepared the way for a successor, Caesar, who had the clearness of vision to see the trend of affairs, and the daring and ability to take advantage of it.

282. Struggle of Marius and Sulla for the Command in the East in 88 B. C. Relieved from the strain of the Social War, the Romans turned their attention to the intrigues of Mithridates in the Orient, and put Sulla in command of an army destined to carry on the war against him. But Marius coveted the appointment, and to attain his object made an alliance with the democratic leader Sulpicius as he had years before with the democratic tribune. The reform measures of Sulpicius and the bill transferring from Sulla to Marius the command of the army destined for the East were pushed through the comitia by the use of force. Sulla was with his army in Campania. He laid before the soldiers the news from Rome. Fearful of losing their share of the Eastern spoils, and indignant at the treatment which their commander had received, they urged him to lead them to the city. Sulla, nothing loath, set out for Rome with six legions. On the way envoys met him and asked him why he was marching with armed forces against the city. "To deliver her from her tyrants," he replied—the same defense which Caesar offered forty years later, when *he* advanced against Rome. The democratic leaders called the mob together, promised the slaves their freedom, and attacked the troops of Sulla from the roofs of houses and temples, but the struggle was short and decisive. Sulla was victor, the new laws were repealed, and Marius and Sulpicius were banished. The meaning of the incident is clear. It was an armed struggle between two leaders for personal supremacy, and success lay with the heavier battalions. But Sulla's troops were eager for the Eastern campaign, and he left the city without firmly establishing his own party in power.

283. Marius and Cinna, Masters of Rome 87 - 84 B. C. Cn. Octavius, one of the two consuls for the next year, 87 B. C. was an aristocrat, but his colleague, L. Cornelius Cinna, belonged to the opposite party. Marius's opportunity had come. Call-

ing out his veterans, he supported the cause of Cinna, drove
Octavius from the city, established the authority of the democratic party, and realized his dream of holding the consulship
for the seventh time. He died in office, having apparently triumphed over his enemy.

284. The Return of Sulla in 83 B. C. But the success
of the democrats was short-lived. We have already followed
Sulla's campaign in the East, and know that within three years
he concluded a hasty peace with Mithridates. Early in 83 he
landed in Italy and advanced toward Rome. The untrained
forces of the democrats under incompetent leaders could
not withstand the assaults of his veteran troops. Sertorius
alone of the Marian leaders escaped with a few troops to set
up later in Spain the standard of the Marian cause. After
crushing out a desperate uprising of the Samnites, who saw
in the civil war a chance to avenge the wrongs of centuries,
Sulla entered Rome as its unquestioned master.

285. Sulla Crushes all Opposition. With grim determination he set himself to work to establish the conservative
party, or the oligarchy, firmly in power again. This involved
in his mind two things: the extermination of the democracy,
and the restoration of the senate to its old position of authority. The first part of his plan was carried through with that
cynical contempt for human life and liberty which was characteristic of him. The horrors of the proscription which followed Sulla's return to Rome never faded from the memory
of the Romans. The murder of his enemies and the confiscation of their property, though carried out without regard to
law or evidence, was reduced to a careful system. The
names of the proscribed were posted in lists; rewards were
publicly offered for their murder and the partisans of Sulla
cut down their victims wherever they could be found. Four
thousand and seven hundred Romans, including forty senators and sixteen hundred knights, lost their lives in this
way. The wrath of Sulla also fell heavily upon the peoples
and towns in Italy which had opposed him, and to hold them

in check in the future, he founded several colonies of veterans. He did all this, not so much from a spirit of animosity against his personal enemies, as with the desire to rid the country of men who might again lead a revolution.

286. How He Entrenched the Senate in Power. He had already received the dictatorship for an indefinite period, instead of taking it for the traditional six months, and, vested with the unlimited powers of this office, he addressed himself to the positive side of his work and showed that his skill as a constructive statesman was as great as his ability in the field. To increase the power of the senate as a law-making body he reverted to the method of procedure which prevailed before 287, by reaffirming the principle that the preliminary approval of the senate was necessary before a measure could be submitted to the plebeian tribal assembly. So long as this conservative system continued in force the tribune was prevented from proposing any measures of which the senate did not approve, for the *concilium plebis*, now held in check by the senate, was the body in which the tribune secured the passage of such bills as he favored. Now the tribune was the acknowledged representative of the democracy. Consequently, by preventing him from proposing any bills without the approval of the senate, Sulla aimed to suppress any organized movement of the democracy. The number of praetors was increased to eight and of quaestors to twenty. Ex-magistrates, by virtue of having held an office, passed directly into the senate. The senate was thus filled automatically; the censor was no longer called upon to draw up a list of senators, and the control of that official over the senate disappeared. Senators were also substituted for knights on the juries. By these measures he freed the senate from the control of the magistrates, and gave it almost exclusive legislative and judicial powers. He felt that the tribune was the mouthpiece of radicalism and reform, and to keep able, ambitious men out of the tribunate he had a bill passed which made the tribune ineligible to any other office in the state. All of these measures, of course, had a political purpose, and were well calculated to restore the old régime, and to put the oligarchy in an impregnable position, but even a Sulla could not hold back the tide setting toward democracy. The changes which we have just noticed were in force but a short time.

287. His Administrative and Judicial Reforms. His permanent achievements were the reforms which he made in the administrative and judicial systems. Hitherto it had been customary for magistrates to command the armies of the state during their year of office. From this time on they were rarely sent to a foreign post until their term of office had expired: that is, an official was really chosen for two years, serving one year as a magistrate in Rome, and the following year as governor in a province. This change was made possible by increasing to eight the number of praetors, who, in the year following their term of office at Rome, could, with the two ex-consuls, take charge of the ten provinces. In originality, permanence, and practical value Sulla's reform of the judicial system was perhaps of more importance still. Hitherto the Romans had had only two standing courts, one to try magistrates charged with accepting bribes or with similar offenses (the *quaestio de repetundis*), and the other to hear cases of murder or attempted murder (the *quaestio de sicariis et veneficis*). Men charged with other crimes were tried before a popular assembly, or else a special judicial commission was established to hear the case, or some other irregular method of procedure was adopted. In the procedure before the comitia, all the people meeting in the assembly heard the evidence brought against a man accused of an offense, and voted upon his guilt or innocence. The method was cumbersome; the evidence could not be properly presented before so large a body, and a great assembly is likely to be swayed by gusts of prejudice or passion. Sulla remedied this defect by providing a number of new courts, each with special jurisdiction over certain classes of crimes. One of the new courts for example, heard cases of forgery, another cases of bribery. Over these courts the

praetors presided.   The juries in Sulla's new courts were made
up of small bodies of picked men, whose deliberations were
directed by a presiding judge, and henceforth justice was dis-
pensed in a speedier, simpler, and surer way than had been
possible before.

288. Sulla's Death in 78 B. C.   Sulla's work was finished.
In 79 he resigned the dictatorship, and retired to his villa at

PORTION OF THE ROSTRA, RESTORED BY HUELSEN

Puteoli.   His death in the following year excited alarm among
his followers and joy among his enemies.   His body was
brought to Rome, and as Appian tells us, "was borne through
the streets with an enormous procession following it.   From
fear of the assembled soldiery all the priests and priestesses
escorted the remains, each in proper costume.   The entire
senate and the whole body of magistrates attended with their
insignia of office.   A multitude of the Roman knights followed

with their peculiar decorations, and in their turn, all the legions
that had fought under him. . . . Some really longed for Sulla,
but others were afraid of his army and his dead body, as they
had been of himself when living. . . . The corpse was shown
in the forum on the rostra, where public speeches were usually
made, and the most eloquent of the Romans then living delivered
the funeral oration, as Sulla's son Faustus was still very young.
Then strong men of the senators took up the litter and carried
it to the Campus Martius, where only kings were buried, and
the knights and the army passed in line around the funeral
pile. And this was the last of Sulla."

289. The Democratic Opposition Under Lepidus. Discontent with the new order of things had not dared to raise
its head during the lifetime of Sulla, but with his death the
opposition began to make itself felt. The knights protested
at their exclusion from the juries; the masses murmured at
the loss of prestige which their representative, the tribune, had
suffered and at the curtailment of the powers of the popular
assembly; the towns whose property had been confiscated for
supporting the democratic cause, and the children of the proscribed clamored for the restitution of their rights and their
property, and the moderates looked forward with misgiving
to the unrestrained and selfish exercise of authority by the
senate. These classes found a temporary champion in M.
Aemilius Lepidus, consul of the year 78, but the armed uprising
which he led was quickly crushed out by his colleague, Q.
Lutatius Catulus, a firm supporter of the Optimates, or conservatives, with the help of Pompey.

290. Pompey and Crassus. It was left for two of Sulla's
own lieutenants to undo his work, and they employed in tearing
down the structure which he had reared the same agency which
he had used in building it up, that is, the army. One of them,
Pompey, had behind him an army fresh from its victory over
Sertorius, the Marian leader in Spain; the other, Crassus,
was supported by the troops which had just suppressed the
dangerous uprising in Italy of the slaves under Spartacus.

291. The Consulship of Pompey and Crassus in 70 B. C. At the close of the year 71 these two men appeared before the city to claim certain political honors, and the moment for making an attack on the constitution of Sulla seemed to have come. Pompey wanted lands for his veterans, which the senate would be loath to give him. Crassus, the rich money-lender, coveted power, and perhaps wished for milder treatment of the taxgatherers in the East. The knights, the democrats, and all the discontented were ready to support their claims, provided concessions were made to themselves. Two victorious armies at the gates of the city furnished an argument which the senate could not resist, and Pompey and Crassus were elected consuls for the year 70. They loyally carried out the bargain which they had made with the democrats and knights, by removing the restrictions placed on the tribunate and by securing the passage of a law which stipulated that the juries should henceforth be composed of senators, knights, and representatives of the commons known as *tribuni aerarii*. By the passage of these two bills the repeal of Sulla's political legislation was complete, and the senate lost the strength which his measures had given it. Only the non-political judicial and administrative changes continued in force. Later the conservatives were still further humiliated by seeing Pompey, in spite of their vigorous opposition, vested with the extraordinary powers which the Gabinian and Manilian laws, as we have already noticed, gave him for the campaigns against the pirates and against Mithridates.

292. The Political Sympathies of M. Tullius Cicero. These two campaigns of course took Pompey away from Rome and removed him from all direct participation in politics up to the close of the year. 62. It is within this period that the Catilinarian conspiracy falls, and it was this conspiracy which brought into prominence the Roman orator, Marcus Tullius Cicero. Cicero was born at Arpinum in 106. By descent he was a knight and a "new man," or *novus homo*, since none of his ancestors had held a curule office. By profession he was an advocate. The influence which these facts had upon him, strengthened by his naturally cautious temperament, made him a moderate in politics, and a strong supporter of

CICERO

the constitution and of constitutional methods. The reactionary programme of Sulla was as little to his taste as the revolutionary methods of the democrats. In fact, he entered public life as a critic of one of Sulla's supporters and won his political reputation by suppressing the uprising of the radicals under Catiline.

293. The Catilinarian Conspiracy, 66-63 B. C. At the outset this movement seems to have had for its object an improvement in the condition of certain classes in Rome and throughout Italy by constitutional, or at least by peaceful, methods. The repeated disappointments which its leaders met in the years 66–64 led to the formation of a secret conspiracy, ready to use any means whatsoever for the accomplishment of its purpose. At this point the timid, the judicious, and in large measure the respectable supporters of the movement fell away, and its further development was left in the hands of moral and financial bankrupts or of honest fanatics and adventurers. Their leader was a patrician, L. Sergius Catiline. He represents a type not uncommon in this period. He was accomplished, brave, dashing, restlessly energetic, and had a charm of manner which attracted others, but he lacked the moral fibre, the mental balance, the largeness of outlook, and the ability to organize and direct which the true leader needs. He came forward in 65 as a candidate for the consulship, but he was charged with extortion in Africa, and not allowed to stand for office. He presented himself again in 64. Much against their will, the senatorial party threw their support to his opponent Cicero. The knights and the middle classes throughout Italy also supported Cicero, because he was one of their own number, and was the champion of law and order. Pompey helped him because he had advocated the Gabinian and Manilian laws, and the orator was returned at the head of the polls. Driven to extreme measures by his defeat, Catiline planned to murder the magistrates and take the city by force. His plans were discovered; he was forced to leave the city, and fell in battle in Etruria. The Catilinarian leaders in Rome were put to death, and Cicero was hailed "Father of his Country."

294. Cicero's Political Methods. Cicero's political course was based upon a new method of securing strength for the social fabric. Gaius Gracchus had exalted the middle classes at the expense of the nobility, Sulla had restored the supremacy of the senate, and thereby antagonized the middle classes. Now Cicero sought to unite both senators and knights in a joint defense of the cause of law and order. His efforts were as futile as theirs had been, because the Roman empire had outgrown the old régime, and because ambitious leaders had been taught by the examples of Sulla, of Marius, and of Pompey to look to the sword, and not to the ballot, as the source of political power.

295. Pompey's Disappointment. The lack of tact and foresight in the methods of the conservative party came out clearly enough two years after the suppression of the Catilinarian conspiracy, on Pompey's return from his campaigns against Mithridates. By treating Pompey generously at that time it could have made him its supportèr, but its failure to gratify his reasonable expectations forced him into an alliance with C. Julius Caesar and Crassus.

296. Gaius Julius Caesar. Caesar had not been a prominent figure in politics up to this time. He had shown his colors plainly enough, however, at the funeral of his aunt, who was the wife of Marius, by displaying in the funeral procession, the bust of that distinguished general and democratic leader, and by setting up again the Cimbrian trophies of Marius which Sulla had removed. While Pompey had been vainly trying to bring the senate to listen to his claims, Caesar had been propraetor of Spain. Pompey and Crassus were not on good terms, but it was not difficult for Caesar to bring them together on the basis of their common needs. Their compact, which was made in 60 B. C., and which is commonly known as the first triumvirate, was merely a private understanding.

297. The Triumvirate Controls Roman Politics. Under it Caesar was elected for the following year to the consulship; lands were given to Pompey's veterans, and his acts in the East were ratified. What Crassus got from the bargain is not clear—perhaps certain tax concessions, or possibly assurance of a future consulship. Provision was made for Caesar's future by a measure which made him governor of Cisalpine Gaul and Illyricum for a period of five years, counting from March 1, 59 B. C., with an army of three legions. To this the senate, perhaps under the influence of Pompey, added Transalpine Gaul and a fourth legion. At the end of his year of office, Caesar was unwilling to depart from the city and leave the interests of the triumvirate in the hands of two such tactless leaders as Pompey and Crassus, without humbling the senate in such a way that it would not dare to upset his plans during his absence. He secured his object by humiliating and sending from Rome two of the ablest senatorial leaders, Cicero and Cato. The methods which he used in accomplishing his purpose had a touch of humor or cynicism in them. Cicero, the champion of the constitution, was banished for having violated the constitution during his consulship by executing the Catilinarian conspirators without granting them an appeal to the people. Honest Cato was sent to Cyprus on the dishonest mission of seizing that island and its treasure. Cicero's recall from exile in 57 raised the spirits of the senatorial party, but its hopes were crushed again by the renewal of the triumvirate the following year, by the extension of Caesar's term of office for another period of five years, and by the assignment of Spain and Syria to Pompey and Crassus respectively for five years. Pompey lingered in Rome, but Crassus set out for the East, where he fell on the field of Carrhæ in a campaign against the Parthians.

298. The Estrangement of Caesar and Pompey. The personal bond which held Pompey and Caesar together had been severed in 54 by the death of Pompey's wife Julia, who was the daughter of Caesar. The death of Crassus in the following year destroyed the balance of power in the triumvirate, and brought Caesar and Pompey face to face as rivals. Pompey, at least, seemed to be waiting only for the right time to strike. The right moment seemed to come in 52, when he was elected sole consul.

299. The Questions at Issue. The senate, which had been watching eagerly for signs of an estrangement between the two men, now began to move boldly against Caesar; and Pompey, after showing the hesitation and duplicity which was so characteristic of him in political matters, at last went over to its side. Caesar's second term of five years would come to an end March 1, 49, but he expected that, in accordance with precedent, his governorship would be extended to the end of the year. Now he was a candidate for the consulship for the year 48, and so hoped to step from the proconsulship to the consulship at the end of the year 49 without a break. This programme he was anxious to carry out, because, if an interval should elapse between his incumbency of the two offices, it would give his enemies at Rome an opportunity to bring political charges against him as a private citizen, which could not be brought against him if he held office.

300. Civil War Breaks Out in 49 B. C. Rumors reached him in Gaul in 50 that the senate was planning to appoint a governor to succeed him before the close of the year 49. Consequently, when the new consuls called the senate together January 1, 49 B. C., a representative of Caesar laid before that body the proposals of his absent master. Their exact character is unknown to us, but they probably covered some or all of the points mentioned above. The senate, however, refused to listen to them, and declared that he would be a public enemy unless he gave up his provinces and his army before the first of July, 49. Two tribunes in the senate who favored his cause and interposed their vetoes to the senate's action, were threatened with personal violence, and set out at once for Caesar's camp at Ravenna, and Caesar replied to the challenge of the senate and Pompey by crossing the frontier into Italy, and marching toward Rome to restore the tribunes to their rightful authority.

301. Summary of Events at Home from 133 to 49

B. C. We noticed in the previous period that the small farmers and free laborers in Italy were being driven into bankruptcy. Tiberius Gracchus sought to relieve them by dividing up the state land among the poor. The senate, which was made up largely of rich men who were occupying this land, opposed and overthrew him. His brother, Gaius, took up the reform and by his legislation united the poor people and the knights against the senate. He, too, was overthrown, but the senate's disgraceful conduct of the war against Jugurtha, gave the democrats an opportunity to advance their leader Marius. The Italians won Roman citizenship in the Social War. The democrats under Marius and Cinna gained control of Rome, but were driven out by Sulla on his return from the war with Mithridates. Sulla was made dictator, and installed the senate in power again, but his arrangements were overturned by the consuls, Pompey and Crassus, who later joined Caesar in forming the first triumvirate. These three men took the government into their own hands, but the death of Crassus, and the quarrel between Caesar and Pompey led to a struggle between them for supreme power, and civil war followed.

CHAPTER X

(49–27 B. C.)

How Caesar made himself master of the Roman world, and was assassinated —How Octavianus, Antony. and Lepidus put down the last effort of the republicans —How Octavianus established the Empire, and thus completed the revolution.

302. Caesar's Chances of Success. To cross the Rubicon into Italy with a single legion, as Caesar did, seemed the height of rashness. He had behind him only the Gallic provinces and an army of nine legions quartered at different points in the North. His enemies controlled all the rest of the civilized world and the Roman treasury, and had a force far outnumbering his. He was a rebel against a state which had placed itself under the protection of the most experienced general of the time. But in Caesar's camp there was one leader and one plan of campaign only. The counsels of his enemies were divided, and even Pompey's authority was not supreme. Caesar's troops were within striking distance of Italy, and were hardened by years of campaigning in Gaul. Pompey had to rely largely upon levies of new recruits or of veterans long out of service.

303. The Campaigns in Italy and Spain in 49 B. C. The course of events proved the wisdom of Caesar's decision. Advancing quickly from Ravenna along the coast of the Adriatic, he threw the Pompeians at Rome into such a panic that they evacuated the city within a fortnight, and withdrew hastily toward the southeast. Pompey saw that it was useless to make a stand in Italy, and hurrying down to Brundisium embarked for Epirus just in time to escape being intercepted by his opponent. Caesar felt himself unprepared to follow the enemy at once, and after a few week's stay in Italy, crossed over to Spain, which was held for Pompey by his three lieutenants, Petreius, Afranius, and Varro. By a clever move on Caesar's part, Petreius and Afranius were cut off from their supplies and forced to surrender, and Varro's submission soon followed. Spain had been won within a month and a half of Caesar's arrival.in the peninsula.

304. Caesar Lands in Epirus in 49 B. C. Then he returned for the real struggle with Pompey. With six legions he made a successful landing at Oricum in Epirus in November, 49, and in April of the following year Mark Antony joined him with four more, but Caesar's legions were depleted by sickness and long campaigns, while Pompey's army had grown to a total of nine legions, supported by a large body of auxiliaries and a strong fleet.

305. The Battle of Pharsalus, August 9, 48 B. C. Caesar placed his army between Dyrrachium and Pompey's camp, and at once began offensive operations in the hope of blockading him; but the Pompeian forces broke through his lines and inflicted so severe a loss upon him that later, when Caesar advanced into Thessaly, Pompey followed him and was induced by his overconfident advisers to risk a battle at Pharsalus. Pompey's horsemen swept down upon Caesar's cavalry, overwhelmed them, and charged Caesar's infantry on the flank, but the tenth legion, supported by cohorts of veterans, which were stationed at this point, stood like a rock. At this moment Caesar threw his reserves into the battle and Pompey's lines broke and retreated in disorder.

306. The Death of Pompey. Pompey himself, who fled for safety to Egypt, was put to death by order of King Ptolemy, as he was landing at Pelusium. "His remains were buried on the shore," as Appian tells us, "and a small monument was erected over them, on which some one wrote this inscription: 'What a pitiful tomb is here for one who had temples in abundance.'" "Such," says the Roman historian Velleius Paterculus, "was the departure from life of a most excellent and illustrious man, after three consulships and as many triumphs, who had ruled the whole world and had reached a position above which it was not possible to rise."

307. Affairs in Egypt and Armenia, and the Battle of Thapsus in 46 B. C. To Egypt Caesar followed the Pompeians, and remained there, held by the settlement of political affairs and by the charms of the Egyptian queen Cleopatra, until the late spring of 47, when he was called to Armenia Minor to check the ambitious projects of Pharnaces, son of the Mithridates who had caused the Romans so much trouble a quarter of a century before. The battle of Zela restored the Roman prestige in that region, and Caesar was free to turn his attention to the massing of the Pompeian forces in Africa. Landing near Hadrumetum, he defeated Scipio the Pompeian leader with his allies at Thapsus, and captured Utica soon after, notwithstanding Cato's vigorous efforts to defend it.

308. The Death of Cato. When Cato saw that the city could be held no longer he took his own life. The story of his death has been told by one of Caesar's own followers: "Cato himself arranged everything with the greatest care and commended his children to his proquaestor Lucius Caesar without exciting suspicion, and without showing any change in his bearing and conversation from what they had been aforetime. Then he withdrew, taking with him secretly into his bedchamber a sword upon which he cast himself. He had already fallen, although life was not yet extinct, when a physician and his friends, whose suspicions had been aroused, rushed into his chamber and applied themselves to the bringing together and the binding up of his wound, but Cato with his own hands ruthlessly tore open the wound, and with a resolute heart brought his life to an end." Cato of Utica, as he was henceforth styled from the scene of his death, was a worthy descendant of his great-grandfather the censor. He may be called the last of the old-time Romans. A man of ostentatious simplicity, of an affected austerity and directness of manner, of the strictest integrity when the Roman state or his fellow-citizens were concerned, but lacking in a sense of justice or mercy to-

ward foreigners, he was still the firm and consistent champion
of the republic, and accepted no compromise with the advocates
of autocracy.   His death was regarded as a dramatic proof
of the end of the republic, and created a profound sensation
throughout the Roman world, so that even Caesar, notwithstanding the pressure of his further campaigns against the
Pompeian forces, took time to reply in his *Anti-Cato* to the
biography of Cato which Cicero wrote, and to defend in it his
own political course.

309. Battle of Munda, 45 B. C.   The remnants of the
Pompeian forces which had collected in Spain Caesar crushed
on the field of Munda, where fell his bitterest foe Labienus,
his Gallic lieutenant, the only officer who had deserted him
when he crossed into Italy.

310. The Assassination of Caesar in 44 B. C.   From
Munda Caesar returned to Rome to carry out the reforms upon
which he had set his heart.   But while he was busily engaged
in these matters, a plot was forming against his life.   The
conspirators were actuated by personal and by political motives.
Many of them were jealous of Caesar, or, like Cassius, dis-
satisfied with the recognition which they had received from
him.   Many members of the senate (for about sixty senators
took part in the conspiracy) were aggrieved at the loss of power
and prestige which that body had suffered at his hands.   Their
smouldering discontent was kindled into flame by the new powers
and honors conferred on Caesar in the early part of 44, and by
the rumors, which were current, that he would be made king
and would transfer the seat of government to Alexandria.
The time and place which they selected for the deed were the
Ides of March and the senate house.   Crowding about him
as if presenting a petition, one of their number, Casca, stabbed
him with a dagger, the others joined in the assault, and Caesar
fell wounded to the death, at the foot of the statue of his great
rival Pompey.

311. Caesar's Purpose Threefold.   The work which
Caesar had set himself to do after the battle of Pharsalus, and

which was left unfinished at his death, was threefold. He
wished to suppress within the limits of Roman territory all
armed resistance to a central authority, to establish in Rome
a permanent government strong enough to carry out a positive
policy in spite of all opposition, and finally to knit together

JULIUS CAESAR

all parts of the Roman empire and give the provinces a good
government. We have already seen him attain his first object.

312. How He Made Himself Master of the State. To
accomplish his second purpose he put himself at the head of
the state and made his position secure, partly by increasing
his own power, partly by diminishing the influence of other

factors in the government. In 48 the tribunician power was given him for life, and in 44 he was made dictator for life. He probably held the proconsulship permanently, and on several occasions he was regularly elected to the consulship. The dictatorship, consulship, and proconsulship gave him all the positive power which he needed, and the tribunician authority enabled him to hold all other magistrates in check. The magistrates for the immediate future were also brought directly under his control by a measure which allowed him to name all officials for 43, as well as the consuls and tribunes for 42. He raised the senate to nine hundred in number, and thus robbed it of its exclusive character, and he took care that his own followers should constitute a majority in it. As for the people, they met as before in the comitia, but the selection of candidates for office by Caesar, and the fact that he alone was directly or indirectly the author of all bills laid before the popular assemblies, made the meeting of these bodies largely a matter of form.

313. How He Unified the Empire. The measures which he took to accomplish his third purpose were excellent. He relieved the congestion of Rome by sending out colonies, and by cutting down the list of those who received free supplies of grain. In his admirable *Municipal Law* he drew up a charter for Italian towns, which gave them their own popular assemblies, senates, magistrates, and courts. Upon the provinces he conferred a great boon by taking into his own hands the appointment of provincial governors. Henceforth provinces ceased to be principalities which were used by officials in filling their pockets or in advancing their political fortunes. Every governor felt his responsibility to a ruler who would hold him strictly to account. Each province became an integral part of the Roman empire, and its interests received some part of the care, which, under the republic, had been given to Italy only. Under the republic, we have said, for it is clear that the republic was now a thing of the past, and that Caesar had really taken into his hands all those powers which in their natural development gave Augustus and his successors their exalted position.

314. Events which Followed Caesar's Death. Although Caesar was dead, both parties, the conspirators and the personal and political friends of the dead leader, rested on their arms. Neither faction knew the strength of the other nor the sentiment of the people. The Caesarian consul Mark Antony thought it best to propose a compromise, and Marcus and Decimus Brutus, Cassius, and the other conspirators accepted it. Caesar's arrangements for the future were ratified, but no inquiry was to be made into the circumstances of his death.

315. Octavius Appears in Italy. An unexpected turn was given to affairs by the arrival in Italy of Octavius, Caesar's grand-nephew, a young man in his nineteenth year, whom the dictator had named as his heir. His fidelity in carrying out the generous provisions of Caesar's will, his tactful course, and the fact that he bore the name of their late leader drew to him so many of Caesar's veterans that Antony, for fear of losing all his troops, hastily left Rome for the North with the forces which were still loyal to him.

316. Mutina, 43 B. C. Antony had secured by law the transfer to himself of Cisalpine Gaul, which had originally been assigned to Decimus Brutus, one of the conspirators. His purpose now was to drive out Brutus and take possession of the province. The senate called Octavius to its assistance and sent him with Hirtius and Pansa, the two consuls of the year 43, to the relief of Brutus. Antony was worsted at Mutina.

317. The Second Triumvirate Formed in 43 B. C. But the victory was dearly bought. Hirtius and Pansa were killed, and Octavius was so aggrieved at the assignment of the vacant position of commander-in-chief to Brutus that he came to an understanding with Antony and his ally Lepidus, and the three men formed a compact, commonly known as the second triumvirate, which was later ratified by law, and gave them even more extensive powers than Pompey, Caesar, and Crassus had exercised twenty years before.

318. Cicero's Part in the Struggle. Their return to Rome was followed by a reign of terror which rivaled that of Sulla. Cicero was one of the early victims of their fury. He had been the head and front of the senatorial opposition, and however vainglorious he may have been of his consulship, however weak during his year of exile, and vacillating when the war broke out between Caesar and Pompey, in this period he rose to the full stature of a brave man of action and a statesman. His scathing denunciation of Antony in his Philippic orations, his brave letters to the governors of provinces, encouraging them to stand firm for the senatorial cause, and his bold leadership of the senate made him the heart and soul of the lost cause. He was put on the list of the proscribed by Antony, and was murdered on his estate near Formiæ in 43 B. C.

319. Velleius's Eulogy of Cicero. His bravery in this last struggle of the republic a century later not undeservedly called forth from Velleius Paterculus this enthusiastic eulogy of him and denunciation of Antony: "Thou hast robbed Cicero, Mark Antony, of the light of life, but of a light obscured by the clouds of trouble—of his declining years, and of a life which would have been more wretched under thee as prince than was death under thee as triumvir, but the fame and the glory which his deeds and words brought him thou hast rather exalted than taken from him. He lives and will live in memory for all time, and so long as this world, ruled by chance or by providence, or however it be governed, so long as this world shall last whose significance, structure, and constitution, he was almost the only Roman to discern, to comprehend, and to set forth in a clear light by means of his eloquence, it will take with it through the ages the praise of Cicero, and in times to come all men will execrate thy crime against him, and the human race shall disappear from the earth before the name of Cicero dies."

320. Philippi, 42 B. C. Meanwhile the two republican leaders, M. Brutus and Cassius, had withdrawn to the East to take possession of their provinces, and were exerting themselves to the utmost to prepare for the struggle which they knew to be inevitable. In the autumn of 42 they had brought together at Philippi a force of nineteen legions of foot soldiers and twenty thousand horsemen. Here they were met by the triumvirs and defeated. Brutus and Cassius took their own lives, and the struggle to reëstablish the republic was at an end.

321. The Roman World Divided between Octavianus and Antony. In the division of territory which followed the victory, Octavius, or Octavianus as he was called after his

A ROMAN GALLEY

adoption by Caesar, took Italy and the West, Antony the East, with Alexandria as his capital. Lepidus had to content himself with Africa, and plays henceforth a minor role.

322. Actium, 31 B. C. The compact between Octavianus and Antony, broken only by temporary misunderstandings, ran for ten years, but the rivalry between the two men was too intense to allow the arrangement to be permanent. It was believed too at Rome that Antony and Cleopatra were

planning to set up a rival power in the East. The great naval
battle near Actium was, therefore, a struggle between the East
and the West, and the victory of Octavianus over Antony and
Cleopatra established once for all the supremacy of the West.

323. The State of Society. The social changes in Italy
which came about in the period preceding the revolution, as
we have noticed in a previous chapter, became still more marked
in the years which intervened between the Gracchi and the

PERISTYLE OF A POMPEIAN VILLA

battle of Actium. The middle class had already disappeared.
Now the aristocracy ceased to exist. Few of the old families
survived the civil wars and proscription. Society was made
up of the very rich and the very poor. The rich men, like
Crassus, had made their fortunes by farming the taxes, by
loaning money in the provinces, and by trading with them,
by speculating in the lands of the proscribed and the bankrupt,
and by cultivating their Italian estates with slave labor. A
great chasm yawned between them and the slaves or the

needy freemen and freedmen who lived upon the charity of
the rich or the largess of the state. To work with the hands
was disgraceful for a freeman because, by doing so, he classed
himself-with the slaves who performed the greater part of the
manual labor. This was one of the evils which slavery had
brought upon Rome. Even so sensible a man as Cicero says
in his *Duties:* "We are to account as unbecoming and mean the
gains of all hired workmen, whose source of profit is not their
art but their labor; for their very wages are the consideration of
their servitude." The lower classes received free corn and
used the money paid them for their votes to buy the other
necessaries of life; for their amusement they demanded dramatic festivals, triumphal processions, and gladiatorial shows.
The rich found their pleasure in spending money. They built
magnificent villas at the seashore, and laid out elaborate parks.
They spent fortunes upon furniture and jewels, and wines
and delicacies for the table were imported from all parts of
the world. It was inevitable that morality should be at a
low ebb in a period when money was the sole object of men's
desires. The restraining influence which religion might have
exerted was lost, because the lower classes were plunged in
unbelief or superstition, while the upper classes took refuge
in some form of Greek philosophy which did little to raise
them out of the slough of materialism.

324. Epic and Dramatic Literature. The utter absence
of epic and tragic poetry throughout the century from Tiberius Gracchus to the battle of Actium is significant of the period.
The times furnished to the writer neither inspiration nor readers
for his works. Even the better types of comedy languished.
Plautus and Terence found no successors, and the stage was
given over to the farce and the mime. Indeed, even these lower
forms of the drama found it hard to hold their place in popular favor in competition with the shows in the amphitheatre.
Only two writers have the flavor of the olden time, Lucretius
in verse and Varro in prose.

325. Lucretius, 96 - 55 B. C. In his great didactic poem,

On the World, Lucretius not only shows the rough literary vigor and fire and the mannerisms even of an Ennius, but the zeal and the dauntless courage of a Naevius. His poem centres about two themes: "Fear not the gods; fear not death," but even in this period of unbelief, it fell upon deaf ears.

326. Varro, 116-27 B. C. Varro wrote books enough for a library, but only his works on *Country Life,* and parts of his *Latin Language* and his *Satires* are extant. Varro's *Satires* Mommsen has aptly characterized as "the last breath of the good spirit of the old burgess-times."

327. Catullus, 87-54 B. C. The temper of the period finds fit expression in the poems of Catullus. They are not lacking in force, in wit, and in sarcasm. They show a fine play of imagination and an artistic form which perhaps no other Latin poet has attained, but their subjects are mainly drawn from the little incidents of polite society, and the verse is that of the decadent Greek period.

328. Oratory Before Cicero. Prose literature fared better in this century. Oratory in particular flourished. Both Tiberius and Gaius Gracchus were effective speakers. Marcus Antonius and Lucius Crassus, at the beginning of the first century, and Cicero's contemporary Hortensius were also distinguished orators, but their orations have not come down to us, and their fame was eclipsed by that of Cicero, Rome's foremost orator.

329. Cicero, 106-43 B. C. His fifty-seven extant orations, some of them written for delivery in courts of law and some composed for political purposes, prove him to have been a great master of style, perhaps the greatest Latin stylist. His activity extended to almost every field of prose literature, to rhetoric, philosophy, law, history, and letter writing. In writing his formal treatises he drew largely from Greek sources, but he adapted the material to his own purposes and gave it a Roman coloring. His *Letters,* eight hundred and more of which are extant, furnish us with an admirable picture of his life and times. Cicero was a prolific poet too, and, if we may judge from the verses which have come down to us, he was a poet of no mean ability.

330. The Historical Works of Sallust, Caesar, and Nepos. History, which, it will be remembered, began with Cato the Censor, takes on a new form during the latter part of this period. Writers no longer compose narratives covering several centuries of Roman history, weaving together legend and fact in hopeless confusion, but they devote themselves to particular episodes, preferably of their own times. Of this sort are Sallust's *War with Jugurtha*, his *Conspiracy of Catiline*, and Caesar's *Commentaries*. Similar in scope also were the biographies which Cornelius Nepos wrote.

331. Summary Account of the Last Days of the Republic. The revolution against senatorial government, which began under the Gracchi, reached its last stage in the struggle for supreme power between Caesar and Pompey, supported by the senate. Pompey's cause was lost on the field of Pharsalus, and Caesar, by his victories at Thapsus and Munda, made himself master of the Roman world. But before he had completed his reorganization of the government he was assassinated, and the republicans made a last effort to ward off the monarchy. They were defeated, however, at Philippi by the triumvirs Octavianus, Antony, and Lepidus, who divided the world between them. The retirement of Lepidus brought Octavianus and Antony face to face, just as Caesar and Pompey had been made rivals by the death of Crassus, and in the naval battle of Actium Octavianus made good his claim to supreme power. The revolution was complete.

CHAPTER XI

How Augustus, sharing his power with the senate, put himself at the head of the state—How he and the other Julian emperors governed the world.

332. The Restoration of Peace. On January 11, 29 B. C., the temple of Janus, whose doors stood open in time of war, was closed for the third time in all Roman history. This symbolical act was a fitting and true omen of the return of peace and prosperity to Rome, for twelve years later the poet Horace in singing the praises of Octavian, writes, "Now faith and peace, and good repute, modesty of the olden time and manly worth, so long forgotten, dare to return, and plenty appears to view, rich with her o'erflowing horn."

333. Augustus, Master of the State. The problem which Octavian set himself to solve on his return to Rome was to retain his position as master of the state, yet at the same time to keep intact the old forms of the constitution. He accomplished his object by retaining the tribunician power for life and by taking the proconsular *imperium* for ten years, counting from 27 B. C. The proconsular power gave him command of the legions, and, as he was allowed to retain the *imperium* within the city, his position at home was equal in rank and authority to that of the consul. The tribunician power authorized him to summon the senate or the popular assemblies for the transaction of business, and to veto the action of almost any magistrate. His preëminence was expressed in the titles of Augustus and *princeps*, or foremost citizen of the commonwealth.

334. How He Kept the Old Forms. While in this way

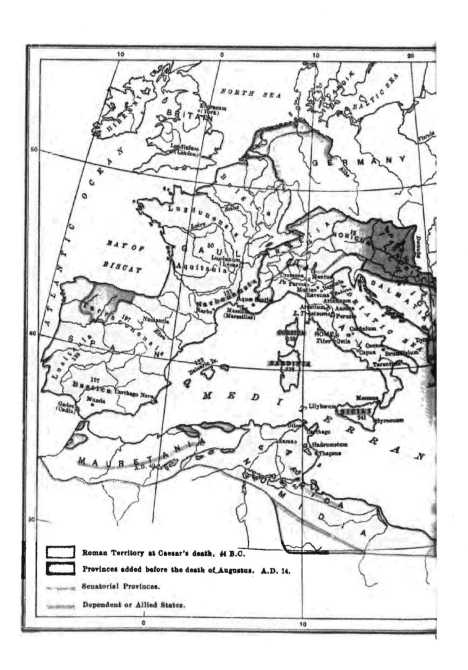

NORTH SEA

BALTIC SEA

Eburacum (York)

BRITAIN

HIBERNIA

Londinium (London)

GERMANY

ATLANTIC OCEAN

BAY OF BISCAY

Lugudunum

GAUL

Aquitania

NORICUM

DALMATIA

SPAIN

Tarraco

Numantia

Narbo

Massilia (Marseilles)

Cremona Mantua
Parma
Mutina
Ravenna

Ariminum
Arretium
L. Trasimenus Perusia

Aesculum

CORSICA

ROME
Tiber Ostia

SARDINIA

Capua
Brundisium

Tarentum

Baetica

Carthago Nova

Gades (Cadiz)

Munda

MEDITERRANEAN

SICILY
241

Messana

Lilybaeum

Syracuse

Utica

Carthago

Zama

Hadrumetum
Thapsus

NUMIDIA

MAURETANIA
A.D. 40

Roman Territory at Caesar's death, 44 B.C.

Provinces added before the death of Augustus. A.D. 14.

Senatorial Provinces.

Dependent or Allied States.

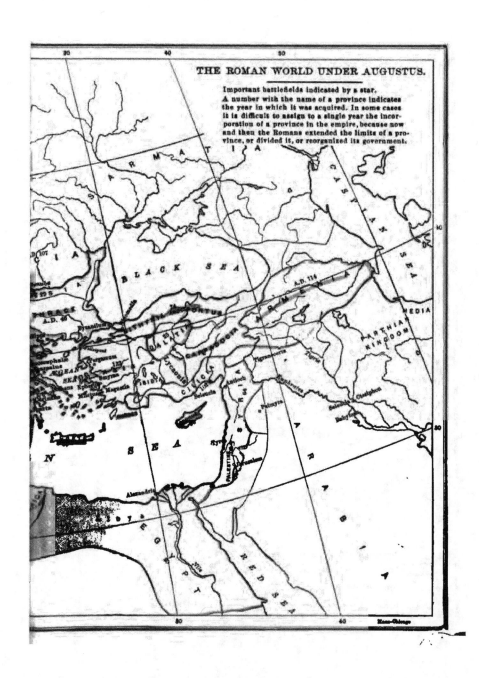

THE ROMAN WORLD UNDER AUGUSTUS.

Important battlefields indicated by a star.
A number with the name of a province indicates
the year in which it was acquired. In some cases
it is difficult to assign to a single year the incorporation of a province in the empire, because now
and then the Romans extended the limits of a province, or divided it, or reorganized its government.

he brought the real power into his own hands, he retained the old offices and machinery of government, and kept the republican forms. The consuls, praetors, and tribunes were still elected as in the past, but Augustus adopted the practice of recommending certain candidates to the citizens, and his recommendation insured an election. The popular assemblies met as before, but the bills submitted to them were drawn up by the emperor, and the candidates bore his approval, so that popular action amounted to nothing more than a formal ratification of the will of Augustus. By these methods Augustus attained the same result which Julius Caesar had reached, the centralization of power in his own hands, but the means which he employed violated the old traditions less, and so did not excite popular opposition.

335. The Senate has a Share in the Government. In one important respect his domestic policy differed from that of Julius. He adopted a conciliatory attitude toward the senate and invested that body with dignity and some real power. This nominal division of authority between the emperor and the senate, for it was largely nominal, has led some writers to style his system a dyarchy, *i. e.*, a joint government by two powers.

336. Government of the Provinces Reorganized. The independence of the senate in this dual arrangement is most apparent in the management of the provinces. The control of Italy and of the settled provinces, like Asia and Macedonia, was intrusted to the senate and magistrates, while the frontier districts, where troops were still necessary, were assigned to the emperor. To no part of the Roman world did the reforms of Augustus bring greater relief than to districts outside of Italy. The governors of imperial provinces were appointed by him on the score of fitness and honesty. They were directly responsible to him, and held office for reasonably long terms, so that they became familiar with their duties and with the needs of their provinces. Even over the senatorial provinces Augustus exercised some supervision, and the excellence of the government in the imperial provinces could not fail to exert a beneficial influence over those not directly under his control. From this time on a governor received a fixed salary and was no longer obliged to rely upon extortion in seeking a reasonable return for his services, and in case he did practice extortion, an appeal could be taken to the emperor with assurance of redress.

337. Augustus Improves Local Conditions. Augustus did a great deal also to improve local conditions in the provinces. In Asia, for instance, he made grants of money to various towns, he improved the system of taxation, constructed public works and opened up the country by building roads. He brought the entire empire also into closer relations with Rome by establishing relay stations along the great military roads at which horses and vehicles were kept to forward official correspondence. These improvements were probably all suggested to him by his personal observation, for during his reign he is said to have visited every province but Sardinia and Africa.

338. The Frontier. One important feature of his foreign policy was to establish a natural and secure frontier. The Euphrates served this purpose to the east. To the south the great desert of Africa formed a natural boundary, and made the provinces in that quarter of the world safe, except from the occasional incursions of nomad tribes. On the west was the Atlantic, and the Rhine and Danube marked the northern frontier.

339. Defeat of Varus in A. D. 9. The most important campaigns carried on during the reign of Augustus were those against the Germans. Tiberius and Drusus, his stepsons, had reduced these people to subjection, but they rose in rebellion against the Romans under a native prince, Arminius, and, falling on the three legions of Varus, the Roman general, in the Teutoberg Forest, destroyed them completely. The Roman standards were captured, and Varus took his own life. The news of the disaster and the disgrace appalled the people at

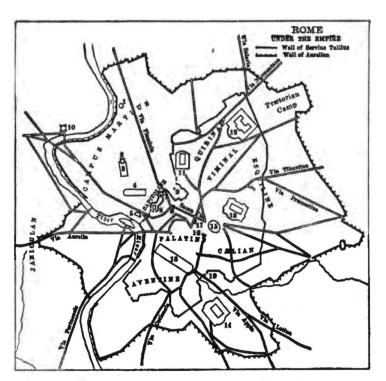

1.	MAUSOLEUM OF AUGUSTUS		10.	MAUSOLEUM OF HADRIAN
2.	PANTHEON		11.	BATHS OF CONSTANTINE
3.	BATHS OF AGRIPPA		12.	BATHS OF DIOCLETIAN
4.	CIRCUS FLAMINIUS		13.	BATHS OF TRAJAN
5.	THEATRE OF MARCELLUS		14.	BATHS OF CARACALLA
6.	ARCH OF SEPTIMIUS SEVERUS		15.	COLOSSEUM
7.	ARX		16.	ARCH OF CONSTANTINE
8.	CAPITOL		17.	ARCH OF TITUS
9.	COLUMN OF TRAJAN		18.	CIRCUS MAXIMUS
			19.	PORTA CAPENA

The gates in the wall of Aurelian received their names from the roads passing through them. Thus the gate through which the via Latina passed was called the porta Latina.

Rome, and so affected Augustus, it is said, that he was heard to cry out in the night: "Varus, Varus, give me back my legions."

340. The City of Rome under the Republic. With all this activity abroad he did not neglect Rome and Italy. Mommsen has described the city of Rome under the republic in the following graphic words: "The streets ascended and descended narrow and angular, and were wretchedly kept; the footpaths were small and ill paved. The ordinary houses were built of bricks negligently and to a giddy height, mostly by speculative builders. Like isolated islands amidst this sea of wretched buildings were seen the splendid palaces of the rich, beside whose marble pillars and Greek statues the decaying temples, with their images of the gods still in great part carved of wood, made a melancholy figure. A police supervision of streets, of river-banks, of fires, or of buildings was almost unheard of."

341. How Augustus Improved It. Julius Caesar made some progress in remedying this state of affairs and in beautifying the city, but it was left to his successor to carry his plans to completion. Agrippa, the minister of Augustus, rebuilt the aqueducts, reorganized the water department, and constructed a number of new baths, bridges, and temples, but the greater part of the work was carried out under the direct supervision of the emperor. As he proudly writes in the memorial of his life which the inscribed record found at Ancyra in Asia Minor, and known as the *monumentum Ancyranum*, has preserved to us: "The Capitolium and the Pompeian theatre— both very costly works—I restored. . . . Water-conduits in many places that were decaying with age I repaired. . . . The Forum Iulium and the basilica, which was between the temple of Castor and the temple of Saturn, works begun and far advanced by my father, I completed. . . . In my sixth consulship, I repaired eighty-two temples of the gods. . . . On ground belonging to myself I built a temple to Mars Ultor and the Forum Augustum, with money arising from the sale of the spoils of war;" and so the record runs through a list which might well justify him in boasting that "he found Rome brick and left it marble." To protect the lives and property of the citizens he established a fire and police department, numbering seven or eight thousand men, and reorganized the system of municipal administration.

342. Improvements in Italy. Improvements similar to these in Rome were made throughout Italy. The via Flaminia, the great highway which ran from Rome to Ariminum, was repaved, guards were stationed at intervals to protect travelers, and military colonies were planted along its course.

343. Social Reforms of Augustus. It is more difficult to change social conditions than material ones. Yet Augustus bravely attacked this problem too. He tried to check extravagance by enacting sumptuary laws which limited the amount to be spent for a dinner on ordinary days and on festivals. He tried to restore the old-time integrity of family life, and to prevent the native stock from dying out, by laying restrictions upon divorce, by putting the childless and the unmarried at a disadvantage in the matter of receiving legacies and otherwise, and by granting favors to men with families. His legislation upon these points, however, did little to remedy the evils at which it was directed. He was more successful in restoring the Roman religion to its old position of dignity. He did this by rebuilding the temples, by celebrating religious festivals with great pomp, and by taking certain priestly offices himself, like the position of pontifex maximus, or chief priest. One of the most interesting of the social changes which he effected consisted in establishing a series of new social classes. They were three in number: The senators, who as ex-magistrates owed their position to his recommendation; the knights, whose social and political standing he definitely fixed; and a local aristocracy, known as the *Augustales*, and made up of rich freedmen in the little towns, who in return for contributing to public purposes enjoyed certain privileges. The interests of these three classes were those of the emperor, and their support did much to strengthen his position.

344. The Results of his Work. If a balance-sheet of the

AUGUSTUS

public ledger were struck it would show a profit and a loss. On the credit side would stand the restoration of law and order, the betterment of material, and to some extent, of social conditions, and in particular a great improvement in the state of the provinces. On the debit side stands the permanent loss of self-government, and of the broadening and educative influence which participation in the management of public affairs exerts upon a people.

345. The Character of Augustus. The likenesses which we have of Augustus reveal clearly enough the essential traits of his character. The clearly-marked features, the strong mouth, and the compact, well-knit figure all point to firmness of purpose and clearness of conception. They indicate a man of balance and self-restraint, and such a man he proved himself to be, both in his public and private life. They suggest also a man of refined tastes, and the encouragement which he gave to art and literature would seem to bear out this interpretation of his physiognomy.

346. Literature under Augustus; Vergil, 70 - 19 B. C. In fostering arts and literature he was ably seconded by Agrippa, his commissioner of public works, who did so much to beautify Rome, by Maecenas his prime minister, who was the patron of Horace, and by Pollio the friend of Vergil, and the founder of the first public library in Rome. To Pollio, Vergil owed his introduction to Augustus, from whom he ultimately received compensation for the farm which he had owned near his birthplace, Mantua, but which the veterans had confiscated, and in grateful recognition of his kindness Pollio is made the chief object of his praise in the *Bucolics*, or pastoral poems which he composed between 41 and 39 B. C. About ten years later Vergil's second great work, the *Georgics*, appeared. The first book of the *Georgics* treats of farming, the second of the planting of trees, the third of the care of cattle, and the fourth of bees. The subject of the poem was suggested to the poet by Maecenas, who reflected the wishes of the emperor in his desire to have the Roman people return to the country, and take up farming again. The *Aeneid*

was not published until after the poet's death. It is the story
of Aeneas and the beginnings of Roman history, which in a
different form had been told in the epics of Naevius and Ennius.

347. Horace, 65 - 8 B. C.   The verses of Vergil's friend
Horace are still more closely connected with the names of
Augustus and Maecenas, because many of his poems are addressed to these two men, or celebrate their achievements.   In
his earliest compositions, the *Satires*, he discusses the different
phases of everyday life, laughing at its vices and foibles.
In making everyday life his theme he follows Lucilius, but his
work is more finished than that of his predecessor, and is free
from the personalities and the biting satire which characterized
the compositions of Lucilius.   To the earlier years of his literary life belong also the *Epodes*.   His most finished productions
are his *Odes* and *Epistles*.   In the last-mentioned poems he
returns to his early study of the life about him.   It is his four
books of lyrical poems, however, which have been most read by
posterity, and upon them Horace himself wished his claim to
immortality to rest.

**348. Tibullus, 54 - 19 B. C.; Propertius, 49 - 15 B. C.;
Ovid, 43 B. C. - A. D. 18.**   Poetry in which the writer turns
his thoughts in upon himself is characteristic of the period.   To
this class belong the elegies of Tibullus, Propertius, and Ovid.
Their poems are called elegies not because they were poems of
lamentation, but because the verses in them were alternately
dactylic hexameters and dactylic pentameters, and the term
elegy was applied to compositions of this metrical form.   Ovid
was a very prolific writer, and left a great body of poetry
behind him.   His best known works are the *Metamorphoses*
and the *Fasti*.   The former deals with the stories of Greek
mythology.   The latter is a Roman calendar of days, into
which are interwoven legends connected with the various
holidays.

349. Livy, 59 B. C. - A. D. 17.   Livy's great history of
Rome was probably planned to contain one hundred and fifty
books.   Of these one hundred and forty-two were completed,

and brought the narrative down from the founding of the city to 9 B. C. Only thirty-five of these books, with very brief epitomes of most of the others, are extant. Livy was not an historical critic, and his purpose was not so much to get at the exact truth in doubtful matters as to present in a graphic form the story of Rome and of the exploits of her great men. In this he has succeeded admirably.

350. The Question of the Succession. Augustus had found no more difficult question to settle than that of the succession. His own powers had been given to him for a fixed term of years or for life. Consequently he could not transmit them to any one else at his death. He could, however, during his own lifetime invest the man of his choice with powers independent of his own and thus do much toward securing the succession for him. This was the plan which he adopted. After the death of his nephew Marcellus and his two grandsons, Gaius and Lucius Caesar, he turned to his stepson Tiberius, and by adopting him and by conferring upon him the tribunician and proconsular powers, invested him with an independent authority which of course did not lapse at his own death in A. D. 14.

351. The Character of Tiberius. Augustus could scarcely have chosen a successor of greater promise. Tiberius was fifty-six years old when his predecessor died, and from his youth on he had been in the service of the state. He had been consul and had held the proconsular and tribunician power His bravery, ability, and success as a military leader had won him the implicit confidence of the soldiers. It is the Tiberius of this period, strong, proud, conscientious, and able, who is painted by Velleius Paterculus, the contemporary historian who served on his staff in Pannonia. A far different picture is that which we have from the pen of Tacitus, a writer of a later date. In point of fact there were two sides to his character, and the better phase of it showed out more clearly in his earlier life and in the early part of his reign.

352. His Mistrust and its Effects. He was naturally very reserved and the intention which Augustus cherished for many years of making some one else than himself his heir and successor developed this quality into a distrust of himself and a suspicion of others. This prevented him from making free use of others in administering public affairs, as Augustus had done. Consequently the burden of state fell upon him alone during the early years of his reign.

353. The Rise of Sejanus. He carried it well, but the strain was too great, and when the clever and unscrupulous Aelius Sejanus had shown himself able to relieve him, Tiberius gave him alone the confidence which he had refused to put in others, and withdrew from a direct participation in public affairs, betaking himself finally to the island of Capri, where he spent the rest of his life. This was what Sejanus desired. He now had a free hand to put out of the way those who opposed him and those who stood between him and the object of his great ambition, the succession to the throne. Drusus, the only son of Tiberius, was poisoned. Agrippina, the widow of Tiberius's nephew Germanicus, and her son Nero were banished, and Gaius, her second son, was marked for attack.

354. Delation. Against victims of less importance Sejanus used the professional informer. The Romans had no public prosecutor, but evidence was collected and charges were brought by private citizens. Cicero won his first brilliant success at the bar in this way by his prosecution of Verres, the governor of Sicily. This practice took on a vicious form under the empire, for men known as *delatores* made a profession of lodging information against others for the sake of sharing in the fines which would be imposed in case of conviction. These professional informers Sejanus, and Tiberius, also, for that matter, freely used against those whom they suspected.

355. The Last Days of Tiberius. The suspicions of Tiberius were at last aroused, and, sending a trusty agent to Rome, he secured the condemnation and death of his former favorite. After the death of Sejanus the mistrust of Tiberius redoubled, and his cruelty knew no limit. He cut himself off still more from the outside world and died in his island home in A. D. 37.

356. The Empire Under Tiberius. It is pleasant to turn from this side of the life of Tiberius to his government of the provinces, and to his administration of financial affairs. He practiced economy himself and insisted upon it in the case of his subordinates, and yet he was liberal when public interests demanded it. In the provinces he held governors strictly to their duties, and punished vigorously those who were guilty of injustice or extortion. In Italy he helped to develop agriculture, and promoted the security of the country districts. The most important constitutional change which he made was to transfer the elections from the popular assemblies to the senate. This change was of course only a formal one, because popular elections had already lost their meaning.

357. Gaius, Nicknamed Caligula, A. D. 37 - 41. Upon the death of Tiberius, Gaius Caesar, the son of Germanicus, the adopted son of Tiberius, was proclaimed emperor by the senate. He is commonly known by the pet name "Caligula" ("little boot") which the soldiers gave him when he was a boy with his father in Germany. Throughout his reign he was the victim of caprice, and represented absolutism in its crudest form. In an incredibly short time he had spent upon extravagant projects of all sorts the sum of seven hundred million sesterces, or about $25,000,000, which his economical predecessor had saved, and proceeded to meet the resulting deficit by confiscation and oppressive taxation. The wrath of the people groaning under this tyrannous government found expression in one conspiracy after another until finally Caligula was murdered by the officers of his own guard.

358. The Personal Appearance of Claudius. He was succeeded by his uncle Tiberius Claudius Caesar. Of the new emperor his biographer Suetonius says: "Either standing or sitting, but especially when he lay asleep, Claudius had a majestic and graceful appearance, for he was tall but not slender . . . . But his knees were feeble and failed him in walking, so that his gait was ungainly on state occasions, as well as when he was taking exercise . . . . He stammered, too, in his speech, and had a tremulous motion of the head at all times, but especially when he was

engaged in any business, however trifling . . . . His mother An-
tonia often called him 'an imperfect man whom nature had begun but had not finished.' And when she wished to upbraid
any one with dullness, she would say, 'He is a greater fool than
my son Claudius.' "

359. How He was made Emperor. It was this man whom
the soldiers found in a balcony in the palace hiding behind the
hangings of the door. Half in mockery and half seriously they
dragged him out, saluted him as emperor, and forced the reluctant
senate to recognize him.

360. His Distrust of Himself and its Effects. The distrust
which Claudius felt of himself and the interest which he had
always shown in antiquarian pursuits determine in large measure
the character of his reign. His lack of self-confidence made him
lean helplessly on others, and as a result he was easily managed
by the members of his household, and the history of the Court
during his reign is a continuous story of intrigue by the women
and the freedmen about him. This state of affairs had its advantages as well as its disadvantages, for some of his favorites,
like the freedman Narcissus, and Burrus, the prefect of the
pretorian guard, were men of affairs.

361. His Patience with Details. The passion for details
which his study of antiquarian matters had developed in him,
made it impossible for him to take a large view of the affairs of
government, but it made him patient and conservative in perfect-
ing the system which he received from his predecessors. It
made him willing to sit for hours in the courts of law, to make
sure that justice was properly administered. In fact, his sympathy with the unfortunate extended even to the slaves, whom
he protected against the cruelty of their masters.

362. His Public Works. His public works were of a sub-
stantial rather than of a showy character. He improved the
water supply of Rome by finishing two great aqueducts, the Aqua
Claudia and the Anio Novus, which his predecessor had begun.
One of these was nearly forty, the other nearly sixty, miles in
length. He insured a steady supply of corn to Rome by con-

structing a commodious harbor at Ostia near the mouth of the
Tiber.

363. His Provincial Policy. There was great military
activity on the frontier during his reign, and he carried out important administrative reforms in the provinces.   The most note-

THE CLAUDIAN AQUEDUCT

worthy of his achievements abroad was the conquest of southern
Britain, an enterprise which he conducted in person. He
watched over the interests of the provinces as Tiberius had
done, and returned to Julius Caesar's policy of granting citizenship freely to the provincials.

364. Nero and his Artistic Tastes. When Nero ascended
the throne in A. D. 54 he was but seventeen years old. He was
the son of the empress Agrippina by her first husband. She was
the daughter of Germanicus, and, therefore, Nero was of the
stock of the Caesars on his mother's side. He thought himself
a great artist, and gave himself up to his acting, painting, and
music, leaving the affairs of state to his two ministers, the philosopher Seneca and the prefect Burrus. For five years, while
these men were in authority, the government was well managed,
but the influence of Seneca was undermined by court intrigues,

and in 62 Burrus died.   Nero now threw off all sense of restraint, and gave free rein to his theatrical and artistic tastes, appearing in public as an actor, a singer, and even a charioteer in the circus.

NERO

The height of his artistic folly was reached toward the end of his reign, when he visited Greece and danced, sang, and competed in chariot races in the principal cities of that country at public spectacles arranged for him. Everywhere he was hailed as a victor, and returned to Rome with eighteen hundred crowns which he had won in these contests.   Meanwhile the court favorites took the reins into their own hands, and by playing upon the jealous suspicions of Nero, persuaded him to put to death his mother Agrippina, his wife Octavia, and Britannicus the son of Claudius.

365. The Great Fire in Rome.   In the summer of 64 a fire broke out in some shops near the Circus Maximus, and, fanned by a high wind, raged for a full week, reducing more than half of the city to ashes.   The story was current in the streets that the emperor had had the city set on fire, in order that he might rebuild it on a more magnificent scale, and gossip said that while the fire was in progress he watched the scene from the palace built by Maecenas, singing meanwhile a passage from a play of his own which described the capture of Troy.   Probably neither of these stories is true, but they illustrate the popular conception of the emperor.

366. The Christians held Responsible for the Fire.   It was perhaps for the purpose of turning suspicion from himself that Nero charged the Christians with having set the city on fire. At least this is what Tacitus tells us, and he goes on to say: "Christus, from whom the name (Christian) had its origin, suffered the extreme penalty during the reign of Tiberius at the hands of one of our procurators, Pontius Pilatus, and a most mischievous superstition, thus checked for the moment, again broke out not only in Judæa, the first source of the evil, but even in Rome, the meeting-place of all horrible and immoral practices from all quarters of the world." The fact that the Christians held secret meetings, and that they would not sacrifice to the image of the emperor and to the Roman gods excited the suspicions of the populace, who looked upon them as enemies of society. Consequently the emperor had the support of the rabble behind him when he condemned many of them to death on the false charge of having set fire to the city. The manner of their death is described by Tacitus: "Covered with the skins of beasts, they were torn by dogs and perished, or were nailed to crosses, or were doomed to the flames and burnt, to serve as a nightly illumination, when daylight had expired."

367. Revolt of Galba and Death of Nero, in A. D. 68. Nero set about rebuilding the city on a very elaborate scale, but before his great schemes were brought to completion the murmur of insurrection was heard in Gaul. It became ominous indeed when Galba the governor of Hither Spain, and a veteran leader, raised the standard of revolt. The news threw Nero into a panic of fear and to avoid death at the hands of the soldiers he took his own life. With his death the Julian line came to an end.

368. The Provinces under Nero. We have followed the course of events at Rome and in Italy during Nero's reign. It remains for us to say a word about conditions in the provinces. Nero, like his predecessors, followed the policy of Augustus in strengthening the frontiers of the empire, but made no serious attempts to push them forward. The early years of his reign were years of prosperity for the provinces, largely because the affairs of state were in the hands of Seneca, who was an able statesman and was familiar with the needs of the provinces, since he was a provincial himself by birth. Even after the influence of Seneca waned, conditions abroad did not grow perceptibly worse until the emperor began rebuilding Rome. To secure funds for this purpose he turned to the provinces, and the oppressive taxes which were laid upon them explain in part the insurrections which led to his overthrow.

369. Representative Assemblies in the Provinces. Perhaps the most interesting political development abroad during this period was the establishment of representative assemblies. These assemblies were closely connected with the worship of the emperor. After his death Julius Caesar was regarded as a god in the provinces. The same honors were paid to Augustus and his successors even during their lifetime, and the practice of paying divine honors to the emperor in the provinces was encouraged and systematized in the hope of developing a spirit of loyalty and a sense of imperial unity. In several of the provinces representatives met annually to arrange the details of the imperial worship, and to impose taxes for its proper maintenance. But these gatherings gradually developed the practice of discussing other matters of general interest to their respective provinces and of sending deputations to the emperor to lay the results of their deliberations before him. The establishment of these provincial councils is interesting because it is one of the earliest attempts to develop on a large scale our modern system of representative government.

370. Literature under Nero. Within the years of Nero's reign falls the principal literary activity of several distinguished men of letters, but the literature of the period reflects in a striking way the spirit of the times. Discouraged or embittered, as the case might be, by the state of society, men sought refuge in philosophy, or railed at the conditions about them, or, turning their thoughts back to the better days of the past, tried to imitate their predecessors, or carefully studied the writings of the past. For these reasons the literature of the period takes the form of philosophy, of satire, of labored imitations of earlier productions, or of learned commentaries upon them.

371. Seneca, 4 B. C.-A D. 65. The most distinguished writer of philosophy was Lucius Annaeus Seneca, a Spaniard by birth, who, as we have already noticed, was for several years the tutor and minister of Nero. He wrote mainly on moral subjects, treating such themes as *Anger, Tranquillity of Mind,* and the *Brevity of Life.* Some of these treatises are in the form of essays; others are letters addressed to his friend Lucilius. His philosophy was neither original nor deep, but he was a man of learning; he had an intimate knowledge of human nature, and originated a style which in large measure supplanted that of Cicero as a model for later writers. He composed a number of plays also, based on Greek subjects, but they are artificial in their style and unsuitable for acting.

372. Persius, A. D. 34-62. Persius the satirist has left us but six poems. He aims to follow Horace, but shows none of his predecessor's kindly humor, delicacy of touch, or felicity of expression. Still many of his fierce attacks upon hypocrisy and immorality reveal his intense sincerity, and have a vigor of style which few other Latin writers have equalled.

373. Petronius, Died A. D. 66. In somewhat the same field is the satire of Petronius. For originality of conception and skill in treatment it surpasses all the other literary productions of the period. It is commonly called a satire, and does in fact hold the follies and vices of society up to ridicule, but it is in reality a romance. In fact it is the earliest known work of prose fiction. It is a story of low life, and tells the experiences of a number of scapegrace freemen and rich, vulgar freedmen. Only a small part of it has survived.

374. Lucan, A. D. 39-65. As Persius tried to imitate Horace, so Lucan followed in the footsteps of Vergil. His epic poem entitled the *Pharsalia*, is a story in verse of the civil war between Pompey and Caesar. The triumph of Caesar is set forth as a great disaster, and Pompey and Cato are the heroes. It shows many of the literary vices of the period, being full of declamation and packed with learned references to mythology. There are fine passages here and there, but when read in sequence it is tiresome.

375. Learned Editions of the Classics. The tendency to dwell upon the great works of the past shows itself still more clearly in the works of learned men like Valerius Probus who brought out editions of Lucretius, Vergil, and Horace and discussed their language and use of words.

376. Summary of Events under the Julian Emperors, 27 B. C. - A. D. 68. In our study of this period we have noticed that the formal establishment of the Empire dates from 27 B. C. when Octavian received the tribunician and proconsular powers, upon which the authority of the emperor was based, and the titles of Augustus and *princeps*. His political policy was to retain the old republican forms, and to divide the authority between himself and the senate. In the provinces he appointed good governors, and gave them long terms of office, and he developed the territory outside of Italy, and fortified the frontiers. In Rome and Italy he constructed many public works, sought to reform society, gave importance to senators, knights, and Augustales, and fostered literature. Before his death he conferred upon his stepson Tiberius the tribunician and proconsular powers and thus assured the succession to Tiberius. The suspicious character of Tiberius made him tyrannical at home, but Italy and the provinces flourished. His successor Gaius, or Caligula, was an unbalanced spendthrift. He was followed by Claudius, who was easily influenced by others, but on the whole was a conscientious, careful ruler. Nero, his successor, governed wisely at first, but soon fell into excesses and ultimately took his own life. In his reign occurred the great fire at Rome and the consequent persecution of the Christians.

CHAPTER XII

FROM VESPASIAN TO SEPTIMIUS SEVERUS

(A. D. 69–193)

How the Empire expanded to its farthest limit under Trajan—How internal evils and the pressure of the northern barbarians began to threaten its life.

377. Galba, Otho, Vitellius, April A. D. 68-December 69. The career of Galba, Nero's successor, was short-lived. The sternness with which he repressed disorder among the soldiers in Germany threw them into mutiny, and they retaliated by naming their commander Aulus Vitellius emperor, while the pretorian guard in Rome, disappointed at the new emperor's lack of generosity to them, proclaimed M. Salvius Otho emperor. Galba was assassinated in January, 69; the senate confirmed the choice of Otho, and the new emperor set out for the North to check the advance of his rival. He was defeated, however, in northern Italy, and Vitellius was at once recognized by the senate.

378. Vespasian Proclaimed Emperor. Meanwhile, this time in the East, a new aspirant for the throne had arisen, in the person of Vespasian. With all possible despatch two of his lieutenants passed over into Italy. Vitellius was defeated in a bloody battle at Cremona, and the troops of Vespasian entered Rome December 20, A. D. 69. On the following day Vespasian received from the senate the tribunician power, and the title of Augustus.

379. His Character and Appearance. The new emperor was of humble birth. His family came from the Sabine town of Reate, the birthplace of that representative of the sturdy Italian stock, Varro. His grandfather had made his livelihood by acting as agent in collecting small debts; his father was a tax-collector. His humble surroundings in early life, and his training as a soldier, had made his tastes simple and his methods direct.

197

He had none of the narrow municipal prejudice of a native
Roman, nor the class prejudice of an aristocrat, which had
hampered his predecessors in their reforms. His squarely built
figure, his thick neck, his broad chin, and his coarse features
revealed his plebeian origin, but spoke volumes for his firmness,
his common sense, and his shrewdness in dealing with the practical affairs of life.

380. The Senatorial Order, an Imperial Aristocracy.
With an emperor of such a type it would be almost possible to
foretell the character of his reign. He applied himself with great
zeal and determination to the complete reorganization of the
finances. He showed his freedom from class prejudice and
from municipal prejudice by freely giving the senatorial rank to
provincials, and with that directness of purpose which characterized him, he did not in all cases require a candidate for senatorial honors to hold a magistracy, but he conferred the dignity
upon him directly. Henceforth the senatorial order ceased to
be an aristocracy of the city of Rome, but became an aristocracy
of the empire, whose privileges were within the gift of the
emperor.

381. Latin Citizenship. In the same spirit of fairness
toward the provinces he gave the rights of Latin citizenship,
which carried with it some of the privileges of Roman citizenship,
to the hitherto subject communities in some of the provinces.
These two practices formed a definite part of the policy of the
Flavian emperors, of whom Vespasian was the first, and perhaps
nothing did more to develop throughout the empire a unity of
interests and a spirit of loyalty to the central government.

382. Attempt to Found a Gallic Empire. Turbulence in
the provinces he repressed with a stern hand. At the beginning
of his reign a Batavian leader named Civilis led an uprising
among the people in what is now Holland. The movement was
joined by many of the auxiliaries serving with the Roman army
in Germany, and by some of the legions. All Germany seemed
to rally to the standard of Civilis in his effort to set up a Gallic
empire, but dissensions sprang up among the leaders, as they

had among the followers of Sertorius a hundred and fifty years before, and the incipient Gallic empire was crushed out as the independent government in Spain had been. The central government was still strong enough to hold the outlying provinces to their allegiance. The time for disruption had not yet come.

383. Revolt in Judæa. The other important military enterprise of the period was the capture of Jerusalem. As far back as the time of Pompey, Judæa had been brought in a measure under Roman control. Just after the beginning of our era it

THE SEVEN-BRANCHED CANDLESTICK FROM THE ARCH OF TITUS

became a province, and a Roman procurator was set over it, but the people were treated with great consideration, and the sanctity of the Temple was carefully observed. But a large party among the Jews resented the presence of the Romans, and their animosity was fanned into a flame of hatred by Caligula's attempt to have his statue placed in the Temple. Consequently they were ready to rise in revolt when, in 66 A. D., a garrison was placed in the Holy City for the first time by Gessius Florus the procurator. Vespasian, who had not yet been called to the throne, was sent to reduce the country. Before he reached Jerusalem, however, he was summoned to Italy to succeed Vitellius.

384. The Capture of Jerusalem. Vespasian's son Titus was left in command, and in the spring of A. D. 70 began the siege of Jerusalem. It is said that a million people had gath-

THE COLOSSEUM OR FLAVIAN AMPHITHEATRE

ered in the city to celebrate the Feast of the Passover. Outside the walls were eighty thousand legionaries and auxiliaries. Starvation reduced the population to the direst extremity, but the city refused to surrender. Men, women, and children fought side by side in its defense. At last the soldiers of Titus forced their way in. The Temple was burned; the city was razed to the ground, and a plough was passed over the site. The victory of

PANORAMA OF POMPEII

Titus was commemorated at Rome by a triumphal arch, which shows to this day carved upon it the seven-branched candlestick of the Temple, the table of shewbread, and the golden trumpets.

385. The Colosseum Dedicated in A. D. 80. This arch and the Colosseum, which was also built in the reign of Vespasian, are two of the most imposing monuments which the Roman world has left us. The Colosseum is in the shape of an ellipse, about six hundred feet long, and five hundred wide. The outer wall, which rises to a height of one hundred and fifty feet, is pierced by four rows of arches, corresponding to the four stories of the building. The seats within are arranged like steps leading up from the arena, and were capable of holding about forty-five thousand people. The building was opened by Vespasian's son and successor Titus, and gladiatorial contests were held in it until A. D. 404, and hunts of wild animals for a century more.

386 Public Baths. In the reign of Titus falls also the construction of the earliest of the public baths of which we have any remains. At the beginning of the fourth century there are said to have been a thousand such establishments large and small in the city. These structures were very elaborate. The larger ones, like that of Titus, had not only rooms for hot and cold and steam baths, but apartments for athletic exercises and for lounging, talking, and lecturing.

387. Titus, A. D. 79 - 81. The reign of Titus was very short. His health was already impaired when he mounted the throne, and within two years he died. He was an accomplished man of great tact and ability. These personal qualities, joined to the lavish way in which he furnished the people amusements, made him the "darling of the world," as Tacitus calls him.

388. The Destruction of Pompeii and Herculaneum in A. D. 79. The most noteworthy event which occurred in his reign was the destruction of Pompeii and Herculaneum by the eruption of Vesuvius. The catastrophe came so suddenly and the cities have been so well preserved by the enveloping layers of ashes, mud, and lava that by digging down to the site of Pompeii we see how the streets were paved, how the houses and shops were built and decorated, and how the common people lived and amused themselves.

389. Domitian is Like Tiberius. The character and reign of Domitian, who succeeded his brother Titus to the throne in A. D. 81, cannot fail to remind us of Tiberius. As Velleius Paterculus thought Tiberius almost more than human, so the

A MOSAIC, SHOWING PARROTS

poets Martial and Statius portray Domitian as godlike. To Tacitus and Pliny, on the other hand, Domitian is only a bloodthirsty tyrant, as is Tiberius in the pages of Tacitus. Domitian was stern and reserved as Tiberius had been, and shut himself up in his palace as Tiberius had cut himself off from the world on the island of Capri. Both emperors felt the responsibility of their position, and did their best to uphold religion and public morality. Each reign falls into two periods. In the case of Tiberius the rise of Sejanus marks the dividing line. In the reign of Domitian it is the rebellion of the governor of Upper Germany. In the first period there is much to praise in each emperor. In the second period both of them fell the victims of their own jealous suspicions, and delation ran riot.

390. His Efforts to Improve Public Morals. In his earnest efforts to improve the morals of the people, Domitian sought to reform the theatre, he enforced the laws which were intended to protect the purity of family life, he restricted the introduction of Oriental religions, he watched over the courts of law, and used his authority as censor to exclude unworthy members from the senate.

391. Domitian Rejects the Theory of the Dyarchy. He broke completely with the theory of the dyarchy that the prince and the senate jointly ruled the state. He was an autocrat by instinct, and consistently followed the policy of keeping the supreme power entirely in his own hands. With this purpose in mind he had himself made censor for life, solely for the purpose of controlling the appointment of senators. In this way he was able to degrade his enemies and to fill the senate with his supporters. He asserted the right also of sitting in judgment on senators charged with capital offenses, and with the help of his *delatores* found it not difficult to put out of the way any senator who aroused his suspicions. We have had occasion to notice the similarity of his character and reign to that of Tiberius. In one important particular their policies differed. Tiberius, and for that matter Nero too, ruled in large measure through ministers. Domitian held the reins of government firmly in his own hands, and tolerated no favorites at court.

392. His Foreign Policy Conservative. His foreign policy was that of Augustus. It lay in strengthening the frontier defenses, and in not advancing the limits of the empire. He continued the work upon a northern line of defense, which, when completed by Hadrian in the next century, extended from the mouth of the Rhine to that of the Danube. It consisted of a wall of earth or of stone with a ditch in front of it, and was protected by fortresses at intervals of nine or ten miles. With the Dacians to the north of the Danube who crossed the river and invaded Roman territory he made a humiliating peace by sending presents annually to their king Decebalus. In Britain Domitian's lieutenant Agricola extended the frontier to the aestuaries of the Clyde and the Forth, and built across the island between these points a wall of defense. Domitian fell in A. D. 96 the victim of a conspiracy organized by his wife Domitia.

393. Literature: Pliny the Elder, A. D. 23 - 79.   Prose literature of the Flavian emperors is represented by the works of Pliny the Elder and Quintilian.   Pliny's book, the *Natural History*, is a great encyclopedia of scientific fact and fiction based upon his observation and reading, and reminds one a little of Varro's treatises.   It deals with geography, anthropology, zoölogy, botany, and mineralogy.   A pathetic interest attaches to his death, since it occurred in A. D. 79 while he was investigating the cause and circumstances of the eruption of Vesuvius.

394. Quintilian, A. D. 35 - 95.   Quintilian was a Spaniard, and, like his fellow-countryman Seneca, a tutor at court.   In his work *On the Training of an Orator*, he describes a complete system of education for one who wishes to enter public life. His book is an admirable treatise on rhetoric, and the literary criticism which it contains is excellent.   He tried to bring the style of Cicero into favor again, but without success.

395. Silius Italicus, A. D. 25-101, and Statius, 40-96. The epic poetry of the period deserves mention, rather because it shows the imitative tendency of the times, than for its own merits.   Both Silius Italicus and Statius have imitated Vergil as slavishly as Lucan did, but their epic poems lack the occasional flashes of genius which Lucan's work shows, and are inexpressibly dull and monotonous.   Statius's *Silvae*, which are brief poems on Domitian's consulship, on the birthday or the death of a friend, and similar subjects, are much more readable.

396. Martial, A. D. 40-102 or 104.   The best known poet of the period is Martial, who left behind him fifteen books of *Epigrams*.   Some of these poems contain two verses only and are written as if they were intended to accompany presents sent at the festival of the Saturnalia, but the majority of them are like our modern epigrams, brief compositions in verse expressing some delicate or ingenious thought.   Martial is a writer of considerable talent, and his poems give us a very interesting, if somewhat unpleasant, picture of the times.   His poetry, like that of Statius and Silius Italicus, is full of servile eulogy of Domitian.

397. Josephus, A. D. 37 - about 100.   In addition to these Latin writers two foreigners, whose works are in Greek, should be mentioned, because they lived for a time at Rome, and dealt in some measure with Roman subjects.   One of these men is the Jewish historian Flavius Josephus, whose *History of the Jewish War* and treatise on *Jewish Antiquities* give us an account of the Roman government of Judæa and of the capture of Jerusalem.   After the fall of Jerusalem Josephus accompanied Titus to Rome, and was treated with great consideration by Vespasian, Titus, and Domitian.

398. Plutarch, A. D. 46 - about 120.   Plutarch, whose biographies of great Greek and Roman statesmen, known as the *Parallel Lives,* have held a well-deserved place in public esteem, was in Rome for a time during the reign of Vespasian and much respected at court, but the greater part of his life was spent in his native country, Boeotia.

399. The Revival of the Dyarchy under Nerva, A. D. 96 - 98. The senate showed its hatred of Domitian after his death by destroying his statues, by erasing his name from public monuments, and by forbidding the people to put on mourning. His successor Nerva was picked out by the senate, and for a short time again the state was under the joint rule of the emperor and the senate.   Trials for treason were suppressed, exiles were recalled, and, as Tacitus puts it, Nerva "harmonized things formerly incompatible, sovereignty and freedom."

400. Relief for the Poor.   The most interesting and important institution which he established was the *cura alimentorum,* or system of relief for the poor of Italy.   He hoped by means of it to prevent the free population of Italy from disappearing altogether.   His plan was to appropriate money to Italian towns, from the interest of which gratuities in the form of money or grain were given each month to a selected number of children of free birth.   The system was developed in an elaborate way by Nerva's successors, and many Italian children were supported by the government.

401. Trajan Made Emperor in A. D. 98. But Nerva was not a man of much physical strength or mental vigor, and feeling the cares of state too great for him, in A. D. 97 he adopted as his son and associate in the government Trajan, the governor of

Upper Germany; and, on Nerva's death in the following year, Trajan succeeded him.

402. He Shows Consideration for the Senate. Trajan was first of all a soldier, and spent a large part of his reign fighting the enemies of Rome. At home he treated the senate with considera tion, and carefully observed the fiction of the dual control of affairs by the emperor and the senate. In fact, during his prolonged absences from Rome, the senate acquired some importance as a legislative body.

TRAJAN

403. Wars with the Dacians, A.D. 101-102 and 104-106. In dealing with foreign affairs he broke with Augustus's policy of maintaining the empire intact without advancing the frontier. In his first great campaign, that against the Dacians, his object may not have been to extend the limits of Roman territory, but rather to protect the northeastern frontier. The people of Dacia, which corresponded nearly with modern Roumania and southeastern Hungary, had given the Romans trouble in Domitian's reign. Now they seemed likely to develop into a strong, united people, and Trajan may well have felt that they threatened the security of the provinces to the south of the Danube. At all events he set out from Rome in 101 to reduce them to submission. The difficulties of the expedition were tremendous. The soldiers had to cross the Danube on a bridge of boats, to cut their way through virgin forests, and to dislodge the enemy from one mountain fastness after another. The Dacians, too, fought desperately and were brilliantly led by Decebalus. But Trajan at last forced his way through the country to the Dacian capital, and Dacia yielded and became a dependent state in the year 102. But her submission was of short duration. Scarcely had Trajan withdrawn from the country, before the people began collecting an army and rebuilding their fortresses. The emperor took up arms against them once more, subdued the country completely, and made it a province, joining it to Roman territory by a great stone bridge across the Danube near Drobetae, the modern Turnu Severin in Roumania.

404. War with Parthia, A. D. 113-117. The second great military enterprise of Trajan was his war with the Parthians. Parthia was the traditional enemy of Rome, and the only great civilized state which maintained its independence. The bone of contention between the two countries was the control of Armenia, just as the control of Bithynia had been the principal question at issue between the Romans and Mithridates two centuries earlier. The dispute had been settled in Nero's reign by a compromise under which the king of Armenia was nominated by Parthia, but received his crown from the Roman emperor. In Trajan's reign the Armenian throne became vacant, and the king of Parthia overthrew the successor to whom the Roman emperor had given the crown. This action of the Parthians led to a long war in which Trajan traversed Mesopotamia and Assyria, and advanced almost to the Persian Gulf.

405. The Results of the War. Mesopotamia, Armenia, and Assyria he made Roman provinces, and in Ctesiphon, the capital of Parthia, the Parthian crown was placed upon the head of Parthamaspates, the son of the Parthian king, and the new monarch acknowledged his dependence on Rome. Trajan even dreamed of invading India, as Alexander had done, but the up-

risings in the country behind him recalled him from this foolish
enterprise.   He had pushed the eastern limits of Roman territory
to the Tigris, and had secured a foothold even beyond this
river, but his new eastern empire was a house of cards, and his
successor within a year of Trajan's death surrendered the territory beyond the Euphrates, and adopted again the eastern
frontier which Augustus had established.   Trajan died in A. D.
117 on his way back to Rome.

406. Trajan's Interest in the Provinces. His acquaintance with the provinces made him take a lively interest in their
welfare.   This fact comes out clearly in his correspondence with
Pliny, the governor of Bithynia.   Pliny consults the emperor
upon all sorts of local matters in his province.   He asks him,
for instance, if the construction of public baths at Prusa and
of an aqueduct at Sinope may be authorized, and if a company of firemen may be allowed at Nicomedia.

407. The Government and the Christians. The most
celebrated letters in the correspondence are one which Pliny
wrote to ask how he should treat the accusations made against
the Christians and Trajan's answer.   To Pliny's inquiry the
emperor replied: "The Christians ought not to be sought out;
if they are brought before you and convicted, they ought to be
punished, provided that he who denies that he is a Christian, and
proves this by making supplication to our gods, however much
he may have been under suspicion in the past, shall secure pardon
on repentance."   This decision expresses clearly the policy of
the Roman government in this matter.   Christianity is an offense
against the state if it is carried to the point of denying the
divinity of the emperor.

408. Trajan's Public Improvements. Trajan spent a
great deal of money on public works in Italy and Rome. He
constructed a road through the Pontine marshes, and improved
the harbor at Ostia.   A new aqueduct was brought into Rome,
two public baths were built, and a magnificent forum was
constructed to unite the old Forum with the Campus Martius.
The most conspicuous monument in Trajan's Forum was the

ris
en
to
riv
suc
rit
fro
11'

an
we
Pli
up
for
of
pa

cel
wi
the
en
if
pu
pr
he
on
the
ag
di

gr
co
th
tw
co
T.

NORTH SEA

BALTIC SEA

GERMANY

Vistula

Elbe

Eboracum
(York)

Londinium
(London)

Lugdunensis

Seine

Loire

GAUL

Lugdunum
(Lyons)

Aquitania

50

NORICUM

Dacia

DALMATIA

Narbonensis

Aquae Sextiae

Narbo

Massilia
(Marseilles)

Cremona
Po
Mutina
Ravenna
Ariminum
Arretium
L. Trasimeno
Perusia

Mantua
Parma
Bononia
Fæsulæ

Ancona

ADRIATIC SEA

Dyrrachium

CORSICA

ROME
Tiber   Ostia

Corfinium

Cannæ
Capua

Brundusium

Ostia

SARDINIA

Baleario Is.

Tarentum

MEDI

Lilybæum

Messana
SICILY
241
Syracuse

Actium

TERRA

NIA

Utica

Zama

Carthago

Hadrumetum
Thapsus

N

E

A

N

sar's death.

eath of Augustus   A.D. 14

A.D. 116.

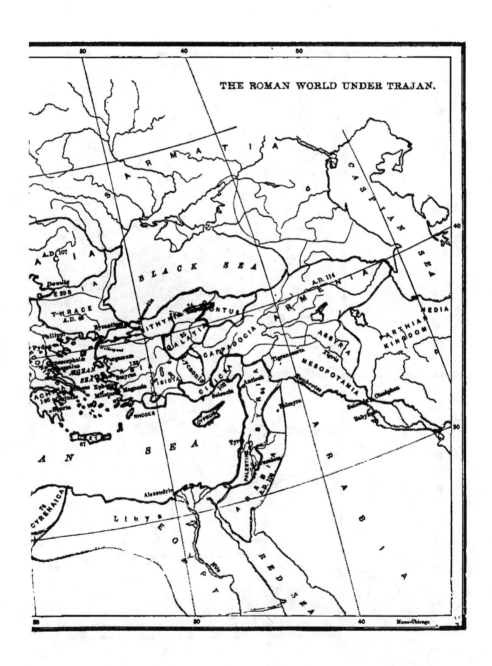

THE ROMAN WORLD UNDER TRAJAN.

×olumn of Trajan, which still stands in a perfect state of preser-
¬ation.   It rises to a height of ninety-six feet, and records in a
series of pictures, cut in relief, and running in a spiral band from
the bottom to the top of the column, the exploits of the Roman
army in Dacia.   The reliefs show us, for instance, Roman troops
setting fire to a town, and the Dacian king submitting to Trajan,
and they give us invaluable information concerning the equipment of a Roman soldier in the second century.

409. Literary History: Juvenal, (about) A. D. 60 - 140.
Juvenal, whose literary activity falls in the reigns of Trajan
and his successor, was the last of the great Roman satirists.
His themes, like those of his predecessors, are the vices and
the weaknesses of the people about him, the pride of wealth,
the vanity of human wishes, the wiles of a fortune hunter,
the hard life of a man of letters, and kindred subjects.   In the
realistic pictures of contemporary life which he paints, all forms
of vice and folly, however repugnant they may be to us, are un-
sparingly portrayed.

410. Tacitus, A. D. 55 - 120.   Tacitus paints life at Rome
in the same dark colors.   Next to Livy he is the greatest Roman
historian, although in matter and manner he is as far removed
from his predecessor as he well could be.   His minor works are
a *Dialogue on Orators*, the *Agricola*, and the *Germany*.   In the
first-mentioned book he gives the reasons for the decay of oratory.
In his *Agricola* he sketches the life of his father-in-law, who was
for several years commander in Britain.   The *Germany* gives
us a brief account of the country and peoples of northern Europe.
His most serious work, however, was his history of the empire
from the death of Augustus to the death of Domitian.   The first
part of this work, covering the years from A. D. 14 to 68, and
known as the *Annals*, contained originally sixteen books, and the
second part, the *Histories*, was divided into fourteen books.
About half of the entire treatise has survived.   The conciseness,
vigor, and poetic coloring of his narrative carry such conviction
to the reader's mind that the estimates which he put upon the
leading men of his time have been the accepted judgment of the

world; but they are often false estimates, because Tacitus was a man of strong personal and political prejudices, which are reflected in his writing.

411. Pliny the Younger, A. D. 62 - 113. We have had occasion already to speak of Pliny's letters to Trajan. Besides the correspondence with Trajan there are nine other books of epistles, full of chatty information about people and things at Rome. Juvenal finds nothing to praise, Pliny little to blame. His letters throw a deal of light upon his times, but he had an eye to publication, and consequently he does not express himself so unreservedly about people and their doings as Cicero does in his correspondence.

412. Hadrian Becomes Emperor in A. D. 117. The right of the emperor to nominate his successor, was so fully recognized by Trajan's time that, although he had not formally associated any one with him in the government, the letter which he sent from his deathbed to Hadrian, the governor of Syria, informing him that he had adopted him as his heir, was accepted as sufficient warrant by the senate for elevating Hadrian to the throne.

413. His Character. The new emperor was a man of quick and restless mind and of wide sympathies and interests. It has been remarked that in his busts "the head is bent a little, as if to catch every sound; the eyes and mouth suggest the quickness and liveliness of an intellect determined that nothing shall escape it." He was liked by the soldiers and the common people because of his simple life and his interest in their welfare, but the senators, who were conservative in their ideas, were hostile to him on account of his fondness for new things.

414. He Reforms the Civil Administration. His reign is important for the changes which he made in the administration of internal affairs. Among other things the civil business of the government was carefully divided among a number of departments or bureaus, and within each bureau officials were graded in a fixed order. In this way business was carried on systematically, and each official was held responsible to his superior.   In these civil offices Hadrian employed knights almost exclusively.   This change of course cut down the number of important positions open to senators, and limited their influence.

415. His Judicial Reforms.   To lighten his duties in deciding cases which came before him he established a *consilium*, or board of advisers, made up of senators and knights who were experienced in the law.   This naturally led him to take another

HADRIAN

step toward making the administration of justice more systematic.   Under the republic and early empire justice had been administered largely by the praetor.   Each praetor on taking office at the beginning of the year published the maxims of law and the forms of procedure by which he would be governed throughout his year of office.   This edict was properly called, therefore, an *edictum perpetuum,* or standing edict.   A praetor commonly adopted the proclamation of his predecessor, making such additions to it and changes in it as seemed to him desirable. Now under instructions from Hadrian an eminent jurist named Salvius Julianus brought together in a single edict all the principles and forms published by praetors and curule aediles, in so far as they were still in force. From this time forth the praetor could make no changes in legal methods, and new law could be made only by the emperor or the senate.

416. His Foreign Policy. Hadrian gave the same systematic attention to the needs of the army. An improved form of the phalanx was adopted; new kinds of armor were introduced, and bodies of troops were trained for special purposes. But Hadrian was a man of peace. He gave up at once the provinces of Armenia, Mesopotamia, and Assyria, and recognized the king of Parthia as a lawful monarch. He spent ten years of his reign travelling through the provinces, so that he became thoroughly familiar with their needs, and no one of his predecessors broke so thoroughly with the republican theory that the provinces were subordinate to Italy, and were to be used for the benefit of Italy.

417. His Curiosity. His extended travels gave him an opportunity to satisfy that curiosity which his contemporaries noted as his most pronounced characteristic. We hear of him going to the point in Asia Minor where the Greeks with Xenophon first saw the sea after their long march homeward. We hear of him visiting the site of Troy, and travelling in Egypt to see the statue of Memnon from which miraculous music was heard at sunrise.

418. His Interest in the Provinces. The provinces profited greatly by his visits. New buildings were erected in many cities of Asia and Greece; the mines in Dacia were developed; colonies were planted in the Danubian provinces; the defenses of the northern frontier were strengthened; a strong wall was built in Britain from Solway Firth to Walls-end, and the collection of taxes was taken out of the hands of private contractors and henceforth managed by the government.

419. The Pantheon and the Castle of San Angelo. Two great monuments of his reign are still standing in Rome, the Pantheon and the Castle of San Angelo. The Pantheon was originally built by Agrippa in the reign of Augustus, but was later destroyed by fire, and the building which one sees to-day in Rome is the work of Hadrian. The Castle of San Angelo, as

THE PANTHEON

the other structure is now called, was built by Hadrian as his mausoleum, and in it his ashes were placed on his death in the year 138.

420. Antoninus Pius, A. D. 138-161. The wisdom which Hadrian had shown in abandoning outlying provinces, like Assyria, which it required a constant effort to defend, and in strengthening the frontier, secured peace throughout the reign of his successor Antoninus Pius. Antoninus was a man of an amiable disposition and of good parts, but he lacked the active temperament and the ability as an organizer which his predecessor had shown. Consequently he made no great changes at home or abroad. His humane disposition was reflected in the administration of justice, for he insisted on applying the spirit rather than the mere letter of the law, and held an accused person

THE MAUSOLEUM OF HADRIAN

innocent, as English-speaking peoples do to-day, until he had been proved guilty.

421. Marcus Aurelius Antoninus, A. D. 161-180. It was a strange whim of fate that, when Antoninus died, the government of the world should be thrust upon a man who would have preferred to spend his life in his study as a philosopher; and that

a man who deplored violence should spend fourteen years of his life in warfare. It was strange, too, that in the reign of one whose main desire it was to see his people prosperous and happy the worst pestilence should break out that the Roman world had ever known. Strangest of all is the fact that the ruler who wrote in all sincerity "tolerance is a part of justice" should be popularly regarded as the first emperor to persecute the Christians systematically; yet all this was true of Marcus Aurelius.

422. War with Parthia, A. D. 162-166. The war which broke out in Parthia shortly after his accession was a legacy from the policy of his predecessor, who had failed to insist upon that respect for Roman authority in the East which Hadrian had enforced. It was again the Armenian question which caused the trouble. The struggle ended with the submission of Parthia, but the victory was dearly bought, for the returning soldiers brought with them a plague which laid waste the empire, and weakened Italy at a moment when she needed her whole strength to repel the inroads of the barbarians to the north.

423. Wars with the Marcomanni, A. D. 167-175 and 178-180. The barbarians who threatened Roman territory were the Marcomanni, Quadi, and other peoples to the north of Raetia and Noricum, who were crowded out of their country by a southward movement of the German tribes beyond them. They swept down into the northern provinces, and even entered Italy, and laid siege to Aquileia. The difficulties of a campaign in so mountainous a country as modern Bohemia, where the Marcomanni lived, and the loss in men and money which the empire had suffered in consequence of the plague made the war a hard one. Nevertheless, it was brought to a successful conclusion, and a later uprising of the Marcomanni and their neighbors was put down. But before he could reduce the newly acquired territory to the form of a province Marcus died.

424. The Development of Serfdom. Before his death, however, he instituted a policy in dealing with the barbarians which had far-reaching social and economic results for many centuries. He assigned land in Roman territory to large numbers of German and Sarmatian colonists. These settlers were really serfs, because, although they were free, they could neither own nor lease their farms. The number of such *coloni*, as they were called, was largely increased by the growing inability of tenants to pay their rent. Such tenants could not, of course, be allowed to move from their farms, and leave behind them

MARCUS AURELIUS IN HIS TRIUMPHAL CHARIOT

unpaid the accumulated charges for rent, and consequently were permanently bound to the land which they occupied, and lapsed into a state of serfdom, which descended from father to son.

425. The Christians. The development of Christianity was causing the government considerable anxiety. The rapidity with which the new religion was spreading is clearly shown by the letters which provincial authorities in Asia, Greece, and Gaul sent to Rome, inquiring how they should deal with its adherents. Marcus adopted the policy of repression, and gave instructions that those who confessed that they were Christians should be put to death. Since many of the Christians voluntarily avowed their faith, the number of martyrs steadily increased.

426. The Reign of Commodus, A. D. 180-192. Commodus, who succeeded his father, revived the evil memories of the later Julian emperors. He gave himself up to the pursuit of pleasure, taking part in the public games just as Nero had taken part in musical contests, and making actors and gladiators his principal associates. The affairs of government were turned over to favorites. Quiet was secured, at home by supplying the populace with food and games at the public expense, on the frontier by making gifts to dangerous chieftains. There was no money to repair public buildings; gold coins disappeared from circulation, and funds for the support of poor children were exhausted. The emperor whose reign had brought on these conditions fell the victim of a plot laid against his life by his concubine Marcia and carried out by an athlete named Narcissus.

427. Pertinax, A. D. 193. The conspirators placed on the throne P. Helvius Pertinax, a distinguished soldier, but he was soon overthrown, and a senator named Didius Julianus, who surpassed all other aspirants for the crown in his promises to the pretorian guard, was invested with the purple.

428. L. Septimius Severus Made Emperor in A. D. 193. But the break in the succession encouraged ambitious leaders to lay claim to the throne, as had been the case on Nero's death. L. Septimius Severus raised the standard of revolt in Pannonia, Pescennius Niger in Syria, and Clodius Albinus in Britain. Septimius Severus had a larger army than his rivals, and without meeting serious resistance, made himself master of the peninsula and of Rome. The frightened senate condemned Julianus to death, and Septimius Severus was proclaimed emperor in the summer of 193.

429. The Dyarchy Given Up. From a survey of the history of the second century it is clear that the independent coöperation of the senate with the emperor had become a fiction. Neither in the choice of an emperor, nor in the management of affairs after he had ascended the throne, could it play an effective part. The theory of the succession rested on two irreconcilable things— heredity, or adoption by the emperor, and on the other hand the free choice of the senate. These two methods of selecting a ruler could not be followed at the same time, and the weaker element in the dual system, the senate, yielded. When it came to the management of public affairs senators found real power centred in the hands of the emperor, and nothing left to them but formalities and details, and even in such matters opposition to the wishes of the emperor was undertaken only at the risk of being prosecuted by one of his pliant tools on the charge of high treason.

430. The Empire Prosperous in the Second Century. It was a fortunate thing for the provinces that two of the ablest emperors of the second century, Trajan and Hadrian, not only travelled extensively through the empire but were of provincial descent. These two facts did much to improve the government and financial conditions, and probably the Roman world, taken as a whole, was never so prosperous at any period of its history as in this century.

431. The Decline of Local Self-government. And yet there were signs of internal weakness both in Italy and abroad. Governors in the provinces and imperial officials in Italy had encroached so much upon the traditional functions of the local magistrates, and those who held local offices were obliged to contribute such large sums to the support of the government, that it was difficult to find candidates for the municipal magistracies, and interest in local politics was almost dead.

432. The State of the Finances. Financial conditions were steadily growing worse and worse. This is shown by the fact that the state had to cancel the payment of large sums due it in the form of taxes, to spend a great deal of money in helping the poor, and to depreciate the currency. On the eve of the war with the Marcomanni, Marcus Aurelius was actually obliged to sell the crown jewels to raise money for the campaign. The trouble lay partly in the extravagance of the court and in a faulty system of taxation, but mainly in the lack of energy and in the incapacity of the people themselves, and in their tendency during times of prosperity to assume financial responsibilities which they could not maintain when unexpected demands were made on their resources. The emperor Hadrian was largely responsible for this last evil. Under his encouragement the small towns all through Italy and the provinces erected costly baths, theatres, and other public buildings and works, whose

construction exhausted their resources at the time, and whose
maintenance became an intolerable burden when some public
misfortune came, like the plague under Marcus Aurelius.

433. The Provinces and the Barbarians. Ominous, too,
were the revolts of Roman generals in the provinces, in which
revolts not infrequently the leader of the insurrection called
upon the barbarians to help him. The southward movement
of the German tribes in the reign of Marcus Aurelius also boded
ill for the future, and the policy of recruiting the army from
the barbarians and of settling large numbers of them in Roman
territory where they could learn Roman methods and some day
turn their knowledge against their masters was of doubtful
wisdom.

434. The Literary Emperors. Of the emperors of the second century Antoninus Pius showed an interest in literature,
Hadrian wrote a little in both prose and verse, while Marcus
Aurelius left behind him in his *Meditations* a little book written
in Greek which has given comfort and courage to many readers
since his day. The work gives us, in the form of simple notes, the
reflections of a sincere, kindly, upright man on duty, life, and
the government of the world.

435. The Literary Style, Artificial. But notwithstanding
this imperial interest in literary matters, pure literature did not
flourish. The literary language, like the people, seemed to be
exhausted, and the best known writers of the period, like
Fronto, Gellius, and Apuleius, tried to infuse new life into it
from the early period by using in their works the words and
phrases of Ennius, Accius, and Cato; but such a style was
bound to be artificial.

**436. Fronto, about A. D. 100-175, Aulus Gellius, born
about A. D. 125.** Fronto was the teacher of Marcus Aurelius,
and his principal work which has come down to us is his correspondence with the emperor. Aulus Gellius compiled what
might be called a scrapbook with extensive comments of his
own. The *Attic Nights*, as he called his book, deals with lan-

guage, literature, law, and philosophy, and contains much valuable information in a disconnected form.

437. Apuleius, about A. D. 125 to about 200. The most interesting and original of the many works of Apuleius is his story of adventure, called the *Metamorphoses*. Lucius the hero is transformed into an ass, and in the form of this animal undergoes a great many marvelous experiences at the hands of magicians, robbers, vagrant priests, and ladies of fashion. Into the main thread of the narrative some twenty or thirty popular tales are interwoven, one of which, the charming story of Cupid and Psyche, has become famous.

438. The Historians Suetonius and Florus. History was cultivated in the second century by Suetonius, who was for a time Hadrian's secretary, and by Florus. In his *Lives of the Caesars* Suetonius has given us in a chatty way, without much regard to the arrangement of the material, biographies of the emperors from Julius Caesar to Domitian. Florus's history is little more than a sketch, in very rhetorical language, of the wars of Rome from the earliest times down to his own day.

439. The Institutes of Gaius. The writings on Roman law are the works of most permanent value which we owe to the second century. Hadrian, by having all existing judicial rules and principles reduced to a systematic and permanent form, prepared the way for the admirable introduction to the study of law which Gaius has left us in his *Institutes*, and this book in its turn was the foundation, three centuries and a half later, of one part of the great code of Justinian, in which Roman law took its final form.

440. The Earliest Christian Latin Literature. To the second century belongs the first piece of Christian Latin literature. It is a pamphlet called the *Octavius*, written in defense of Christianity, by Marcus Minucius Felix. At about the same time there appeared in Greek, Justin Martyr's celebrated apologies for Christianity, in which he explains the mysteries of the faith, and upholds the truth of Christianity and the innocence of its adherents.

441. Revival of Greek Letters. The second century in fact witnessed a revival of Greek letters, and Greek became the literary language of the empire. Lucian of Samosata, the most distinguished figure in the movement, shows the absurdities of the old theology in his inimitable *Dialogues of the Gods*, and doubtless helped to clear the way for Christianity. Aristides of Mysia, like Apuleius, travelled through Greece and Asia Minor, lecturing in the principal cities. Fifty or more of his discourses, which deal mainly with incidents in ancient history, have come down to us. Arrian of Nicomedia in Bithynia is best known for his *Anabasis of Alexander*, which is in imitation of Xenophon's work, but is more comprehensive in its scope than Xenophon's *Anabasis*, since it contains a complete biography of its hero. From Appian's histories of the foreign wars and the civil wars of Rome we have already had occasion to quote. The *Foreign Wars* furnishes an invaluable source of information for the contests with Syria, Illyria, Carthage, and with Mithridates. Appian's book on the *Civil Wars* is an equally important work on internal affairs in Italy from 133 to 35 B. C., on the war between the triumvirs and the republicans, and on the struggle between Antony and Octavian. In this period also falls Pausanias's *Itinerary of Greece*, in which he aims to describe all the important buildings and works of art to be seen in Greece in his day, and the great treatises on astronomy and geography of Ptolemy of Alexandria belong to the same time.

442. Summary of Events from Vespasian to Septimius Severus, A. D. 69-193. Vespasian was chosen emperor, as we have noticed, after a year of confusion. He reformed the finances, constructed the Colosseum, gave Latin citizenship freely to the provinces, and with the help of his eldest son Titus, who succeeded him, captured Jerusalem. His second son Domitian, who followed Titus, lessened the importance of the senate, and made himself an absolute ruler. Abroad he added Britain to the Empire. Nerva and his successor Trajan tried to build up the free population of Italy by supporting children of free birth. Trajan's wars with Dacia and Parthia added the provinces of Dacia, Armenia, Mesopotamia, and Assyria to the empire, and gave it a greater extent than it ever had before or after his time. Hadrian, who succeeded Trajan, is distinguished for his legal, administrative, and military reforms, and for his interest in the provinces. He gave up the newly acquired territory in Asia. The peaceful reign of Antoninus Pius was followed by the wars with Parthia and the Marcomanni which vexed the reign of Marcus Aurelius, and led to the establishment of barbarian colonies on Roman soil, and the development of serfdom. The decline of self-government in the second century, the bad state of the finances, and the prevalence of insurrections are symptoms of Rome's decline.

CHAPTER XIII

FROM SEPTIMIUS SEVERUS TO CONSTANTINE

(A. D. 193–337)

, How Aurelian and Diocletian saved the Empire from dissolution—How Diocletian reorganized and divided the Empire—How Constantine moved the seat of government from Rome to Byzantium, and how he came to recognize Christianity.

443. Three Prominent Emperors in the Third Century. In the confusion which reigns throughout the empire in the third century three figures stand out clearly—Septimius Severus at the beginning of the period, Aurelian and Diocletian toward its close. Each of these three emperors checked the downfall of the empire, and gave it a new lease of life, by suppressing insurrections in the provinces, by driving back the barbarians, and by reforming abuses in the government.

444. Military Reforms of Septimius Severus. Septimius Severus distinguished himself especially by the changes which he made in the civil and military administration and in the laws. He rendered service in the army more attractive by making the position of the minor officers more honorable, and by granting new privileges to private soldiers in the auxiliary troops. Foremost among the privileges granted were Roman citizenship, after a short term of service, and recognition of the marriages which soldiers had contracted with native women in the provinces. Septimius Severus added three legions to the army, and brought it to a high degree of efficiency, as is shown by his successful war against Parthia and by the reconquest of Mesopotamia, which, it will be remembered, Hadrian had given up. These achievements were commemorated in the great arch which still stands in the Forum. But perhaps his most noteworthy service in defense of the empire consisted in his reorganization and improvement of the roads and in their extension along the northern frontier.

445. His Legal Reforms. This reign is most fruitful in the establishment of important legal principles and in the reduction of Roman law to a logical system. The leader in the movement was the distinguished jurist Papinian who was for a time prefect of the pretorian guard. Under his direction the great rules of law governing inheritances, contracts, loans, and similar matters were developed into the form which so many modern nations have adopted.

446. The Levelling Process. The reduction of Italy to

THE ARCH OF SEPTIMIUS SEVERUS

the level of the provinces goes steadily on. Troops are now for the first time permanently stationed in Italy, and the emperor assumes the military title of proconsul in Italy as well as in the provinces. The levelling process is brought to completion by Bassianus, nicknamed Caracalla, the successor of Septimius Severus, who by an edict in 212 makes all freemen of the empire Roman citizens. Henceforth Italians and provincials are equal before the law.

447. A Century of Anarchy. On his deathbed Septimius

Severus had stated with truth: "I received the commonwealth in disorder; I leave it in peace." But peace and order were of short duration, for they rested on the fickle support of the troops. By the army Caracalla was overthrown, and his successors Macrinus, Elagabalus, and Alexander Severus. It is unnecessary for our purpose, however, to trace the fortunes of all the emperors who followed one another in rapid succession during this century.

448. The Reign of Gallienus Typical. The reign of Gallienus from 260 to 268 is in some respects typical, and a sketch of it will give one a clear, though perhaps an exaggerated, picture of the state of affairs during the entire period which is under consideration.

449. The Incursions of the Barbarians. In these eight years no part of the Roman world, with the possible exception of Africa and the islands, escaped the devastating raids of the barbarians. In the East the Persians had made a prisoner of Valerian, the father of Gallienus and his former colleague, and had overrun the province of Syria. In the valley of the Danube the Goths entered Roman territory from the north, supplemented their land campaign by an attack from the sea on the east, ultimately pushed down as far as Achaia, and plundered Corinth and Athens. In the north the Alemanni broke through the barriers along the Rhine, and penetrated as far as Ravenna without meeting serious opposition. The Franks entered Gaul, pressed down into Spain, and even made their way across the Mediterranean to Africa. These incursions were essentially marauding expeditions, and when the lust for booty had been satisfied, the barbarians usually withdrew as speedily as they had come. No serious loss of territory, therefore, resulted from them, but cities were destroyed, the country was laid waste, and commerce in many cases was ruined. The result was that the resources of the people, already scarcely sufficient to support the burden of taxation laid upon them, were still further impaired.

450. The Rise of Independent Rulers. Another evil of the century which reached its climax during the reign of Gallienus and seemed to portend the speedy dismemberment of the empire was the rise of provincial governors to the position of independent rulers, and the recognition of their claims by the central government. These nationalist movements, if we may so term them, grew very naturally out of the state of affairs in many of the provinces. In their origin and character they were not unlike the partially successful attempt which Sertorius made in the first century before our era to set up a government of his own in Spain. The interests of the people within a given province or group of provinces were the same; their foes were the same, viz., the barbarians along their frontiers, and, since the central government could not protect them effectually, they felt it necessary to organize for their own defense. Both the provincials and the soldiers looked to the governors of their respective provinces for leadership. Under a weak or unpopular emperor, therefore, it was an easy thing for an ambitious general to ignore the authority of Rome, and to usurp the powers and titles of an independent ruler.

451. Gaul and Palmyra Assert their Independence. The most notable cases of the sort are those of Postumus in Gaul and Odaenathus in Palmyra. Postumus set up a government of his own in Gaul, established a court, and took the titles of consul and pontifex maximus. As for Odaenathus, he was given entire charge of Asia with the unrestricted right to appoint governors and generals. He and his wife Zenobia assumed the titles of king and queen of Palmyra, and, after her husband's death, Zenobia threw off all semblance of submission to Roman authority, and even went to the extent of invading and subduing Egypt.

452. Aurelian, 270-275, Restores Unity. It was Aurelian, the second of the great emperors of the third century, who saved the empire from the dissolution which threatened it. Egypt was recovered; Palmyra was captured after an heroic resistance; its people were given to the sword, and the city so completely destroyed that even its site was unknown for centuries. With Roman authority recognized once more in the East, the emperor directed his attention to Gaul. Tetricus, who, after a brief period of confusion, had succeeded Postumus as emperor of Gaul had added Britain and northern Spain to his dominions, but the army got beyond his control and committed such excesses that both he and the people of the province received Aurelian with open arms. In the magnificent triumph which Aurelian celebrated on his return to Rome, Zenobia and Tetricus both appeared in the train of the conqueror. The East and the West acknowledged once more the authority of Rome, and the unity of the empire was again asserted. And yet it was ominous for the future that this same emperor who had repelled the barbarians, and put down pretenders throughout the Roman world, thought it necessary to protect the city of Rome itself against the possible incursions of barbarians by building about it the great wall which still stands to commemorate his reign.

JULIA DOMNA

453. Some Brilliant Women of the Third Century. No account of the third century would be complete without some mention of the brilliant women who played so conspicuous a part in the history of the period. Foremost among them was Julia Domna, her sister Julia Maesa, and her niece Julia Mamaea.

454. Julia Domna. Julia Domna the wife of Septimius Severus, was a native of Syria, of low station, but she was a woman of such intellectual power and political ability that she acquired a great influence over her husband, and on his death directed in large measure the affairs of state under her son, the emperor Caracalla. Caracalla was overthrown by his pretorian prefect Macrinus, and Julia Domna was banished.

455. Julia Maesa. Partly to avenge her sister, and partly to advance the fortunes of her grandson Elagabalus, Julia Maesa put forth all her efforts to encompass the downfall of Macrinus. Within a year she accomplished her purpose and also secured the succession for her grandson. Throughout his reign she was the power behind the throne, going so far as to take part even in the deliberations of the senate. When she saw that the downfall of Elagabalus was imminent, she persuaded him to adopt her other grandson Alexander Severus, the son of Julia Mamaea. In this way the real power in the state, which had passed from Julia Domna to Julia Maesa, was by her transmitted to Julia Mamaea.

456. Julia Mamaea. Mamaea was a worthy successor of her two kinswomen. She devoted herself energetically to the education of her son. Later, when he assumed the reins of government, she directed his political policy, and her likeness appears with his on the coins of the period.

457. Victorina. The three women of whom we have just been speaking distinguished themselves by their skill in statecraft. Victorina and Zenobia, while not lacking in political capacity, were also military leaders of marked ability. Victorina was the mother of the predecessor of Tetricus, and really governed Gaul during her son's reign. On his death she advanced Tetricus to the throne. Her influence with the Gallic army is shown clearly by the affectionate titles which the soldiers gave her, and by the fact that, after her death, Tetricus, as we have already noticed, was utterly unable to hold them in control. Her fame had penetrated even to the Orient, and Zenobia at one time planned to form an alliance with her.

458. Zenobia. Zenobia herself is the most picturesque figure of the century. She was as famous for her beauty as she was for her accomplishments and for her political and military

talents.   She spoke readily Greek, Latin, and the languages of
all the peoples about Palmyra.   She took a lively interest in
literature and philosophy as well as in the sterner pursuits of
war and the chase.   She made Palmyra a great commercial
centre.   At one time her empire included even Egypt, and no
military enterprise which Aurelian undertook proved so difficult and hazardous as her overthrow and the capture of her
capital.

459. Diocletian Abandons the Theory of the Dyarchy.
If we stop to consider the political history of the period we shall
find that the position of the senate was what the emperor chose
to make it.   The senate was still nominally a partner in the government, but in reality exercised only such powers as he was
willing to delegate to it.   Diocletian, who ascended the throne
in 284, boldly discarded even the theory that it ruled jointly
with the emperor, and frankly embodied in the constitution
the changes which three centuries had wrought in the body
politic.

460. The Senate Reduced.   He gave up the practice of
consulting it on matters affecting the empire, and issued all laws
and edicts in the name of himself and his colleague.   It became,
therefore, nothing more than the common council of the city of
Rome, and those who held the magistracies were reduced to
the position of municipal officials.

461. The Two Augusti.   Under Diocletian's scheme of government the empire was to be ruled jointly by himself and Maximian, whom he made his colleague.   They bore the title of
Augusti, and all edicts were issued in the name of both, and all
appointments to office were thought of as coming from them
conjointly.

462. The Two Caesars.   Shortly after his accession he and
Maximian chose two Caesars who stood just below the Augusti
in point of dignity.   The purpose of this arrangement was to
provide for the succession, since it was a part of Diocletian's
plan that, when one of the Augusti died or resigned, his position
should be taken at once by one of the Caesars.

463. The Augusti Rule in Different Parts of the Empire.
According to the theory of Diocletian's scheme of government
the two Augusti were to rule the Roman world jointly, but in
point of fact Diocletian made Nicomedia his capital and, with
his Caesar, ruled the East; while Maximian, making Milan his
seat of government, with the assistance of his Caesar, governed
in the West.

464. The Civil Administration. An essential part of
Diocletian's plan was the more complete separation of the civil
and military administrations. At the head of the civil administration were four pretorian prefects who resided respectively at
Constantinople, Sirmium, Milan, and Treves, or Trier. Their
prefectures were divided into dioceses, and these sub-divided into
provinces.

465. The Military Administration. At the head of the
military administration there were from five to ten officials, and
under them were the territorial commanders, styled *duces* or *com-
ites*, but the *ducatus*, or unit of military administration, did not in all
cases correspond with the *provincia*, or unit of civil administration.

466. The Old and the New in Diocletian's Government.
Diocletian did two things. He gave up the fiction that the
government was anything else than a pure monarchy, and he
developed into a well-balanced system methods of administration
which his predecessors had introduced. It is clear that there
was very little in his scheme which was essentially new. The
senate and the magistrates had at one time ruled the Roman
world. Diocletian limited the exercise of their powers to the
city of Rome, but in doing this he was merely bringing to completion a process which had been going on from the time of
Augustus. He shared his authority with a colleague, but this
plan had been tried as early as the reign of Marcus Aurelius.
It may even be regarded as a revival, under a different form,
of the dual system of the consulship. The separation of the
civil and military administrations was a natural outgrowth of
the carefully graded system of offices which Hadrian introduced,
and was probably not unknown in some parts of the Roman

empire at least a half century or more before the time of Diocletian. The practice of conferring the title of Caesar on the intended successor to the throne also goes back to the reign of Hadrian. Diocletian made the provinces very much smaller than they had been, largely to diminish the power of provincial governors, but in doing so he was only carrying out a policy which Domitian and his successors had adopted. In all these matters he was merely developing institutions which his predecessors had established. The new point of greatest importance which he introduced was the division of the empire into two parts. Theoretically such a division was not contemplated in his plan, as we have noticed, but when one Augustus established his headquarters in the East, and the other in the West, a partition of the empire or a struggle for supremacy was reasonably sure to be the outcome of the arrangement. Such a turn of affairs came at once, for in 307, two years after Diocletian's abdication, there were six rulers claiming the title of Augustus.

467. Constantine Sole Emperor, A. D. 324-337. After sixteen years of civil war and dissension Constantine the Great restored harmony by uniting the whole empire under his sway. For two other changes of great importance also his reign is noteworthy—for the recognition of Christianity as a legal religion, and for the transfer of the seat of government from Rome to Byzantium.

468. The Growth of Christianity. Christianity spread most rapidly in the Orient and in Italy. In the East the Scriptures were widely circulated in Greek, which was the tongue of cultivated people, and in Syriac, which the lower classes used. For the West translations had been made into Latin. In the early part of the third century Tertullian boasts: "We are a people of yesterday, and yet we have filled every place belonging to you—cities, islands, castles, towns, assemblies, your very camp, your tribes, companies, palace, senate, forum. We leave you your temples only." This is undoubtedly an exaggeration, but the new religion made rapid progress. It was introduced into Gaul in the middle of the second century, and into Spain in the following century. It had made such headway in Africa that a synod held in northern Africa about A. D. 255, was attended by seventy-one bishops and presbyters. It has been estimated that there were from fifty thousand to sixty thousand Christians in Rome in the middle of the third century, and not much later we hear of missionaries along the Rhine, on the Danubian frontier, and even in Britain.

469. The Christians Suffer Persecution. The government made spasmodic efforts to check the growth of Christianity, and church historians reckon ten general persecutions, the first one being under Nero, and the last and most severe one under Diocletian. At first the state contented itself with the destruction of Christian books, with the banishment of the Christians, the confiscation of their property, and the infliction of corporal punishment. These measures not proving effective, many who persisted in their refusal to offer incense to the gods were put to death.

470. Reasons for the Government's Hostility. Some of the reasons for the hostility of the government we have already noticed. As time went on, other characteristics of the new faith excited distrust, notably the unwillingness of the Christians to serve in the army, and the development of the church into a compact, well-organized institution. The communicants were gradually organizing everywhere into societies which met in basilicas, or large halls set apart for meetings. These churches acquired property which the clergy administered. Over the clergy were the bishops who were appointed for life, and the bishops in a province were in turn under the jurisdiction of the bishop who had his seat in the capital of the province, and was known as the metropolitan, or later as archbishop, while finally the metropolitans were coming to acknowledge the superior authority of the bishop of Rome.

471. Galerius's Edict of Toleration in A. D. 311. It was undoubtedly this development of a state within the state which excited the alarm of many of the emperors. But, since Christianity kept on growing in spite of the efforts which the government made to hold it in check, the emperors of the fourth century decided to reverse their policy, and to recognize Christianity publicly. They hoped to secure its support for the throne, or perhaps we may say that it was for the mutual interest of the emperor and the Christians to come to an understanding. The first definite step in this direction seems to have been an edict which Galerius issued in 311 permitting the Christians to worship undisturbed and to rebuild their churches.

472. Constantine's Conversion to Christianity. But

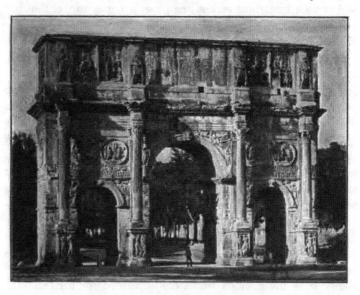

THE TRIUMPHAL ARCH OF CONSTANTINE

persecution of the Christians still continued in some parts of the empire, and it was left for Constantine to secure for them complete toleration, and by adopting its creed himself to make Christianity in a way the religion of the state.   Tradition attributes his friendly attitude not to considerations of state but to a vision which he saw.   Eusebius his biographer tells us that on the day before the great battle which he fought with his rival Maxentius, at the Mulvian bridge near Rome, he beheld in the heavens the figure of the cross, with the legend, *Hoc vince,* "By this (sign) conquer." In the night which followed, Christ appeared to him, showed him the same sign, and directed him to have it displayed on a banner.

473. The Labarum. Whether the story of the symbol and the vision is true or not, such a standard, known as the *labarum,* was carried by the troops on the following day in the battle which gave Constantine the mastery of Italy, and was adopted by him and his successors as the imperial device. It is conceivable, therefore, that the success of his troops under the emblem of the cross may have led him to favor Christianity. The standard, which is shown upon his coins, consisted of a spear supporting a transverse rod, from which hung a purple embroidered banner. The spear was surmounted by a golden crown encircling the monogram of Christ's name in Greek letters.

474. The Council at Nicæa, A. D. 325. The new attitude which the government had taken toward Christianity, the growth of the new religion, and the development of a compact organization in the church are alike shown in the great council held at Nicæa, over whose first meeting the emperor himself presided, seated upon a golden throne. This first council of the world, or Ecumenical Council, which was attended by about three hundred bishops and by a thousand or fifteen hundred presbyters and others, had been called together to settle the doctrine of the church concerning the nature of Christ. Arius, an African presbyter, had been long maintaining with great learning and eloquence that the Son was created by the Father, and was inferior to Him. The chief opponent of Arius was Athanasius, an Egyptian, who maintained the absolute equality of the Father and the Son. The council by a vote, almost unanimous, rejected the teachings of Arius, banished him, ordered his books publicly burned, and adopted the Nicene Creed which continues to be used by most churches to-day.

475. Constantine Makes Constantinople a Christian City. The changed attitude of the government in religious matters found expression in the appearance of the city of Byzantium, which Constantine chose as his residence. Among the many public buildings which he constructed, there was not a single pagan temple, for, instead of the temples and altars which were the glory of Rome, Byzantium or Constantinople, as the city was rechristened by Constantine, had its churches and its crucifixes. The location of the new capital was admirably chosen. It was the central point of the eastern half of the empire, on the border-line between Europe and Asia Minor, and the meeting-place of all the great highways from the East

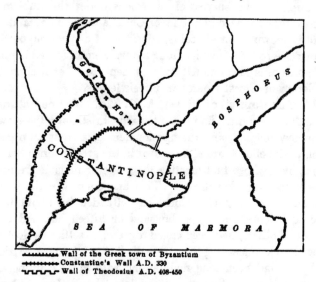

▲▲▲▲▲▲ Wall of the Greek town of Byzantium
✛✛✛✛✛✛ Constantine's Wall A.D. 330
ᴜᴜᴜᴜ Wall of Theodosius A.D. 408-450

and the West. The town, which was triangular in shape, was bounded on two sides by water and on the third side by land. It was, therefore, easy to defend, and well adapted for traffic by sea, for it had an excellent harbor; the Straits of Bosphorus opened northward into the Euxine and southward ships could pass through the Propontis and the Hellespont into the Aegean and the Mediterranean.

476. The Outlook for Rome. The transfer of the em-

peror's residence to Constantinople was a sad blow to the
prestige of Rome, and at the time one might have predicted
her speedy decline.   But the development of the Church, and
the growing authority of the bishop of Rome, or the pope, gave
her a new lease of life, and made her again the capital—this time
the religious capital—of the civilized world.

**477. Summary of Events from Septimius Severus to
Constantine, A. D. 193-337.**   In reading the history of this
period it is clear that the reign of Septimius Severus, who was
distinguished for his military and legal reforms, was preceded
by a period of civil war, and was followed by a century of anarchy
during which independent governments sprang up in Palmyra
and Gaul, until Aurelian restored unity to the Empire toward
the end of the third century.   The theory of the dyarchy—that
the emperor and senate ruled conjointly—established by Augustus, was frankly given up by Diocletian, who made himself
and his colleague Maximian autocratic rulers, one of them
establishing his capital in the East, the other in the West.
Their successors quarreled, but Constantine united the Empire
again under his control.   He recognized Christianity as a state
religion, had its creed formulated at Nicæa, and transferred his
residence to Byzantium.

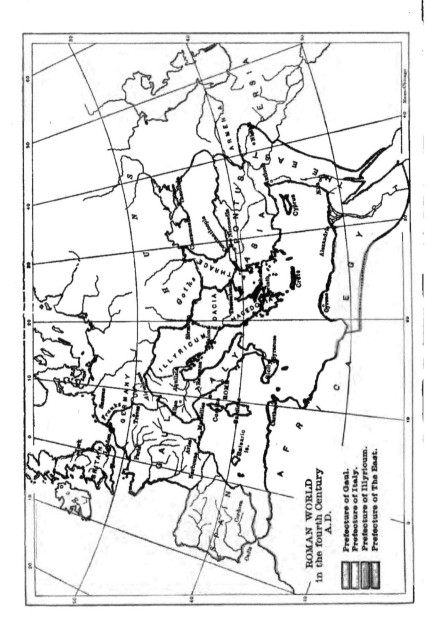

ROMAN WORLD
in the fourth Century
A.D.

Prefecture of Gaul.
Prefecture of Italy.
Prefecture of Illyricum.
Prefecture of The East.

CHAPTER XIV

THE BARBARIAN INVASIONS AND THE WESTERN WORLD

IN THE FIFTH CENTURY

(A. D. 337–500)

How the German peoples entered the Empire and divided it among themselves—How Christianity finally triumphed over paganism—How monasteries were established, and how the Bishop of Rome became the head of the church in the West.

478. Constantine's Immediate Successors. Constantine at his death in 337 divided the empire between his three sons and two nephews. They promptly quarreled with one another, and the empire was rent by civil feuds until 350 when Constantine, the second son, succeeded in making himself master of the whole Roman world.

479. Julian Tries to Revive the Old Religion. At his death the army chose his nephew Julian as his successor. Julian the Apostate, as he is commonly called, had been brought up as a Christian, but his study of Greek philosophy led him to prefer the old Roman religion as a system, while the harsh treatment which he had received as a young man from his Christian relatives developed in him a personal dislike for Christianity. Consequently, when he ascended the throne in 361, he proclaimed himself a pagan, and used every peaceful means in his power to bring the people back to the old faith. He confiscated the revenues of the churches, restricted the right of the Christians to teach, and rebuilt many of the temples. But his efforts were of little avail, and under his successors Christianity resumed its place as the dominant religion of the empire.

480. Rome and the Barbarians to the North. Julian died while on a campaign against the Persians, and if the Romans of his day had been asked where the danger to the empire lay, they would have located it in that quarter. But before the close of the century trouble of a much more serious nature than the Persian wars broke out on the northern frontier. The Romans had long dreaded the barbarians to the north. The invasion of Italy by the Gauls in the fourth century B. C., the descent of the Cimbri and Teutones into the peninsula toward the close of the second century before our era, and the wars which Marcus Aurelius had waged against the Marcomanni and Quadi at such fearful cost had taught the Romans that the northern frontier must be defended at all hazards.

481. The Northern Line of Defense. With this purpose in mind, Domitian and Hadrian, as we have already noticed, had constructed a line of defense, which, following in part the course of the Rhine and the Danube, extended from the mouth of the one river to that of the other. To the west and south of this frontier lived the Romans and the provincials who had accepted Roman civilization. Just beyond it were the Germans.

482. Our Information Concerning the Germans. Julius Caesar's campaigns in the North brought him into conflict with the Germans, and in his *Commentaries* he has given us some information about them. This is supplemented by the accounts which the historians Velleius Paterculus and Tacitus of the first century A. D. have left us, notably by Tacitus's interesting sketch of the country and the people; and finally writers of history of the fourth century have told us the story of the relations of the Germans with the Romans in later days. These different sources of information furnish us with a fair knowledge of the people, of the changes which they were undergoing, and of their dealings with the Romans.

483. Their Appearance and Character. They were a people of great stature, with fierce blue eyes and blonde hair. Their life in the open trained them to endure cold, hunger, and fatigue. They were addicted to gambling and immoderate drinking, but they retained their courage and manly vigor in a much higher degree than did the more civilized peoples south of the frontier line.

484. Their Occupations and Life. They lived in villages, cultivating the land, and tending their flocks and herds. There were few roads to connect these little communities with one another, so that commerce was almost unknown, and the small amount of trade which flourished was carried on by means of barter. But their delight was in hunting and war. They fought without much regard to discipline or military formation, but with a dash and a vigor which made it difficult to resist their attacks, for, as Tacitus tells us, "it was shameful for the prince to be outdone in courage, shameful for his followers to be unequal in courage to their prince."

485. German Confederations. As time went on, their common interests and common mode of living led the petty tribes within a given district to enter into alliance with one another. In the fourth century of our era the most important of the confederations thus formed were those of the Franks near the mouth of the Rhine, of the Alemanni to the south of them, of the Visigoths, or West-Goths, north of the Danube and near its mouth, and, still farther east, of the Ostrogoths, or East-Goths.

486. The Germans Become more Civilized. In the three centuries which had elapsed between the time of Tacitus, from whose description of the Germans we have quoted above, and the period which we are discussing, the character of some of the German tribes and their relations with Rome had undergone serious changes. Those who had been brought into contact with the Romans had adopted a more settled and civilized mode of life. Christianity even had made considerable progress among them, since a converted Visigoth of the fourth century, named Ulfilas, had invented an alphabet for them, translated the Bible into the Gothic tongue, and induced some of them to accept Christianity.

487. Their Gradual Migration into the Empire. Some of the Germans had already crossed the frontier peacefully, and of their own accord, and settled on Roman soil. Others had been brought in by force to occupy land laid waste in war. Still others had forced their way into Roman territory, and made themselves masters of it. The last-mentioned process had taken place in the province of Dacia, which was now controlled by the Visigothic king. The Germans were received readily as soldiers, and some of them were advanced to important positions in the Roman army. Two circumstances had contributed largely to bring about this slow and essentially peaceful invasion of the empire: the increase of population in the North, which made migration necessary, and the attraction which the fertile lands and the greater wealth of the South held out.

488. The Huns Appear in Europe. But at the moment which we have now reached in our story a new factor of an entirely different sort gave a sudden impetus to the southward movement. A people hitherto unknown in history, called the Huns, of an Asiatic race, entered Europe just north of the Caspian Sea, and descended upon the Ostrogoths. "They were men of great size," as Ammianus Marcellinus, a historian of the fourth century, tells us, "and had such short legs that you might fancy them two-legged beasts, or the stout figures which are hewn out in a rude manner with an ax, and stand on the posts at the ends of bridges. . . . They had no settled abode, but were homeless and lawless, perpetually wandering with their wagons, which they made their homes; in fact, they seemed to be a people always in flight."

489. The Visigoths Flee across the Danube. These people overran the country of the Ostrogoths, and descended upon the Visigoths like a whirlwind. The Visigoths fled before them, and, coming to the banks of the Danube, begged Valens, the emperor at Constantinople, to permit them to cross the river into Roman territory. Their request was granted, and, as Ammianus says, "so soon as they had obtained permission of the emperor to cross the Danube and to cultivate some districts in Thrace, they poured across the stream day and night, withou▸ ceasing, embarking in throngs on board ships and rafts and on canoes made of the hollow trunks of trees."

490. The Battle of Adrianople in A. D. 378. The settlement of such a host of barbarians in one body within the limits of the empire was a dangerous experiment in itself. The danger was aggravated by the ill-treatment which these immigrants suffered at the hands of the Roman officials of the province of Moesia, and finally the new-comers broke out into revolt against Roman authority. Valens marched against them with a large force, and the two armies met at Adrianople. The barbarians defeated their opponents and slew the emperor. The battle of Adrianople is, therefore, a turning-point in history, because a barbarian force has defeated a Roman army in a pitched battle on Roman soil.

491. The Visigoths Hold Roman Territory. Theodosius, the successor of Valens, came to an understanding with the Visigoths, however, and allowed them to settle in the provinces to the south of the Danube, under their own rulers, and as allies of the Romans. He even enrolled forty thousand of them as soldiers, and to some of the German leaders he gave commands in his army.

492. Stilicho Holds Them in Check. One of them, Stilicho, a Vandal by birth, was made commander-in-chief of the army, and to him the emperor on his deathbed entrusted the guardianship of his two boys, Honorius and Arcadius. Honorius took the West, and Arcadius the East, and thereafter the two parts of the empire were never reunited in any true sense of the word. The Visigoths, taking advantage of the fact that the throne in the West was occupied by an incapable young man, not yet twenty years of age, left their newly-acquired territory and marched southward into Greece, under their brilliant young leader Alaric. The Greeks implored help from Italy; Stilicho came to their assistance, and the strange spectacle presents itself of the empire attacked by one barbarian and defended by another. The Goths, checked by the move of Stilicho, withdrew on condition that Alaric should be made governor of Illyricum. Alaric's next move was against Italy, but again Stilicho forced him back. Stilicho's enemies, however, had poisoned the mind of Honorius; the great Vandal was charged with being a traitor, and put to death.

493. Alaric Takes Rome in A. D. 410. The one bar which had stood between Alaric and Rome was removed, and the Gothic king was not slow to take advantage of the opportunity. Sweeping down from Illyricum at the head of his forces, he appeared before Rome, and demanded its surrender. The city could not withstand the assault made upon it; a breach was made in the great wall that Aurelian had built about it a century and a half before, and the Goths entered. They treated the city, however, with wonderful forbearance. Contenting themselves with the spoils which they could carry with them, they departed, leaving the temples and public buildings practically untouched. While continuing his raid in southern Italy, Alaric was seized with fever and died, and his brother-in-law Ataulf, who succeeded him, withdrew from the peninsula.

494. The Visigoths Occupy Spain and Gaul in A. D. 415. As Alaric on a former occasion had retired from Greece on condition of being recognized by the Roman state as governor of Illyricum, so as the price of his withdrawal from Italy Ataulf exacted the appointment as commander of the forces intended for the campaign in Spain. Spain had been overrun five years before by the Suevi and the Vandals from the valley of the upper Danube, and it was Ataulf's mission to recover the province for Rome. This task he and his successor accomplished, but instead of turning over the recovered territory to the emperor Honorius, the Visigoths established there a kingdom of their own, comprising the greater part of Spain, and Gaul as far north as the river Loire. Their capital was Toulouse.

495. The Vandals Invade Africa in A. D. 429. Having seen the Visigoths settled at last after forty years of wandering in search of suitable homes, let us turn to the Vandals who had been displaced by them. Being driven southward by the advancing Visigoths, they naturally crossed over into Africa. To this enterprise, in fact, their king Gaiseric was invited by Boniface, the Roman governor of Africa, who was offended at the treatment which he had received at the hands of the Roman court.

Boniface quickly repented his invitation, and opposed the invaders, but without success.

496. St. Augustine and the African Church. The most vigorous resistance which the Vandals encountered in Africa was offered by the fortress of Hippo, where the celebrated theologian St. Augustine was bishop. He died during its siege, which lasted for fourteen months or more. Not the least of the misfortunes, to his way of thinking, which the invasion of the barbarians brought in its train was the fact that the Vandals, though Christians, had accepted the heretical teachings of Arius, which St. Augustine had been vigorously opposing for many years. The anxiety which he felt for the future of the church in Africa was well founded, for it never regained its previous strength and importance. The recovery of Africa by the Eastern Empire in 534 resuscitated it for a short time, but in the middle of the seventh century Christianity and the remnants of Roman civilization in Africa fell, never to be restored, before the sword of Islam.

497. The Vandals Sack Rome in A. D. 455. With the capture of Carthage the Vandals completed their conquest of northern Africa. The city had regained the old splendor and power which she had enjoyed before her destruction by Rome, and under the Vandals she prospered and became the commercial and piratical capital of the Mediterranean. It fell to the lot of Vandal Carthage, in fact, to take vengeance on Rome for the wrongs which Punic Carthage had suffered centuries before at the hands of her Italian rival; for Gaiseric, her great ruler, crossed to Italy and captured the city, but like Alaric, he spared the buildings, although he carried off great quantities of spoils and hundreds of captives.

498. The Burgundians in Southeastern Gaul. While these events were happening in Africa, the Burgundians, another tribe of Germans, from the shores of the Baltic, passed over into Gaul and occupied the valleys of the Saône and the lower Rhone. Short-lived as their kingdom was—it lasted but a century—they have left us in the Burgundian laws and in the *Nibelungenlied* two of the most interesting literary monuments of this period.

499. The Burgundian Laws and the Nibelungenlied.
The Burgundian laws, which were codified by king Gundobald,
are interesting because they show very clearly the treatment
which the Romans received at the hands of the German settlers
or invaders. The *Nibelungenlied*, or *Song of the Nibelungs*,
is the finest piece of early German literature. The story comes
from the north, but took definite form in Burgundy, and was
handed down by word of mouth until the thirteenth century,
when it was committed to writing.

500. The Huns Grow in Importance. For fifty or seventy-five years after they had driven the Visigoths across
the Danube the Huns played a small part in European affairs.
In fact, the emperor in the East had purchased peace by ceding
to them a part of Pannonia and by paying them large sums as
tribute. Their territory had greatly increased, and in the fifth
century, their king Attila ruled over all the wild tribes from the
Don to the Danube, and waited for a plausible pretext to invade
the fair fields of the empire.

501. Attila Invades Gaul. Such an opportunity offered
itself in 451. We need not stop to consider the reasons which
Attila gave for his advance to the south. His real purpose was
to plunder the country. Gaul was the object of his attack, and
he advanced into the centre of that province, laying the country
waste with fire and sword. All southwestern Europe would
probably have suffered the same fate had it not been for the
vigorous action of Aëtius, the governor of central Gaul, and the
loyal support of Theodoric, the king of the Visigoths.

502 Attila is Defeated at Châlons in A. D. 451. They
checked Attila's advance on the field of Châlons in 451, where
it is said that from one hundred thousand to three hundred
thousand of his warriors fell, and thus they turned back the tide
of barbarian invasion. Many writers have held that by winning
this victory Aëtius saved Gaul and Spain for the cause of civilization, and that, had Attila defeated the Romans and Goths, the
new German state would have been smothered in its infancy.

It would seem more probable that the restless Huns, after sweeping through Gaul and Spain, would have departed and returned
to their own part of the world with their plunder, and that the
developing German civilization would have recovered from the
shock.

**503. Romans and Germans Recognize their Common
Interests.** However that may be, the Romans and Germans
saw clearly that they had common interests, and that their cause
was the cause of civilization against barbarism, and the battle
of Châlons, in which they fought side by side, was typical of the
welding together of the two peoples into one.

504. Attila Threatens Rome. Turning back from his
campaign in Gaul, Attila entered Italy with the intention of
marching upon Rome. Fortunately, before he had carried out
his threatened purpose, he was induced to withdraw, partly
through the representations of an embassy, led by Pope Leo the
Great, which went to his camp in northern Italy. Attila himself
died in the following year, and with his death the Huns pass out
of European history.

505. Ricimer Makes and Unmakes Emperors. Although
Italy was saved from the ravages of Attila and his Huns, she had
fallen on sorry times. The army was again master of the situation, as it had been two and three centuries before, and for sixteen
years its leader, the Suevian general Ricimer, made and unmade
rulers, as he pleased. To his position Orestes, a former secretary of Attila, succeeded, and raised his own son, a child of
six, to the throne with the title of Romulus Augustulus.

**506. Romulus Augustulus, the Last Emperor in the
West.** It was a strange whim of fate that "the little Augustus,"
who by chance had derived from his grandfather the name
which the first king of Rome had borne, should have been the
last emperor in the West, but so it proved. The soldiers, disappointed at not receiving from Orestes the expected grants of
land, overthrew him, and made Odoacer, or Odovakar, one of
their number, their leader. Romulus Augustulus was forced
to abdicate in A. D. 476, and an embassy was sent to Con-

stantinople to announce to the emperor in the East that the people of Italy accepted him as the sole ruler of the empire. The embassy further stated that it had perfect confidence in the virtues and ability of Odoacer, and it begged the emperor to give him "the title of patrician and the government of the diocese of Italy." With this event the empire in the West came to an end.

507. Continuity of the Roman Empire. It is clear that "the fall," so-called, "of the empire in the West" did not involve the disappearance of the Roman empire. The continuity of its history was unbroken. The successors of Augustus and Constantine still sat upon the throne. They had only transferred their capital from Rome to Constantinople, and at Constantinople they continued to reign until this city fell before the assaults of the Turks in 1453.

508. What Really Happened in A. D. 476. One other point is clear in this connection. The event which happened in 476 was not an unexpected and dramatic catastrophe. It was merely the candid recognition of the existing state of affairs, and formal occupation of Italy by the Germans was simply the last step in the process of dissolution which had definitely begun a century earlier at the battle of Adrianople.

509. The Condition of the Western World. The western half of the Roman world was now under the control of the German invaders. The Danubian provinces had long since been given over to the Ostrogoths, Britain had become the prey of the Picts and Scots, and soon fell into the hands of two German tribes, the Angles and the Saxons. The Franks occupied Belgium and the country bordering on the lower Rhine. The Burgundians had established themselves in the valleys of the Rhone and the Saône; the Visigoths had seized southwestern Gaul and Spain, and the Suevi the northwestern corner of the Spanish peninsula. Across the Strait of Gibraltar in northern Africa were the Vandals. Now finally Italy passed under the control of Odoacer.

510. The "Fall" of the Empire in the West: Internal Causes. We have already observed, in following the narrative of eveuts, some of the forces which effected the gradual dismemberment of the empire in the West. Weakness within and pressure from without combined to bring it about. Foremost among the internal causes we have noticed slavery, which reduced to poverty the farmer and the free artisan, and put a stigma on manual labor. Partly for this reason, and partly from other causes, the mass of the people, in Italy at least, lost their moral fibre, and became incapable of defending themselves, or of managing successfully their own private and public affairs. The population declined; trade and commerce had almost died out; too much was taken from the people by a vicious system of taxation and by dishonest officials, and the emperors in the West were too incapable to use even the means at hand to repel the invaders.

511. External Causes. While social and political degeneration was going on within, the barbarians outside the empire were growing stronger by combining into great confederations, and were learning Roman methods of warfare, so that when the need of more land or the pressure of the wild tribes behind them pushed them southward, or when the wealth of the empire tempted them across the frontier, they were not wholly unprepared to make good their claims to Roman territory. Many of them, too, had been allowed to settle in a more or less peaceful fashion on Roman soil, so that a large part of the western world came into their possession largely by way of gradual occupation rather than by conquest.

512. Relations of the Germanic Kingdoms to the Empire. We must not think of all the newly-established Germanic kingdoms as technically independent. Ataulf, the Visigoth, it will be remembered, received from the emperor a commission to regain Spain for the empire, and he and his successors recognized the supremacy of the central government. In fact, the Visigothic and Frankish kings in Spain and Gaul did not throw off their allegiance to the empire until toward the close of the sixth century. Odoacer in Italy claimed to hold his position as the representative of the emperor at Byzantium. Only the Vandal king in Africa asserted himself as an independent sovereign. And yet in no one of these cases did the supremacy of the emperor amount to much. He was too far away and too weak to assert it, and the German ruler imposed taxes, appointed officials, declared war, and made peace without regard to the occupant of the throne at Byzantium.

513. How These Relations Came About. This difference between the theoretical and practical relations of the Germanic kingdoms came from the application to a large area of practices which had been followed on a small scale for nearly a century. In the early years of the southward movement, for instance, a tribe would cross the Danube with the consent of the emperor and settle on Roman soil. The chief would style himself an official of the empire, and would govern in that capacity, but as the Roman administrative system grew laxer, he would gradually govern without much regard to the emperor. If we think of this system as prevailing over an extensive territory like Spain or Italy, we have a fairly clear idea of the relation of the Germanic kingdoms to the empire in the latter part of the fifth century.

514. How the Germans Treated the Romans. We should probably be wrong in supposing that social conditions in the western world were suddenly and radically changed by the barbarian invasions. The various German peoples differed greatly from one another, of course, in character and in civilization. The Vandals, for instance, were fierce and intolerant; the Burgundians mild and ready to take up a settled life. Consequently the treatment which Roman provincials experienced at the hands of their conquerors was different in different sections, but on the whole their life did not undergo such a sudden or marked change as one would at first suppose.

515. Reasons for Their Tolerant Attitude. The reasons are not far to seek. Many of the German tribes had been for some time more or less closely associated with the Romans in the relations of everyday life, and in the army, where German auxiliaries are found from the time of Augustus. The new-

comers añd the natives had come to know each other; they had
begun to assimilate, and some of the German tribes had become
partly civilized, so that, after settled conditions had been established, the two peoples seem to have lived amicably together, and
the Romans were treated with reasonable fairness. That they
did appreciate their common interests, in some cases at least, was
shown by their united action in Gaul against Attila and his
Huns. Furthermore the sentimental respect which the Germans
and their leaders had for the empire contributed not a little to
develop in them a tolerant attitude toward Roman institutions
and the Roman people.

516. The Struggle Between Christianity and Paganism.
It was a fortunate thing for the Christian church that it had sent
its missionaries into Germany and converted many of the Germans to Christianity. As a result Christianity suffered no serious
check from the invasions. By this time it had nearly driven out
paganism, although the struggle had been a long and hard one.
The state and the old faith, with the centuries of history behind them, were indissolubly bound together in the imagination
of the Roman. The old religion had struck its roots so deeply
into the ceremonies, the festivals, and the amusements of public
life, into literature and art, into the family relations and everyday
life that it could be torn out only with great difficulty.

517. The Triumph of Christianity. As the Christians
gradually became the dominant element in society and the state,
they turned against the pagans the same weapons which the
pagans had used against *them* in their earlier days. In 392, for
instance, people were forbidden by law to offer sacrifices and to
visit the temples, but paganism was evidently not stamped out
at once, because in the next century we find edicts issued against
those who observed pagan rites.

518. Arianism and Orthodoxy. Although it was fortunate
for the Christians of the Roman world that many of the barbarians had been converted to Christianity before the invasions
began, it was unfortunate that they had adopted Arianism.
This circumstance probably did more than anything else to keep

the Gauls, Spaniards, and Africans, who were orthodox, from amalgamating readily with the invaders. The Vandal kings even confiscated the churches of the Catholics and in some cases punished their members with imprisonment and death. This element of discord was removed, however, in the sixth century, when Africa was regained by the Eastern empire, and the Visigoths became Catholics.

519. The Development of Asceticism. Two institutions of the church which exerted an immense influence on the western world during the Middle Ages—monasticism and the papacy—come into prominence during this period. The beginnings of monasticism, so far as Christianity is concerned, are to be found in the East. Some men reasoned, "It is the weakness of the flesh and the pleasures of the world which tempt us to sin. Therefore we will withdraw from the world, we will mortify the flesh, and we will give ourselves up to prayer and meditation." It was this sentiment which led St. Anthony in the third century to retire to a solitary place in Egypt, and spend there nearly eighty years of his life. It was this feeling which led him to wear a hair shirt and a sheepskin girded about him, to sleep upon the bare ground, and to fast for days at a time. The persecutions which the church suffered in the third century lent an impetus to the ascetic movement by driving men temporarily at least into the desert.

520. Monasteries Established. To others who wished to renounce the vanities of the world, the life of the hermit did not appeal. Such people did not think it necessary to forego altogether the society of their fellow-men. Men of this way of thinking withdrew to some retired spot, and associated themselves together in a religious community, whose members subjected themselves to a more or less rigorous discipline. These monastic organizations, like the hermits, first become common in Egypt, in the fourth century. This method of retiring from the world was better suited to the climate of Europe and to the less fanatical temperament of the people of that part of the world.

521. The Life of the Monks. The monks gave themselves

THE MONASTERY OF MONTE CASSINO

up to their religious duties; they taught the barbarians Christianity, and engaged in agriculture and other forms of manual labor.   In course of time life in the monasteries came to be regulated in accordance with a carefully developed system.

522. The "Rule" of St. Benedict. The form which it finally took, and which it kept in the main through the Middle Ages was given to it by St. Benedict in the early part of the sixth century.   He drew up a constitution to govern the celebrated monastery of Monte Cassino, which he founded, and his "Rule," as it is called, was adopted by almost all the monasteries in the

FROM A MANUSCRIPT OF VERGIL (AENEID, BK. II. 689-699) OF THE FOURTH
CENTURY.   NOTICE THAT THE WORDS ARE NOT SEPARATED

West.   Under it a monk was required to give up all his property, to promise implicit obedience to his superior, and to agree never to marry.   The time which he had free from his religious duties he was expected to devote to acts of charity, to manual labor, and to the copying of books.

523. Services which the Monasteries Rendered. To this last provision of St. Benedict's Rule we owe the preservation of the Latin classics, for if they had not been preserved in the monasteries, and if copies of them had not been made by the monks, the greater part of them would have been lost altogether.

In the monasteries, too, the traveller found shelter; the persecuted and even the criminal found protection; the poor and sick went to them for food and care, and those who sought escape from the turbulence of the world without, found within the sheltering walls of the monastery an opportunity to lead a life of peace, or to pursue the studies to which their tastes inclined.

524. Reasons for the Growth of the Papacy. The other institution of the church which began to exert a great influence upon Europe before the close of the fifth century was the papacy. A variety of circumstances contributed to this result. As we had occasion to notice in the last chapter, the church was rapidly developing into a compact institution, with a carefully graded system of ecclesiastics, running from the clergy through the bishops to the metropolitans. It was natural for the practical-minded Romans to organize the church in the same careful way as they had organized the state. In fact, the ecclesiastical organization was in large measure suggested by and modelled after the political organization. Now unity was given to the state by making the emperor the final source of authority. Consequently it was natural to round out the ecclesiastical system in a similar way by making some one person the head of the church.

525. The Bishop of Rome as the Successor of St. Peter. Several things combined to confer this dignity upon the bishop of Rome, or the pope, as that official exclusively was called shortly after the fifth century. In the first place he was commonly regarded as the successor of St. Peter, and, therefore, the primate of the Church, since several passages in the New Testament were interpreted as testifying to the fact that the Founder of Christianity had designated this apostle as head of His Church. Notable among these passages was that one in which Christ says: "And I say also unto thee, that thou art Peter, and upon this rock I will build My Church; and the gates of hell shall not prevail against it. And I will give unto thee the keys of the kingdom of heaven; and whatsoever thou shalt bind on earth shall be bound in heaven; and whatsoever thou shalt loose on earth shall be loosed in heaven." That St. Peter came to Rome is made highly probable by evidence from various sources, and that he organized the church there, presided over it, and transmitted his authority to his successors, was commonly accepted by the Catholic Church from an early period. As early as the second century, Irenaeus, the bishop of Lyons, draws from this fact the conclusion "that it is a matter of necessity that every church should agree with this church (*i. e.*, the church of Rome), on account of its preëminent authority."

526. Rome the Traditional Centre of the Western World. The tendency, which resulted from these facts, to recognize the superior authority of the head of the Roman church, was materially strengthened by the position which Rome had held for centuries as the political capital of the world. Roman citizens had been accustomed to refer to her all difficult questions for final settlement.

527. Church Questions Submitted to Rome. Now disputes inevitably arose among the churches of Europe on points of doctrine, morality, and church government, and these questions were naturally referred to Rome for adjudication. Thus on important matters the opinion of the church at Rome was sought from an early period, and in the middle of the fourth century the Council of Sardika decreed that bishops deposed by a synod should have the right to appeal to the bishop of Rome, and in the same century we hear of certain difficult questions submitted by a Spanish bishop to the bishop of Rome for decision.

528. The Great Ability of Certain Popes. The great ability which certain of the popes of the period showed extended the influence of the papacy and gave its decisions that recognized authority which they enjoyed later. Conspicuous among them were Leo the Great, who occupied the papal chair from 440 to 461, and Gregory the Great, pope from 590 to 604.

529. Leo the Great, A. D. 440 - 461. It was Leo whose influence helped to save Rome from the hands of Attila. His authority in church matters was accepted in Italy, Gaul, Spain, and Africa, and it was while he was at the head of the Church at Rome that Valentinian III, the emperor of the West, decreed that the decisions of the pope should be regarded as final throughout the western world, and that bishops should be forced by the provincial governors to come to Rome in response to his summons.

530. Gregory the Great, A. D. 590 - 604. The life of Gregory carries us into the next century, but, while we are speaking of the growth of the papacy, it will be convenient to mention the services which he rendered to the church and the state. Like his great predecessor, Leo, Gregory turned back from central Italy a barbarian horde, made up this time of the Lombards. Like Leo he asserted the supremacy of the Roman See. His authority in northern Italy must have been weakened by the settlement there of the Lombards, some of whom were pagans and others Arians, but this temporary loss was more than offset by the successes of the orthodox Franks in Gaul, by the conversion of the Visigoths to Catholicism, and by the extermination of the Arian kingdom of the Vandals in Africa,—all of which events took place in the sixth century. These new elements of strength were supplemented by the conversion of Britain to Christianity, which began during his incumbency of the papal office. In fact, thanks to his missionary spirit, his piety, tact, sound judgment, his literary gifts, and his administrative ability, the papacy made a long step in advance toward acquiring that dominant position which it held later in the western church and the western world.

531. Summary Account of the Barbarian Invasions, to A. D. 500. The danger from the barbarians to the north, which, as we observed in a previous chapter, threatened the empire under Marcus Aurelius, took definite form in this period. The Visigoths, one of the German tribes which had been crowding into the empire, were forced across the Danube by the incursions of the Huns, an Asiatic people, defeated the Romans at Adrianople, and were allowed to settle in Roman territory under their own rulers. At last they established themselves permanently in Gaul and Spain. Other German peoples moved southward, the Vandals occupying Africa, and the Burgundians, southeastern Gaul. The Huns reappeared under Attila, and threatened the civilization of western Europe, but were defeated at Châlons. The Danubian provinces were now held by the Ostrogoths, Britain by the Picts and Scots, the lower Rhine by the Franks, and Italy by a native prince. In other words, the West was divided up and occupied by the Germans. As for the Empire, the final division of it into the East and the West was made in 395, and the last emperor in Rome abdicated in 476. The German kingdoms nominally acknowledged allegiance to the emperor in the East, but really paid little heed to his authority. At the same time they treated the Romans well, and adopted much of Roman civilization. In particular, Christianity spread rapidly among them, and two of its institutions—monasticism and the papacy—came into prominence in this period.

CHAPTER XV

REORGANIZATION OF THE EMPIRE IN THE WEST

(A. D. 500–800)

How the German kingdoms, after Justinian had temporarily regained some of them for the Empire in the East, established themselves, defended themselves against the Mohammedans, and were united into an Empire by Charlemagne, king of the Franks.

532. Theodoric Conquers Italy in A. D. 493. In the last chapter we left Odoacer in control of Italy as its patrician or governor. Of this position he was deprived toward the close of the fifth century by a host of several hundred thousand Ostrogoths, who moved southward from their old home on the Danube, entered Italy, and made their king Theodoric undisputed master of the whole peninsula. We have had occasion to notice in another connection the restraint which many of the German kings showed in their dealings with the Romans. In Theodoric's treatment of the Italians this enlightened and beneficent policy is conspicuously illustrated. Except that they were not enrolled in the army, and that they were forced to give up a part of their land, the Italians enjoyed the same rights and privileges as the Germans. Even the fact that they were Catholics, while Theodoric was an Arian, was not counted to their disadvantage.

533. His Domestic Policy. The system which he adopted for the government of the two peoples was a singular one. Each people had its own courts and administrative system, so that, when two Goths were at variance with each other, the question at issue was heard by a Gothic judge; when two Italians fell out, they brought their case before an Italian judge; while an Italian and a Goth sat in judgment where both Goths and Italians were involved. Theodoric's policy was equally enlightened on the side of the material welfare of the people. He made a vigorous effort to revive agriculture in the peninsula; he had the roads

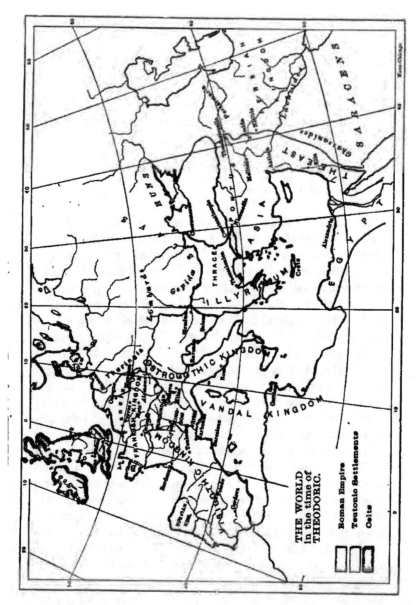

THE WORLD
in the time of
THEODORIC.

Roman Empire
Teutonic Settlements
Celts

and aqueducts repaired, and spent large sums in restoring public monuments at Rome and elsewhere.

534. His Patronage of Letters. Although he was illiterate himself, he was the patron of letters and honored with high office Boëthius, the last Latin writer in whose works the true classical spirit found expression. The principal work of Boëthius, a treatise *On the Consolation of Philosophy*, was much read during the Middle Ages, and had an immense influence on the thought of the period.

535. His Foreign Policy. Theodoric's foreign was as wise as his domestic policy. Noricum and Raetia were brought under his control; he married the sister of Chlodovic, the ambitious king of the Franks; one of his daughters he gave in marriage to a Burgundian prince, another to Alaric, king of the Visigoths, and his sister he wedded to the king of the Vandals. By these means he secured alliances with all the principal Teutonic states. A turn in fortune made his influence still greater. His son-in-law Alaric was slain in battle, and, during the minority of Alaric's son, he assumed the regency of the Visigothic kingdom in Spain and southern Gaul.

536. Fate of the Ostrogothic Kingdom. In fact, the western world seemed on the point of being united once more under a single ruler, but the times were not yet ripe for such an outcome. Europe had still three centuries to wait for its Charlemagne, and within thirty years of Theodoric's death the great Ostrogothic kingdom, which had been built up largely by his efforts, was overthrown by Justinian, the eastern emperor, and the Ostrogoths, as a people, disappear from the pages of history.

537. Why the Empire in the East Survived. In tracing the course of events in Europe we have lost sight of the Empire in the East. That this part of the Roman world maintained its integrity, while the Empire in the West was disrupted, was due to a variety of causes. The city of Byzantium was too well placed and too strongly fortified to be taken readily by undisciplined troops with few engines of war. Its access to the sea made it diffi· ult for a German force to reduce it by starvation, for none of the Germanic peoples, save the Vandals, had a navy. Furthermore, the tide of the barbarian invasions turned rather toward the southwest, and the empire in the East suffered less from this source of danger than did Europe; and, when the East was threatened, the eastern emperors showed more diplomacy or more energy than the vacillating, jealous rulers of the West. The system of government and the social and economic conditions were better in the East than in the West. These causes with others combined to save the eastern world from the fate which befell the other half of the empire.

538. Justinian, A. D. 527 - 565. In the century which followed the death of Theodosius, the last ruler of the whole Roman world, no one of the emperors at Byzantium is a man of much ability; but Justinian, who ascended the throne in 527, deservedly holds a most distinguished place in Roman history. His lively interest in philosophical questions reminds one of Marcus Aurelius, his passion for building, of Trajan, his tireless activity and his interest in the law, of Hadrian. In addition to the other qualities which he possessed, Justinian had a faculty which is most essential in a ruler—the ability to pick out the right men for the business in hand. Such men he found in Belisarius his general, in Tribonian the great jurist, and in Anthemius the architect of the church of St. Sophia.

539. His Conquest of Africa. His most dramatic enterprise was his plan to reunite the Roman world by reconquering the Mediterranean provinces of Italy, Spain, and Africa. His principal agent in this great undertaking was Belisarius. The conquest of Africa was effected with a force of but fifteen thousand men, the Vandal kingdom was brought to an end, and the authority of the emperor was reëstablished.

540. He Regains Italy in A. D. 535. In 535, just two years after the conquest of Africa, Belisarius landed in Sicily with the apparently insignificant force of seventy-five hundred men, and crossed to Italy. Notwithstanding the small size of his army, however, his advance into Italy was almost a triumphal march. The Italians, disaffected toward their Gothic rulers, opened the gates of the cities in southern Italy to him, the Goths made only a feeble resistance, and within a year and a half Rome fell into his hands.   But the Goths were strong in northern Italy, and from this quarter in the following spring came a force of one hundred thousand men under the Gothic king Witiges to recapture the city.   For its defense Belisarius had but five thousand, and yet with this handful of men he held the city against the towers and rams of the enemy, against their desperate onslaught, and in spite of the terrors of hunger.   For a year the siege continued.   Then news reached the camp of the besiegers that an imperial army had entered northern Italy and was threatening Ravenna.   These tidings called the Gothic king to the north, and Belisarius, following him, assumed command of the reinforcements from the east, and ultimately took Ravenna and captured king Witiges.   The conquest of Italy seemed to be effected, and Belisarius returned to Byzantium to celebrate his triumph.   But the fortunes of the Goths at this low ebb found a champion in their young king Baduila, who for his chivalry, his generosity, and his unselfish devotion to the cause of his people, has been styled "the first of the knights of the Middle Ages."   He recovered northern Italy, captured Naples and Rome, held in check Belisarius, who had been sent back to Italy, and for twelve years upheld the Gothic cause in the peninsula.   His defeat at last by the imperial general Narses and his death crushed all danger of further resistance and Italy became once more a part of the empire.

541. Southern Spain is Added to Justinian's Realm. Scarcely had the conquest of Italy been completed when civil war in Spain gave Justinian an opportunity to interfere there. Tiberius, the imperial governor of Africa, crossed to Cadiz on the invitation of the rebels, and established himself in southern Spain. Notwithstanding the fact that the Visigoths quickly composed their difficulties, they could not dislodge the imperial troops, and for a half century the southern coast of Spain with its important towns was held for the eastern emperor. With the conquest of Africa, Italy, and southern Spain, Justinian's dream of bringing the Mediterranean under his control was realized.

542. The Persian Wars, A. D. 540 - 545. The check which Justinian put on the ambitious designs of the Persian monarch Chosroes was perhaps of more permanent significance than his conquests in Europe. The eastern potentate, taking advantage of the fact that Justinian was occupied in Italy, found a pretext for a quarrel with him, declared war, invaded northern Syria and captured Antioch. Belisarius served his master to good purpose in this war also, for the eastern monarch was ultimately brought to sign a treaty of peace in which he agreed to retire to his own territory and to give up his designs of conquest. Only once in later years did the Persians threaten the empire, and then the decisive victory which the emperor Heraclius won over them at Nineveh removed all danger from that quarter. Justinian and Heraclius, therefore, not only saved the empire, but they saved Europe also from the danger of Persian invasion.

543. The Significance of Justinian's Code. Yet Justinian is best known to us, not through his military exploits, notable as they were, but through his code of laws. The code of Justinian constitutes perhaps the most enduring, the most characteristic, and the most valuable legacy which the Roman people have left to us. It brings together legal principles and rules covering all the dealings of man with his fellow-man, which the most practical people of antiquity had developed in its experience of more than a thousand years. This body of law, which forms the basis of the legal system of a great part of Europe, would probably not have survived had it not been put in a systematic, permanent form by Justinian.

544. The Contents of the Code. To carry out his great enterprise of codifying the law, he appointed a commission of jurists under the leadership of Tribonian, and after working several years this commission published the result of its labors. The code which it drew up consists of four parts, the *Pandects* or *Digest*, which contains opinions on important points in law, taken from the treatises of all the great writers of legal literature from the first century B. C. to the fourth century A. D.; the *Institutes*, a handbook for the study of law; the *Codex*, which brings together the edicts, official instructions, and judicial decisions of all the emperors, and the *Novellae*, or new imperial laws, issued after the first three parts had been finished.

545. Justinian as a Builder. Like Trajan, Justinian spent

ST. SOPHIA AT CONSTANTINOPLE

immense sums of money in building churches, aqueducts, and bridges, in fortifying towns and in constructing forts in all parts of the empire. An entire volume by Procopius, an historian of the time, is devoted to the emperor's buildings and public works. The most noteworthy of these is the church of St.

Sophia in Constantinople, which he rebuilt after its destruction by fire.

546. The Fall of Constantinople in A. D. 1453. It is not essential to our purpose to follow the history of the empire in the East beyond the reign of Justinian. The Persians were obliged by Heraclius in the seventh century to give up their plans of conquest, as we have already noticed; the Saracens were forced to abandon the siege of Constantinople in the following century, and the city held out against all the assaults from the East until it was taken by the Turks in 1453.

547. Constantinople and the Greek Classics. The fact that it did not fall until the date just mentioned was of immense significance for the culture of Europe. The fourteenth century in Italy was the dawn of a new life. The world emerged from the intellectual darkness of the Middle Ages, and a great impetus was given to the new development by the discovery in monasteries, where they had long lain neglected, of the works of the great Latin writers. But the Latin classics abound with references to Greek literature. Vergil suggests Homer; Cicero points to Demosthenes and Plato. Their acquaintance with Latin literature made scholars eager to know something of Greek, but, unhappily, Greek books were not to be found in the West, and the Greek language was unknown. It was a most fortunate thing for civilization, therefore, that Constantinople was able to hold out until the western world was thus prepared to receive the Greek classics. Had she fallen even a century or two earlier, quite possibly Greek literature would have been lost with her. As it was, Greeks came to Italy from Constantinople in the fifteenth century, bringing with them the Greek classics and a knowledge of the Greek tongue, and in this way the priceless treasures of Greek literature have been preserved to us.

548. The Lombards Invade Italy in A. D. 568. We left Italy under the domination of the emperor in the East, but this régime was short-lived. In the army with which Narses, the imperial general, had completed the conquest of Italy were five thousand Lombards under the command of their king. The Lombards were at this time living in Pannonia, and at the close of the war returned to their own homes.   But they did not forget the fertile fields of Italy and when Narses had grown old and feeble, and no longer had the full confidence of the emperor, their king led them down into Italy, and settled them, without meeting serious resistance, in the valley of the Po.   In the course of a few years they extended the limits of their kingdom to include the greater part of northern and central Italy.

549. Political Divisions in Italy. The Lombards were less civilized than the Ostrogoths, and curiously disinclined to act together and in a systematic way, so that the Lombard chiefs established a number of essentially independent duchies, as they were called, in the peninsula, and the Lombard troops, without any very apparent reason, passed by one district to conquer another and settle there.   Thus Italy was parcelled out into a number of Lombard duchies, and into half a dozen other districts, noteworthy among these being Rome and Ravenna, which still recognized the authority of the emperor.

550. How the Pope Acquired Temporal Authority. It was at this time that Gregory the Great ascended the papal throne, and henceforth the temporal authority of the papacy, that is, its influence in secular affairs, becomes an important factor.   The development was very natural.   Rome was cut off from Constantinople by the Lombards, and the principal representative of the emperor had left Rome and taken up his residence at Ravenna.   The pope was, therefore, the most influential personage in Rome, and upon his shoulders gradually fell the responsibility for the maintenance of law and order, and the conduct of political affairs.   Then, too, large tracts of land in various parts of the empire had from time to time been given to the pope, and these he had to administer through his agents.   In this way he acquired the position of a political ruler.

551. Britain Conquered by the Angles and Saxons. It is to Gregory the Great that the conversion of Britain to Christianity is due.   The lot of the islanders for two centuries had been a very unhappy one. Under Roman rule the Britons had become so dependent upon their masters for protection that when the Roman troops were recalled from the island in 407 the natives were utterly incapable of defending themselves, and the Picts and Scots to the north of the great wall overran the whole country. In their desperation they appealed for help to the Angles, the Saxons, and the Jutes. In the fifth century these peoples, who lived in Denmark and the country to the south, came, but not so much to help the Britons as to seize their land. The invaders were even more uncivilized than the Lombards. Consequently Roman civilization was stamped out entirely, and the new civilization which developed in the island was of pure Germanic origin.

552. Conversion of the Britons to Christianity. The newcomers were pagans, and so they continued to be until the time of Gregory. His admiration was aroused one day at Rome by some fair-haired British captives in the slave-mart, and, grieving to think that they and their countrymen were still heathen, he sent forty monks to the island under a prior named Augustine to evangelize it. Of their experiences in Britain we hear in the *Ecclesiastical History of England* written in the next century by an English monk named Baeda: "In this island landed the servant of our Lord, Augustine, and his companions. . . . The king, having heard their message, ordered them to stay in that island where they had landed and that they should be furnished with all necessaries till he should consider what to do with them." His decision was a favorable one, for we hear that "he permitted them to reside in the city of Canterbury, which was the metropolis of all his dominions, and pursuant of his promise, besides allowing them sustenance, did not refuse them the liberty to preach." Canterbury has ever since been regarded as the religious centre of England, and from this point the Christianization of the whole island was ultimately effected.

553. Few Conquests of the Germans Lasting. We have followed the history of seven branches of the Germanic peoples.

We have seen Africa seized and occupied for a century by the Vandals, Spain and a part of Gaul conquered by the Visigoths and the Burgundians, Britain overrun by the Angles and Saxons, and Italy held by the Ostrogoths until they were dispossessed by the Lombards, who in their turn were ultimately overthrown by the Franks. Of all these conquests, only those of the Angles and Saxons were permanent. The Vandals were driven out of Africa, as we have noticed, by the eastern emperor. The Ostrogoths lost Italy, and finally the followers of Mohammed took Spain from the Visigoths, and the Franks conquered the Visigoths and Burgundians in Gaul, and later the Lombards in Italy. It is to these last two events—the conquests of the Franks and of the Mohammedans—that we have now come in our narrative.

554. The Franks not a Roving People. Unlike the other Teutonic peoples the Franks were not of a roving disposition. We recall the raids of the Angles and Saxons, and the long wanderings of the Vandals, the Visigoths, and the Ostrogoths, before they settled permanently. But the Franks never went far from their original homes. They contented themselves with gradually pushing forward their frontiers, until they had made themselves masters of the territory about them, and in this enlarged domain they took up their permanent abode.

555. Their Early Conquests. The two branches of this people, the Salians and the Ripuarians, lived along the lower Rhine when they become known to us. In a battle near Soissons in 486, when their career of conquest begins, they defeated the Roman governor Syagrius and thus gained control of northern Gaul as far as the river Loire.

556. The Franks Become Christians. Their leader in this successful war was Clovis, with whom one may say that the Frankish kingdom begins. His next campaign was against the Alemanni who lived across the Rhine in the Black Forest. Clovis himself was a heathen, but Queen Clotilda, his wife, was a Christian; and, when Clovis found himself hard pressed by his enemies in a battle near Strassburg, he took a vow that he would become a Christian if the God of the Christians would give him victory. The event turned out as he wished, and Clovis had himself and three thousand of his followers baptized into the Christian faith.

557. Results of Their Conversion. This event did not lead to any noteworthy change in the character of Clovis and his men. He continued to be as savage and unscrupulous as he had been before, but the political results of his conversion were far-reaching. The other Germanic peoples were Arians, as we have already noticed, while the Roman peoples in whose territory they settled were orthodox. This difference in creed kept the two elements of the population at variance with each other. Now, fortunately for the future of the Frankish ambitions, Clovis became an orthodox Christian. This circumstance not only brought him the support of his own Roman subjects, but also enlisted in his behalf the secret sympathy of the orthodox Romans who lived in southern Gaul, for both the Visigothic and the Burgundian kings were Arians. This situation of course favored Clovis's plans of conquest. His acceptance of orthodoxy also made him the natural champion in the West of the papacy, and led in time to an alliance between the pope and the Franks which was of great significance for western Europe.

558. Clovis Conquers Gaul. The heretical belief of his Burgundian neighbors furnished Clovis with a ready pretext for the invasion of their territory, and his desire to teach the true faith at the point of the sword led him to make war upon the Visigoths also. In both campaigns he was successful. The Burgundians were obliged to acknowledge his overlordship, and the Visigoths were forced to give up Gaul and retire into Spain. Before his death in 511 he had brought under his control almost all of Gaul from the Rhine to the Garonne.

559. Kingdom of the Franks under the Merovingians. His kingdom at his death was divided among his four sons. They were soon at variance with one another, and for a period of a hundred years intrigue, murder, and civil war ran riot. Notwithstanding this dissension among themselves the vigor of the Franks was such that their territory steadily increased in extent, until under Dagobert in 628, when the Merovingian dynasty, as the family of Clovis was called, reached the highest point of its power, the Frankish kingdom included Belgium, Holland, France, and western Germany.

560. The Mayor of the Palace. Although the entire Frankish territory was united under Dagobert, it was made up of three states which at various times in the past had been independent of one another, Austrasia the eastern kingdom, Neustria the western kingdom, and Burgundy, and each of these had its own administrative officers. Now it happened that Dagobert, when he ascended the throne, was a very young man, and he relied largely for advice upon Pippin, one of the court officials in Austrasia, known as the Mayor of the Palace. The long period of years during which Pippin really directed the government and the ability which he showed made him more powerful in Austrasia than the king himself. Pippin's son managed to succeed to his father's authority, the position of Mayor of the Palace became hereditary in the family, known as the Carolingian, and in Austrasia the king became a mere puppet in the hands of this official.

561. Pippin Becomes Ruler of all the Franks in A. D. 687. The Mayor of the Palace in Neustria, on the other hand, supported the king against the nobility, and the nobility appealed to Austrasia for help. This was granted by Pippin, the Austrasian Mayor of the Palace, the grandson of Dagobert's councillor, and after a hard struggle the Neustrians were defeated, and all three kingdoms—Austrasia, Neustria, and Burgundy—passed under the control of Pippin. At his death his position was inherited by his son Charles, known later as Charles Martel.

562. The Last of the Merovingians. How completely the Mayor of the Palace had taken to himself the functions of the king is shown very clearly in a celebrated description which Einhard, a contemporary chronicler, has given us of the "do-nothing kings," as they were called, of the Merovingian line: "Nothing was left to the king. He had to content himself with his royal title, his flowing locks, and long beard. Seated in a chair of state, he was wont to display an appearance of power by receiving foreign ambassadors on their arrival, and on their departure, giving them, as if on his own authority, those answers which he had been taught or commanded to give. . . . When he went anywhere, he travelled in a wagon drawn by a yoke of oxen, with a rustic oxherd for charioteer. In this manner he proceeded to the palace, and to the public assemblies of the people held every year for the despatch of the business of the kingdom, and he returned home again in the same sort of state. The administration of the kingdom, and every matter which had to be undertaken and carried through, both at home and abroad, was managed by the Mayor of the Palace." Such a useless office could not continue indefinitely, and with the death of Childeric in 752 the dynasty of the Merovingians came to an end.

563. Mohammed and the Koran. It was well for Europe that the Franks were united and were led by a strong man. Otherwise the newly developing Germanic civilization might have been engulfed by the tide of Mohammedan conquest. To understand the rapid spread of Mohammedanism we must glance at the conditions in Arabia nearly two centuries before the period which we have reached in following the history of the Franks. Mohammed, the founder of the new faith, was born in Mecca in 570. In early manhood he showed a religious bent, and withdrew frequently to lonely spots for meditation. On one of these occasions, as he slept, an angel seemed to stand before him holding a scroll from which he was bidden to read and on the scroll was written what Mohammed accepted as a revelation from above. This was the first of the revelations which he received from time to time thereafter, and which were put together after his death into the Koran, or sacred book of the Mohammedans.

564. His Teachings are Accepted in Arabia. Mohammed taught that God is one, that he is all-powerful, and that the individual must surrender himself completely to his will. The people of Mohammed's native city, Mecca, were hostile to these teachings, because her prosperity was due to the pilgrimages which the faithful made to her idolatrous shrines, and they obliged him to flee from the city, but the Arabians elsewhere eagerly accepted his doctrines. In the end even Mecca was obliged to yield to him, and in 630, or eight years after his flight from the city, he returned as its master. His flight from Mecca in 622, or the Hegira as it is called, is the event from which the Mohammedans reckon all dates.

565. They Make the Arabs Resistless Warriors. His success over the people of Mecca was the beginning of the religious and political conquest of his native land, and before his death Mohammed began to cast his eyes even beyond the limits of Arabia. The religion which he taught was well adapted to make brave warriors of its adherents. It is the duty of the believer to spread the new faith, by the sword if need be. All things, even the length of a man's life, are ordained of God. Consequently one cannot die until the appointed time has come, and, therefore, is as safe on the field of battle as in his own home, and death in battle with infidels ensures the believer admission to paradise. We can get some notion of the sort of warriors which such teachings nurtured by calling to mind the fierce courage with which the Arabs of the Soudan, in our own day, armed only with primitive weapons, have rushed to certain death against the Gatling guns and repeating rifles of disciplined European troops.

566. Conquests of the Mohammedans. It was an army made up of men like these which went forth from Arabia to conquer the world. Syria and Mesopotamia were wrested from the Roman empire, and Persia was subdued. Then the tide of conquest moved westward. Egypt was taken, and the province of Africa which Justinian had regained from the Vandals was lost forever to the empire. Arab hordes pushed along the northern coast of Africa, and in 711 crossed the Strait of Gibraltar into Spain, and one after another the great cities of Spain, Seville, Cordova, Valentia, and Saragossa fell into their hands, until the entire Visigothic kingdom, except the mountainous region in the north, had been occupied by them.

567. The Battle of Poictiers, or Tours, A. D. 732. In 732, under their great leader Abderahman, seventy thousand or more Saracens crossed the western Pyrenees into Gaul. Charles, the son of Pippin, felt the gravity of the danger which threatened his country, and brought the whole force of the Franks into the field to drive back the invader. The two forces met on the field of Poictiers. All day long the battle raged. The Saracen cavalry charged the enemy again and again, but they could not break through the solid lines of the Franks, and when darkness came on they withdrew from the field, and returned across the Pyrenees, never to enter France again. By this victory Charles Martel ('The Hammer'), as he was henceforth called, saved Europe for Aryan civilization and for Christianity. Had he been defeated, Gaul would probably have fallen into the hands of the Mohammedans, all central Europe would have been threatened with a like fate, and the whole course of civilization would probably have been changed.

568. Pippin, Mayor of the Palace, Becomes King. At his death Charles Martel divided his powers between his sons Pippin and Carloman. The insurrections which followed his death were put down by the two new Mayors of the Palace and in 747 unity was again secured by the abdication of Carloman, who withdrew into religious seclusion. Pippin, who now ruled alone, felt himself strong enough to depose the king Childeric, and a message was sent to Rome to secure the pope's approval of his course. The pope replied: "It is better that the man who has the real power should also have the title of king, rather than the man who has the mere title and no real power."

569. He Comes to the Assistance of the Pope. The new king soon had an opportunity to show his gratitude for this friendly decision from Rome. We have already noticed that the Lombards were Arians and the least considerate toward the Romans of any of the Germanic invaders. They had long harassed the pope by encroaching upon his territory. No help was to be had from Constantinople, because the pope and the emperor had quarreled over certain ecclesiastical matters, and the pope had gone to the point of excommunicating the emperor. In this emergency the pope appealed for help to his Catholic champion in the West, the king of the Franks. Pippin responded readily.   He entered Italy, forced the king of the Lombards to submit to him, took from him a strip of territory about Ravenna, and bestowed it upon the papacy. This addition of territory made the pope an important political ruler, and the significance of his temporal power may be thought of as dating from this gift made by Pippin.

570. The Appearance and Dress of Charlemagne. It is fortunate for us that we have a biography of Pippin's son and successor Charlemagne, or Charles the Great, from the hand of a contemporary. Although this sketch, which is often attributed

CHARLEMAGNE

to his secretary Einhard, is probably too friendly an account of Charlemagne and his deeds, it gives us some invaluable glimpses of the life of the times.   This is the picture which Einhard gives us of the new king: "He was stout and vigorous, of good stature, although his neck was short and thick. . . . His step was firm and the whole carriage of his body was manly.   He wore the dress of his native country, that is, the Frankish; next his body, a linen shirt and linen drawers; then a tunic with a silken border and stockings.   He bound his legs with garters and wore shoes on his feet. . . . He wore a blue cloak, and was always girt with his sword, the hilt and belt being of gold and silver."

571. He is Crowned King of the Lombards in A. D. 774. He has won a place in history as a warrior, a patron of letters, a statesman, and a champion of the church, and we may briefly look at his career to advantage from these four points of view. His long reign of forty-six years, from A. D. 768 to 814, is full of wars, but his most important campaigns were in Italy, Germany, and Spain. He had been on the throne but five years when the pope called upon him to prevent the Lombard king from seizing the cities which Pippin had given to the papacy. Charlemagne promptly marched into Italy, overthrew the Lombard ruler, and had himself crowned king of the Lombards. Thus the kingdom of the Lombards passed away, as had those of the Ostrogoths, the Visigoths, and the Vandals.

572. Conquest of Saxony, A. D. 772 - 803. Charlemagne's campaigns in Germany against the Saxons were not brought to a successful conclusion with so much ease. These people who dwelt upon his northeastern frontier had not been much affected by the civilization of the South, and were probably in a state of culture not much farther advanced than that of the Germans when the Romans were first brought into contact with them, and Charlemagne's campaigns in their country were not unlike those of Caesar in Gaul. They rarely met him in open battle, and no sooner had one district been brought into subjection than trouble broke out in another. And, just as had been the case in Caesar's campaigns, when quiet seemed to prevail throughout the land the appearance of a popular leader, like the Saxon hero Widukind, would set the country ablaze with patriotic fire. It was thirty years before the land was thoroughly pacified.

573. Annexation of Bavaria in A. D. 787. Charlemagne's other territorial acquisition in Germany, Bavaria, was secured with less difficulty. By a mere show of force the Bavarians were induced to yield; their duke was obliged to retire into a monastery, and Charlemagne took the government into his own

CHARLEMAGNE'S EMPIRE and its growth.

hands.   The addition of Bavaria to his realm was very important because it secured him a direct line of communication through his domains from Saxony in the North to Italy in the South, and gave him a better frontier defense against the Slavs on his eastern border.

574. Conquest of Northern Spain, A. D. 778 - 812.   While Charlemagne was engaged in the war with Saxony, ambassadors came to him from some of the Saracen chiefs in northern Spain—for the whole peninsula was now held by the Mohammedans—offering to accept him as their overlord.   He accepted the offer, crossed the Pyrenees, and received the submission of Barcelona and Gerona.   On the way back his forces suffered a disastrous defeat in the mountains at the hands of the Basques.   In this battle, at Roncesvalles, fell Roland, count of Brittany, to whose name wandering minstrels attached the story of warlike deeds and chivalrous adventures which three centuries later was set down in writing as the *Chanson de Geste de Roland*, one of the finest of the epic poems of the Middle Ages.   In spite of this disaster, this campaign and those which followed it secured for the Franks, and, therefore, for Christendom, a strip in northern Spain as far south as Barcelona, and was the first step toward the expulsion of the Mohammedans from Spain, which was finally accomplished in 1492.

575. Charlemagne as the Patron of Letters.   It would be wrong, however, to think of Charlemagne, as simply a warrior. He took a very lively interest also in letters and art.   He called to his court some of the most distinguished scholars of his time, Einhard his secretary, Alcuin the Anglo-Saxon, and Paulus Diaconus the Lombard.   Thanks to his influence, the monasteries took up again the practice of making copies of the manuscripts of the Latin classics which they possessed, and in consequence many works of antiquity were preserved which otherwise would probably have perished.   Just as our New England ancestors established colleges primarily for the proper training of ministers of the gospel, so Charlemagne's first purpose in the encouragement which he gave to learning was the education of the clergy.

576. His Famous Letter on Education. In a famous letter written by him on this subject he says: "In recent years when letters have been written to us from various monasteries to inform us that the brethren who dwelt there were offering up in our behalf holy and pious prayers, we noted in most of these letters correct thoughts but uncouth expressions. . . . Therefore, we exhort you not only not to neglect the study of letters, but also with most humble mind, pleasing to God, to pursue it earnestly, in order that you may be able more easily and more correctly to penetrate the mysteries of the divine Scriptures. . . . Be it known, therefore, to your Devotion pleasing to God, that we, together with our faithful, have considered it to be expedient that the bishoprics and monasteries intrusted by the favor of Christ to our government, in addition to the rule of monastic life and the intercourse of holy religion, ought to be zealous also in the culture of letters, teaching those who by the gift of God are able to learn, according to the capacity of each individual."

577. How He Organized the Government. Charlemagne's statesmanship showed itself clearly in his organization of the administrative system and in his foreign policy. In Saxony, for instance, he allowed the people to retain their customary law, which had been handed down by word of mouth. In fact he had it collected and set down in writing. At the same time capitularies, or royal orders, were issued, applicable to all parts of the realm, and the authority of the king in each district was represented by a count or other official, who in return for this grant of authority, and for the privileges and emoluments which he received, acknowledged himself to be the vassal of the king. This royal official in turn chose subordinates on the same basis, who became his vassals, and in this way the feudal system came into being.

578. His Alliance with the Church. The most characteristic part of his domestic policy was the close alliance which he fostered between the church and the state. The Saxons, for instance, were heathen, and Charlemagne's first thought was to convert them to Christianity, and a large part of his capitularies were intended to protect the church, and to promote its dignity and influence.   In this way the clergy and the secular officials worked harmoniously to further their common interests.

579. He is Crowned Emperor of the Romans.   This side of his policy comes out in a more striking way in his direct relations with the papacy.   We have already noticed that in 774 he came to the rescue of the pope in his struggle with the Lombards.

ST. PETER'S AT ROME

Again, in the year 800, he was called to Rome to compose a difficulty between Pope Leo III and his opponents.   The matter was satisfactorily arranged, and in celebration of its settlement a service was held in St Peter's on Christmas Day.   What happened on this occasion we learn from Einhard's narrative. "On the most holy day of the birth of our Lord, the king went to mass at St. Peter's, and as he knelt in prayer before the altar, Pope Leo set a crown upon his head, while all the Roman populace cried aloud, 'Long life and victory to the mighty Charles,

the great and pacific Emperor of the Romans, crowned by God!'
After he had been thus acclaimed, the pope did homage to him,
as had been the custom with the early rulers, and henceforth he
dropped the title of Patrician, and was called Emperor and
Augustus." With this act, the empire in the West, known later
as the Holy Roman Empire, was reëstablished.

**580. Summary Account of the Reorganization of the
Empire in the West, A. D. 500 - 800.** As we have followed
the course of events outlined in this chapter it is clear that the
cardinal points in the period from Theodoric to Charlemagne
were the attempts of the emperor at Constantinople to reëstablish
his authority in western Europe, the readjustment of the German
kingdoms, their struggle with Mohammedanism, the development of civilization and the spread of orthodox Christianity, and
the reorganization of the West under a single government. For
a time it seemed as if Justinian, the Eastern emperor who is
famous for his codification of Roman law, might regain the West.
In fact, he recovered Italy, northern Africa, and southern Spain,
but the Lombards drove the garrisons of his successors out of
Italy, and a wave of Mohammedan conquest swept over Africa
and Spain, and would probably have engulfed western Europe,
had it not been for the defeat of the Mohammedans at Poictiers
by Charles Martel. Charles Martel was Mayor of the Palace
for the Franks, and this people, beginning its conquests under
Clovis, had subdued all of western Europe except Spain, which
was held by the Mohammedans, and Britain, which was occupied
by the Anglo-Saxons. Pippin, the son of Charles Martel, was
made king of the Franks, and transmitted the sceptre to Charlemagne, who conquered Italy, Saxony, Bavaria, and northern
Spain, and thus became master of western Europe. He promoted learning, supported the Church, and was crowned emperor
of the Romans by the Pope.

ATLANTIC OCEAN

NORTH SEA

BALTIC SEA

Northmen

Swedes

Hamburg

Frisians

Saxons

Paderborn

AACHEN Austrasia

Frankfurt

Bohemia

Paris

Soissons

Tours

Bavaria

Neustria

FRANCE

Navarre

BAY OF BISCAY

Aquitania

Geneva

Lyons

Valentia

Milan

Pavia

Ravenna

ADRIATIC SEA

Cantabria

Gascony

Roncesvalles

Spanish March

Narbonne

Nimes

Arles

Zaragoza

Gerona

Barcelona

CORSICA

ROME

Spalato

Gaeta

Bari

E m i r a t e

o f

Lisbon

Toledo

SARDINIA

Naples

Amalfi

C O R D O V A

CORDOVA

Seville

Cadiz

MEDITERRANEAN

Palermo

SICILY

Syracuse

Kairouan

London

Canterbury

A F R I C A

	Roman Empire in the East.
	Empire of Charlemagne.
	Western Caliphate
	Eastern Caliphate

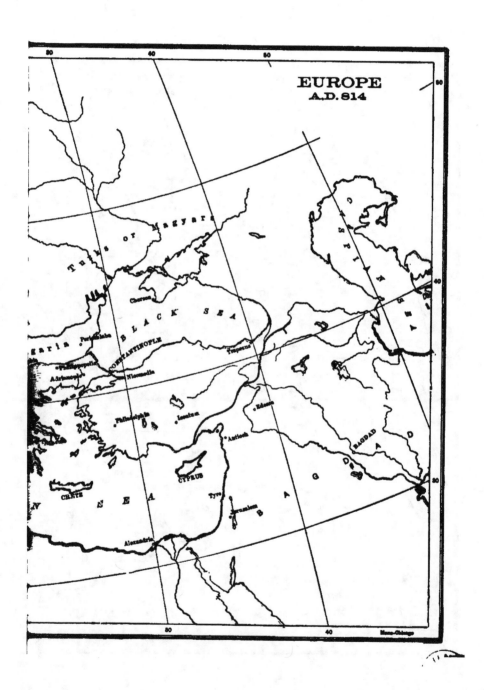

EUROPE
A.D. 814

CHRONOLOGICAL LIST OF IMPORTANT EVENTS *

THE REGAL PERIOD
753–509 B. C.
(See Chap. III)

THE REPUBLIC
509–264 B. C.

The conquest of Italy (Chap. IV)
The struggle between the patricians and plebeians (Chap. V)

---

* The dates and events in bold face type should be memorized.

† The dates of the regal period and of the early republic are very uncertain.

THE REPUBLIC

264–133 B. C.

The conquest of the Mediterranean Lands (Chap. VI)
and its effect on Rome (Chap. VII)

B. C.	
256	Battle off Ecnomus
	Regulus besieges Carthage
249	Roman defeat at Drepana
247	Hamilcar Barcas commands in Sicily
241	**Treaty made**
	Sicily acquired
241 (?)	Centuriate comitia reformed
240	**Livius Andronicus brings out first Latin play**
239	Birth of Ennius
238	Rome takes Sardinia and Corsica
238–222	Gallic wars
237	Hamilcar develops Spain
234	Birth of M. Porcius Cato
229–228	Illyrian war
227	Number of praetors increased to four
219	Hannibal takes Saguntum
218-201	**Second Punic war**
218	Hannibal enters Italy
	Battles of the Ticinus and the Trebia
217	Battle of Lake Trasimene
216	**Battle of Cannae**
215	Alliance between Hannibal and Philip
215–205	First Macedonian war
212	Marcellus takes Syracuse
211–206	P. Cornelius Scipio subdues Spain
207	Battle of the Metaurus
204	Scipio crosses to Africa
202	**Battle of Zama**
201	Treaty made
200–	Literary activity of Plautus
About 200	**Cisalpine Gaul and Liguria Romanized**
200–196	Second Macedonian war
197	Battle of Cynoscephalæ
197	**Provinces of Hither and Farther Spain established**
196	Independence of Greece proclaimed
195	Cato's unsuccessful defence of the Appian law against extravagance
192–189	War with Antiochus III
190	Battle of Magnesia, followed by treaty
171-167	**Third Macedonian war**
168	**Battle of Pydna**
159	Death of Terence

THE REPUBLIC

133–49 B. C.

The conquests completed by Caesar and Pompey abroad (Chap. VIII)

and

The revolution at home (Chap. IX)

B. C.

73–71	War with Spartacus
70	**Sulla's laws repealed by the consuls Pompey and Crassus**
	Vergil born
67	**The Gabinian law**
66	**The Manilian law**
65	Horace born
66–62	Pompey's campaigns in Asia
63	Death of Mithridates
	Cicero suppresses the Catilinarian conspiracy
60	First triumvirate formed
59	Caesar consul
	Livy born
58–50	**Caesar's campaigns in Gaul**
56	Renewal of the triumvirate
53	Crassus slain by Parthians

THE REPUBLIC

49–27 B. C.

The death struggles of the Republic (Chap. X)

49–45	**War between Caesar and the Pompeians**
48	**Battle of Pharsalus**
46	**Battle of Thapsus**
45	**Battle of Munda**
44	Caesar made dictator for life
44	**Caesar assassinated**
44–43	War about Mutina
43	**Second triumvirate formed**
	Cicero murdered
42	**Battles of Philippi**
31	**Battle of Actium**

THE EMPIRE

27 B. C.—A. D. 68

The establishment of the Empire and the Julian Emperors (Chap. XI)

27	**Octavianus receives proconsular power for ten years and the title of Augustus.**
27 B. C. - A. D. 14	**Reign of Augustus**
17 B. C.	Publication of the Aeneid
35–13 B. C.	Literary activity of Horace

THE EMPIRE

A. D. 68–193

From Vespasian to Septimius Severus (Chap. XII)

THE EMPIRE

A. D. 337–476

*The Barbarian Invasions and the Western World in
the Fifth Century* (Chap. XIV)

A. D.

415	The Visigoths settle in Gaul and Spain
429	The Vandals invade Africa
440–461	Leo the Great, pope
443	The Burgundians occupy south-eastern Gaul
449	The Saxons invade Britain
451	Attila defeated at Châlons
455	The Vandals sack Rome
476	Romulus Augustulus, the last emperor in Rome, abdicates
	Odoacer called patrician of Italy by Eastern emperor

THE EMPIRE

A. D. 476–800

Reorganization of the Empire in the West (Chap. XV)

486	Clovis defeats the Romans at Soissons
493–553	The Ostrogothic kingdom in Italy, established by Theodoric
496	Clovis accepts Catholic Christianity
527–565	Justinian emperor in the East
	The Code compiled
533–534	Belisarius regains Africa
553	Italy restored to the Eastern empire
568	The Lombards invade Italy
590–604	Gregory the Great, pope
	The Christianization of Britain begins
610–641	Heraclius drives back the Persians
622	The Hegira
687	Pippin becomes ruler of all the Franks
711	The Mohammedans enter Spain
732	Battle of Poictiers
751	The Mayor of the Palace made king
768–814	Reign of Charlemagne
774	Charlemagne made king of the Lombards
772–803	Saxony conquered
787	Annexation of Bavaria
778–812	Conquest of northern Spain
800	Charlemagne crowned emperor at Rome

FAMILY OF THE JULIAN EMPERORS

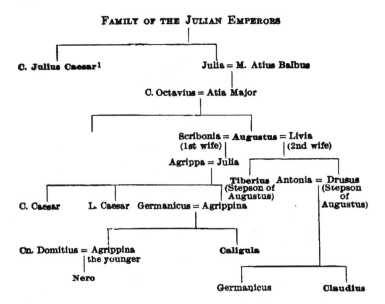

[1] The names of Julius Caesar and of the five Julian emperors are printed in bold face type. Only those members of the imperial family in whom we are interested are shown here. Notice that there are two branches: one through Livia, the second wife of Augustus, whose son Tiberius by a former husband succeeded Augustus, the other through Scribonia. There were two emperors in each branch. The parallel horizontal lines connect the names of husband and wife.

SPECIMEN OF A DESCRIPTIVE SUMMARY OF ROMAN POLITICAL INSTITUTIONS*

THE MONARCHY

The Chief Magistrate: the King. The government of the primitive state by the elders of the clans gave way to the rule of the *rex* or king. He was chief executive, chief priest, lawgiver, and judge. He was assisted by *quaestores parricidii*, or detective officers, and by *duumviri perduellionis*, or officials who prosecuted those charged with treason.

The Senate. The senators, or *patres*, were representatives of the different clans, and constituted the advisory council of the king.

The People. There were three elements in the population: the patricians, or nobles, the plebeians, or commons, and the clients, who were dependents. The people were divided into thirty *curiae*, and were called together by the king in the *comitia curiata*, which met to consider matters concerning the several clans, the question of war or peace, etc. For service in the army they were organized on the basis of landed property in the *comitia centuriata*, made up of 193 centuries.

THE REPUBLIC

THE MAGISTRATES

The consuls, two in number, chosen annually, took the place of the king in 509 B. C. The consul presided over the senate and *comitia*, acted as judge, and as commander-in-chief.

A **dictator** was chosen by the consuls in times of great danger. He had supreme power over officials and private citizens, and no one could veto his action. The **magister equitum,** his lieutenant, commanded the cavalry.

The **tribunes,** first chosen in 493 B. C., were intended to protect citizens, especially plebeians, from the arbitrary action of a magistrate. The tribune could punish a magistrate who refused to yield, and his person was inviolable. The number of the tribunes, probably five at first, was increased to ten in 457 B. C.

---

* See explanatory paragraph at the end, on p. 290.

The **decemvirs** (451–449 B. C.) were officials temporarily appointed to collect and publish the laws.

The **consular tribunes** (445–367 B. C.) were six military officials vested with the powers of the consul, and could be chosen from the ranks of the plebeians.

The **censors** (443 or 435), two in number, relieved the consuls of the duty of assessing the property of citizens, of drawing up the lists of senators and citizens, and of managing the finances.

The **quaestors,** of whom we hear in the regal period, became the keepers of the state funds, and after 447 were elected by the people. The quaestorship is the first regular magistracy to which the plebeians were made eligible. The number of quaestors was raised from two to four in 421 B. C., to eight in 267, to twenty by Sulla, and to forty by Caesar.

The **praetors,** first chosen in 366 B. C., were all judges at first. After 227 B. C. some of them acted as judges, others as provincial governors. After 81 B. C. every praetor served one year at Rome as a judge, and the following year as governor of a province. At the outset there was only one praetor. In 242 B. C. the number was raised to two, in 227 B. C. to four, in 197 B. C. to six, under Sulla to eight, under Caesar to ten, and later to fourteen, and to sixteen.

The **plebeian** and **curule aediles** acquired in time similar functions. The former office dates back to the early years of the republic, and was connected with the tribunate. The curule aedileship was established in 366 B. C. The aediles had the supervision of public places, the care of the corn supply, the superintendence of the games, and certain judicial powers. Each of the two colleges of aediles had two members.

The **proconsul,** first chosen in 326, held in a province the authority of a consul, without being under the constitutional restrictions put on the consul in Rome.

The **vigintisexviri,** or twenty-six men, were minor officials, and comprised the "ten men" who acted as judges in special cases, the four prefects, or judges, for certain districts of Italy, the three police magistrates, the three officials of the mint, the four street commissioners, and the two commissioners for roads outside Rome.

The **interrex** was an extraordinary official who came into office when the chief magistracy became vacant.

The **triumvirs** were three extraordinary officials, Octavius, Antony, and Lepidus, chosen in 43 B. C. for a period of five years, with supreme power "to put the state in order." The compact made by Caesar, Pompey, and Crassus, commonly known as the First Triumvirate, was never sanctioned by law.

Methods of Election. Consuls, praetors, censors, and probably the decemvirs were elected in the *comitia centuriata*; curule aediles, quaestors, the *vigintisexviri*, the consular tribunes, and the triumvirs of 43 in the *comitia tributa*; the plebeian tribunes and plebeian aediles in the *concilium plebis*. An interrex served for five days only. How the first interrex was chosen is unknown. Each subsequent interrex was appointed by his predecessor. Consuls became proconsular governors at the end of their year's term at Rome. They usually cast lots for their provinces. The *magister equitum* was appointed by the dictator.

The certus ordo. The order in which the offices were to be held was fixed in course of time, partly by law, partly by custom, as follows: *tribunus militum* (one of the six officers attached to a legion), one of the *vigintisexviri*, quaestor, *tribunus plebis*, aedile, censor, *magister equitum*, praetor, interrex, consul, dictator.

Age Requirement. After the time of Sulla probably the minimum age requirement for the quaestorship was thirty-one years, for the praetorship forty, and for the consulship forty-three.

The imperium included the power to take the auspices, to represent the state in its dealings with foreign countries, to command the army and navy, to judge and inflict even the death penalty in the provinces, to issue proclamations, to preside over the senate and popular assemblies, and to act as the general executive officer of the state. The dictator, consul, praetor, and *magister equitum* of the regular officials had this power. The others did not.

Curule magistrates. The magistrates in the *certus ordo* above the quaestor, but not including the plebeian officials, had the right to sit in a curule chair on official occasions.

Eligibility of Plebeians. Plebeians only were eligible to the tribunate and aedileship of the plebs. They were also eligible to the consular tribunate, to the quaestorship after 421, to the consulship after 366, to the dictatorship after 356, to the censorship after 339, to the praetorship after 338, and about the same time to a place in the college of curule aediles.

Term of Office. The dictator was expected to resign when the task for which he was appointed was finished. At the most his term was limited to six months. The censor held office for one year and a half; the interrex for five days, the triumvirs of 43 b. c. for five years. All other officials held office for one year, except that the consuls and praetors served for a second year, and in some cases for a longer time, in the provinces.

Veto Power. Any magistrate could veto the action of his colleague, or of an official beneath him in rank. A tribune could veto the action of a colleague, or of any magistrate, but his action could not be vetoed by any other official save by one of his colleagues.

Attendants. A dictator was attended by twenty-four lictors, a consul by twelve, the city praetor by two, and a praetor or propraetor in a province by six.

The foregoing descriptive summary deals with the three elements in the state, viz., the magistrates, the senate, and the people for the regal period, and with the magistrates for the republican period. Make a similar summary for the senate and people under the republic, and for the emperor, the imperial officials, the senate, and the people under the early and later empire. For details see Abbott's *Roman Political Institutions*, pp. 220–264 and pp. 341–398. In analyzing the position of the senate during the republican period, for instance, give the number of senators and the method of choosing them at different times, the property and age requirement, the powers of the senate and its method of exercising them, etc. For other specimen Summaries, and for Studies, Questions and other "Helps," see the *Handbook* which is issued simultaneously with this *History*.

Brief List of Books for a School Library *

Bury, *History of Rome to the Death of M. Aurelius*, American Book Co., N. Y. $1.50. A good sketch of imperial history from the battle of Actium to the date indicated in the title.

Emerton, *Introduction to Study of the Middle Ages*, Ginn & Co., Boston, $1.12. Well written account of the period from A. D. 375 to 814. Useful bibliographies.

How and Leigh, *A History of Rome to the Death of Caesar*, Longmans, Green & Co., N. Y., $2.00. Very attractive style.

Pelham, *Outlines of Roman History*, Putnam, N. Y., $1.75. A scholarly treatise, running to 476 A. D.

Abbott, *Roman Political Institutions*, Ginn & Co., Boston, $1.50. A history and description of the Roman constitution and government for high school and college students.

---

* A more extended list of books for teachers and advanced students will be found in the *Handbook*, which is issued simultaneously with this *History*.

Gow, *Companion to School Classics*, Macmillan, N. Y., $1.75. An excellent little treatise on the Roman army, law, philosophy, etc.

Johnston, *The Private Life of the Romans*, Scott, Foresman & Co., Chicago, $1.50. The best manual on the subject.

Kiepert, *Atlas Antiquus*, Sanborn, Boston, $1.75. Maps and plans of the ancient world, with index to places.

Munro, *A Source Book of Roman History*, Heath, Boston, $1.00. A well-chosen collection of extracts from the sources, with excellent bibliographies.

Robinson, *Readings in European History*, Vol. I, Ginn & Co., Boston, $1.50. Covers the later period.

Appian, *Roman History*, translated by White, 2 vols., Macmillan, N. Y., $3.00.

Einhard, *Life of Charlemagne*, American Book Co., N. Y., $0.30.

Livy, *History of Rome*, 2 vols., American Book Co.

Muir, *The Coran*, Society for the Propagation of Christian Knowledge, $0.60.

Plutarch, *Lives*, the Dryden translation, so-called, revised by Clough. Little, Brown & Co., Boston, $2.00.

Polybius, *Histories*, translated by Shuckburgh, 2 vols., Macmillan, N. Y., $6.00.

The books whose titles are given above may be purchased for $27.00. If possible, the following books should be added.

Mommsen, *A History of Rome*, 5 vols., Scribners, N. Y., $10.00.

Dill, *Roman Society from Nero to M. Aurelius*, Macmillan, N. Y., $2.00.

Dill, *Roman Society in the Last Century of the Western Empire*, Macmillan, N. Y., $2.00.

Platner, *The Topography and Monuments of Ancient Rome*, Allyn & Bacon, Boston, $3.00.

Putzger, Historischer Schul-Atlas, Velhagen & Klasing, Leipzig, $1.00.

Sallust, Florus, and Velleius Paterculus, translated by Watson, Macmillan, N. Y., $1.00.

Suetonius, *The Twelve Caesars*, translated by Thompson, Macmillan, N. Y., $1.50.

INDEX

To assist in the pronunciation of the foreign words found in the following list the primary accent has been marked, and the words have been divided into syllables. The division of final *-cius*, *-sius*, and *-tius* into two syllables (pronounced *-shi-us*), adopted by most books of reference, has been followed here, although in most of these cases some teachers may prefer the more nearly monosyllabic pronunciation, *-shyus*. Where it seemed necessary, vowels have been marked as long or short. Other devices used to indicate the sound of a letter are the following: ä, like *a* in *far*; ọ, like *c* in *nice*; ẹ, like *c* in *call*; ȩh, like *ch* in *character*; g̣, like *g* in *gender*; ṣ, like *s* in *has*. The French nasal (somewhat like *ng* in *gong*) is indicated by n̂. Underscored letters are silent. A full set of rules governing the pronunciation of Latin proper names, when used in an English sentence, has been formulated in an admirable way by Professor Walker, and may be found in his forthcoming edition of Caesar's *Gallic War*. For topical studies based on the Index see the *Handbook for Teachers*.

(References are to sections.)

Ae'ci-us (or At'ti-us), writer of tragedy, 238

A-chae'ans (or A-chai'ans), 186, 194; Achaean league, 196

Ae'ti-um, battle of, 323

Ad-ri-a-no'ple, battle of, 490

Ad-ri-at'ic Coast, 18, 19

Ae'dile-ship, Cu'rule, established, 124; open to plebeians, 126; see also p. 288

Ae-ge'an Sea, 185

Ae-mil'i-an Way, 137

Lu'ci-us Ae-mil'i-us Pau'lus, at Cannae, 172

Ae-ne'as, 36

Ae'qui-ans, the, location of, 13; wars with Rome, 63

Ae-ser'ni-a, 85

Ae-tō'li-ans, 186

A-fra'ni-us, 303

Africa, made province, 204; occupied by the Vandals, 495, 496; reconquered by Justinian, 539; taken by the Mohammedans, 566

Agrarian Questions, control of state land, 48, 104; growth of estates, 135; employment of slaves, 135; law of Tiberius Gracchus, 259-262

A-gric'o-la, 392, 410

Agriculture, principal early indus-

try, 21; influence on character, 47; ownership of land, 23, 47, 48; low state of agriculture, 257

Ag-ri-gen'tum, 155, 174

A-grip'pa, 341

A-grip-pi'na, 353, 364

Äl'a-ric, 492, 493

Al'ba Fu'cens, 75, 76

Al'ba Lon'ga, 36-38

Al'cu-in, 575

Al-e-man'ni, 449, 485

A-le'si-a, 245

Al'li-a River, battle of the, 64

Allies, (see Socii)

Alps, the, geographical boundary, 17; political boundary, 165

Am-mi-a'nus Mar-cel-li'nus, 488

A-mu'li-us, 37

Amusements, 10, 236, 238, 323

Ancus Mar'ti-us, 38

An-dris'cus, the pretender in Macedonia, 195

Li'vi-us An-dro-ni'cus, "father of Roman literature," 238

An'ge-lo, San, castle of, 419

Anglo-Saxons, their conquest of Britain, 551; their conversion to Christianity, 552

An-the'mi-us, architect of St. Sophia, 538, 545

An-ti'o-chus III, (See Syria)

292

www.ingramcontent.com/pod-product-compliance
Lightning Source LLC
LaVergne TN
LVHW012205040326
832903LV00003B/140